NEGLECTED

STORIES

NEGLECTED STORIES

THE

CONSTITUTION

AND

FAMILY VALUES

PEGGY COOPER DAVIS

HILL AND WANG

A division of Farrar, Straus and Giroux

Hill and Wang
A division of Farrar, Straus and Giroux
19 Union Square West, New York 10003

Printed in the United States of America
Designed by Abby Kagan
First published in 1997 by Hill and Wang
First paperback edition, 1998

The Library of Congress has catalogued the hardcover edition as follows:
Davis, Peggy Cooper, 1943–
    Neglected stories : the Constitution and family values / Peggy
Cooper Davis. — 1st ed.
        p.   cm.
    Includes bibliographical references and index.
    ISBN 0-8090-7241-6 (alk. paper)
    1. Civil rights—United States—History.   2. Parents—Civil
rights—United States—History.   3. Free choice of employment—
United States—History.   4. Freedmen—Civil rights—United States—
History.   5. Family—United States—History.   6. Social values—
United States—History.   I. Title.
KF4749.D48   1997
342.73'085—dc21   97-3898

A concerted effort has been made to obtain permission to quote from copyrighted works.
Grateful acknowledgment is made to the following:
Bantam Doubleday Dell. Excerpts from *Loving Warriors: Selected Letters of Lucy Stone and Henry
    B. Blackwell, 1853–1893* by Leslie Wheeler. Copyright © 1981 by Leslie Wheeler. Used by
    permission of Doubleday, a division of Bantam Doubleday Dell Publishing Group, Inc.
Curtis Brown, Ltd. Excerpts from *Lay My Burden Down: A Folk History of Slavery* by B. A.
    Botkin. Published by University of Chicago Press. Copyright © 1945 by B. A. Botkin,
    renewed. Reprinted by permission of Curtis Brown, Ltd.
Cambridge University Press. Excerpts from *Freedom: A Documentary History of the
    Emancipation, 1861–1867, Series 1: Vol. 2: The Wartime Genesis of Free Labor: The Upper
    South*, Ira Berlin, Steven F. Miller, Joseph P. Reidy, and Leslie S. Rowland, eds. Copyright
    © 1990 by Ira Berlin. Reprinted with the permission of Cambridge University Press.
Wynton Marsalis. Excerpt from *Blood on the Fields*. Copyright © 1997 by Wynton Marsalis.
    Reprinted by permission of the author.
James Mellon, ed. Excerpts from *Bullwhip Days: The Slaves Remember: An Oral History*.
    Published by Weidenfeld and Nicholson. Copyright © 1988 by James Mellon. Reprinted by
    permission of the author.
William Morrow & Co. Excerpts from *Once a Slave* by Stanley Feldstein. Copyright © 1971 by
    Stanley Feldstein. Reprinted by permission of William Morrow & Co., Inc.
W. W. Norton & Company, Inc. Excerpts from *Ahead of Her Time: Abby Kelley and the Politics
    of Antislavery* by Dorothy Sterling. Copyright © 1991 by Dorothy Sterling. Reprinted by
    permission of W. W. Norton & Company, Inc.
Pantheon Books. Excerpts from *The Black Family in Slavery and Freedom, 1750–1925* by
    Herbert Gutman. Copyright © 1976 by Herbert Gutman. Reprinted by permission of
    Pantheon Books, a division of Random House, Inc.

The illustrations that open each chapter have been reproduced with permission: for Chapter 1,
by permission of the Chicago Historical Society; for Chapters 2–5, by permission of the
Photographs and Prints Division, Schomburg Center for Research in Black Culture, The New
York Public Library, Astor, Lenox and Tilden Foundations.

for Elizabeth Cooper Davis,

the growing edge of her family and a source of hope for the large and small communities in which she moves

ACKNOWLEDGMENTS

• ⟺ •

Some readers of my account of the role and promise of families may suspect a bias resulting from fortunate family circumstances. They will not be wrong. My first and deepest thanks go to the Cooper and Davis families—to my parents, George and Margarett Cooper, who exemplify the best of family values (and whose genealogical research has informed my work); to my husband, Gordon Davis, who has perfected the trick of being both a constant source of support and a constant source of intellectual challenge; to Elizabeth Cooper Davis, who has learned her father's tricks; and to an inspiring extended family that has helped and taught me in more ways than I can say.

The New York University School of Law has nurtured this project for several years. Under the leadership of Norman Redlich and John Sexton, two brilliant, scholarly, and scholar-friendly deans, it has provided mind-stretching company, among whom I am especially grateful to Anthony Amsterdam, Jerome Bruner, Sarah Burns, Ronald Dworkin, Nancy Morawetz, and David Richards; research support (funded, in part, by the Filomen D'Agostino and Max E. Greenberg Research Fund); and a spirit of public responsibility and intellectual excitement.

I have been blessed with two superb editors: Arthur Rosenthal, who talked patiently and wisely with me through the early phases of this work, and Elisabeth Sifton, who lived with me inside the text and wrought magical improvements, both in my thinking and in my prose. I thank them both, and I thank Martin Segal for helping to bring us together.

Jean Carey Bond and Jean Strouse, each a friend and each a more experienced and much admired writer, were generous with advice and encouragement. Eric Foner was a patient and immensely helpful tutor in the management of historical material. El-Hajj Malik El-Shabazz is an uncited intellectual influence, for his characterization of the civil and social diminishment of his family by orders institutionalizing his mother and committing her children to state care awakened me to the relationship between family autonomy and antislavery.

The editors of the Cardozo, Harvard, Michigan, and Yale law reviews and the Harvard Civil Rights–Civil Liberties Law Review published earlier versions of some of what follows and provided, in the process, thought-provoking discussion and painstaking editorial work, as did student research assistants at New York University.

CONTENTS

• ⬌ •

NEGLECTED

STORIES

"Freedom's in the trying."

—*Wynton Marsalis*, Blood on the Fields

A PATH TO APPRECIATION
OF FAMILY RIGHTS

• ⟺ •

his is a book of stories. They are of two kinds.

    Some are stories that lawyers and judges have constructed to explain why the Fourteenth Amendment of the United States Constitution protects the independence and integrity of families. I shall call these Doctrinal Stories.

ABOVE: 1819 marriage bond of Elijah East, with permission from the bride's owner

Others are stories of enslaved families in the United States—families composed of people who were denied, in law and often in fact, the right to create and maintain ties of affection and responsibility to spouses, to children, to parents, or to extended kin. They could not marry; they had no legal tie to their parents; and they had no legal tie to the children born of their bodies. People who lived or were touched by the stories of enslaved families became deeply conscious of the enormity of these deprivations. They therefore developed a commitment to family freedom and, with their victory in the Civil War and the passage of the Thirteenth, Fourteenth, and Fifteenth amendments, made family freedom a constitutional right. Because they inspired this constitutional commitment, I shall call the stories of enslaved families Motivating Stories.

Both kinds of stories have been neglected, and in several senses. We are not long past the time when matters having to do with families and children were regarded as "women's stuff" and given only glancing attention in professional disciplines. Doctrinal Stories of family rights jurisprudence therefore warrant rearticulation and careful interpretation. Nonetheless, they are not unknown to constitutional scholars or considered unimportant, and they frequently figure in public political debate. The Motivating Stories have suffered greater neglect. They are stories of a subordinated people, and we are not long past the time when histories were stories only of the superordinate. In addition, the Motivating Stories figure in the drama of Reconstruction after the Civil War; the Thirteenth, Fourteenth, and Fifteenth amendments are expressive in important respects of Reconstruction's ideology of antislavery and universal civil freedom. For a variety of reasons having to do with majoritarian biases and interest politics, the period of Reconstruction was for many years shamelessly maligned by historians, its ideology demeaned, and its importance to the United States' political and constitutional history minimized. Nonetheless, in recent years, the Motivating Stories have been rescued from obscurity as historians of slavery, of the family, and of Reconstruction have exposed and corrected the revisionism of earlier accounts.[1]

This book does not, then, present new or unknown stories of constitutional doctrine, slavery, or Reconstruction. But it does do something unprecedented. Despite the urgency and clarity with which people involved in antislavery struggle and in Reconstruction politics spoke of family rights, the connections have never been drawn between the Motivating Stories and the meaning of the Fourteenth Amendment. The contribution of this book is to draw those connections. My argument is that family rights jurisprudence and the political discourse which it both reflects and shapes are enriched and clarified by Motivating Stories of slavery, antislavery, and Reconstruction.

THE DOCTRINAL STORIES

The Constitution of the United States does not contain the word "family." It makes no explicit mention of marriage, parenting, contraception, procreation, or abortion. People in the United States nonetheless invoke the Constitution when rights of family liberty and autonomy are threatened. When interracial couples were told that they could not marry, they appealed to the Supreme Court.[2] When the state of Oklahoma ordered a man sterilized for having committed the crime of embezzlement, he raised a constitutional claim.[3] When Nebraska and Oregon told parents that they could not have their children instructed in "foreign" tongues or in private schools, parents claimed that their constitutional rights of liberty and family autonomy had been trampled.[4] When Illinois removed children from a father's care without any showing that he had been neglectful, he claimed a constitutional right of family integrity.[5] When the dispensation of contraceptive devices and the performance of abortions were crimes, people protested the loss of a constitutional right to choose when and whether to bear or beget a child.[6] Legislated restrictions upon marriage, official seizures of children, and suppression of individual choice in child rearing and procreation have inspired outrage—a sense that if constitutional limitations are too feeble to protect against state control of family life, they are too feeble to reconcile fundamental liberty with the need for social order.[7] In most of these cases, the Supreme Court has read the Constitution as providing a measure of protection: working from the Fourteenth Amendment's assurance that life, liberty, and property cannot be taken without due process of law, it has elaborated a constitutional doctrine of family liberty. The doctrine recognizes a domain of personal and family life and holds that within this domain governmental interference with private choice must be specially justified.

All legal doctrines are stories, structured upon formal but ambiguous texts and nourished by history and culture. They owe their existence to collective recognition which comes as a result of their resonance with the culture and traditions of the people who announce and live by their terms.[8] Doctrinal stories inevitably reflect perspective. They take *selectively* from history and culture. This is only natural. History and culture cannot be captured in all their richness and complexity. It is necessary to summarize. It is necessary to put some things in the foreground, to put some in the background, and to ignore others.[9] It follows that when judges draw upon history or culture, they necessarily draw upon partial accounts, accounts that accentuate certain historical or cultural forces and minimize or ignore others. The Supreme Court's doctrine of family liberty is no exception.

The Court's story of family liberty has thus far been written from a perspective that obscures important evidence that a range of "freedom of personal choice in matters of marriage and family life"[10] is fundamental to American constitutional democracy. It is therefore undeveloped and unconvincing. It does not teach as well as it might why the Constitution, read in the context of the forces that produced it, protects the right of families to function with a significant measure of autonomy. Perhaps for this reason the Court's doctrine of family liberty has been criticized persistently.

Dissenting members of the Supreme Court and critics of the Court have assailed the doctrine of family autonomy as an illegitimate construction, unjustified by reference to the constitutional text or to United States history and traditions. Felix Frankfurter, before he became a member of the Court, condemned the first of the Court's decisions to protect parental autonomy, arguing that although they overturned legislation born of intolerance, they represented an interference, unjustified by the terms of the Constitution, with initiatives undertaken by elected representatives of the people.[11] When Frankfurter subsequently became a member of the Court, he continued to urge that state interferences with family liberty were constitutional so long as "legislators could in reason have enacted [them]."[12] Justice Hugo Black resisted every attempt to infer a right of family liberty from the language and history of the Constitution. The thinking that led to constitutional protection of family rights was, in his view, a manifestation of "natural law due process philosophy,"[13] which, for Black, was an unacceptable basis for constitutional decision making and served only to mask the whims and predilections of Justices seeking to invalidate laws with which they disagreed.

Lawyers in the academy have had similar reservations about the legitimacy of family rights doctrine. Robert Bork compared the right of a married couple to use contraception to the right of a utility company to emit pollutants and found them of "identical" constitutional weight. In his view, the Constitution provides no principled basis for preferring the claims of those who seek to control pollution over the claims of those who would pollute—or the claims of those who seek to control the use of contraception over the claims of those married couples who would practice contraception. These matters must be left for legislative judgment; "the judiciary has no role to play," and the Constitution is irrelevant.[14]

The extraordinary public and congressional debates that culminated in Professor Bork's rejection for appointment to the Supreme Court were part of a process that may, over time, result in political ratification of the long-standing Supreme Court practice of recognizing and enforcing (albeit somewhat sporadically) individual and family liberties to which Bork thought the Constitution irrelevant.[15] A powerful centrist block of the Court strongly reaffirmed the practice in 1992 when it declared, in the case of Planned Parenthood v. Casey, that "marriage, procreation, contraception, family relationships, child rearing, and education . . . involv[e] . . . choices central to personal dignity and autonomy, [and] are central to the liberty protected by the Fourteenth Amendment."[16] But Casey's reaffirmation of the doctrine of family liberty evoked bitter dissents from two Justices, and the debate continues, both on and off the Court.

Communitarian thinkers have rejected the doctrine of family autonomy on the ground that it valorizes an individualism that precludes healthy social exchange. Michael Sandel, to take a noted example, offers a philosopher's review of family rights jurisprudence and concludes that it is grounded in nothing more profound than the idea that individual selves should be "unencumbered." He therefore concludes that the doctrine of family liberty is both morally empty and inconsistent with the United States' political traditions.[17]

Feminist scholars have had special cause to resist family rights doctrine, for it had its origins in a male-centered ideology that asserts, vis-à-vis the state, the primacy of the claims of male heads of households to act as they please with respect to wives and children, whom the law first conceptualized as men's property. Feminists call attention to abuse and exploitation of women and children and argue that support of rights-based doctrines of liberty and privacy amounts to complicity in private systems of abuse. They have therefore been motivated to rethink the right of abortion choice as a matter of equal opportunity rather than family liberty[18] and to call for collectivist and protectionist strategies of family governance.[19] Seeing government as responsible for protecting the welfare of subordinated or otherwise vulnerable people and guarding against private as well as public tyrannies, many feminist scholars have joined ranks with communitarian thinkers to de-emphasize rights-based jurisprudence and public-private dichotomies.[20] They are concerned more with government's duty of care and less with the individual's right "to be let alone."[21]

Even as controversy over family rights has escalated, the contending sides have agreed on certain basic principles for understanding how the Constitution speaks to the question. Every member of the Court, and most analysts of the Court, agree that the Constitution's failure to mention family rights explicitly does not end the matter and that the Constitution's broader protections of civil liberty properly encompass at least some measure of family liberty. Supreme Court Justices and scholars across the ideological spectrum seem also to agree that history and tradition should inform interpretation of the Constitution's general guarantees of civil liberty.

But what do history and tradition teach about rights of family? Is Michael Sandel correct when he argues that recognition of rights of family autonomy is a breach of United States' political traditions? John Hart Ely, perhaps the most respected opponent of family rights doctrine, once said that the doctrine is not only unmentioned in the

constitutional text but "not inferable from the language of the Constitution, the Framers' thinking . . . , or the nation's governmental
structure."[22] When Professor Ely made that claim, he conceded that
someday a theory might link individual and family liberty to the
thinking of the Framers or the structure of our government.

This book takes Ely's concession as a challenge. It draws upon the
history that produced the Fourteenth Amendment—upon Motivating
Stories—to demonstrate that those who sponsored and shaped that
amendment understood rights of family as aspects of liberty, fundamental to proper definitions of freedom and citizenship and necessary
to the governmental structure envisioned for a reconstructed Union.
These lessons of history establish the constitutional legitimacy of family rights doctrine and suggest its proper limitations. They also provide
a helpful frame of reference for social and political discourse about
liberty, autonomy, and family values.

THE MOTIVATING STORIES

For much of our history, rights of family were simply assumed; there
were few occasions to debate them or to seek to have them enforced.
The idea that family rights are aspects of national citizenship was,
however, unambiguously asserted in the aftermath of the Civil War.
Like so many great ideals of the United States' political system, the
ideal of family liberty was refined and deepened by the struggle against
slavery and caste oppression.[23] Professor Akhil Reed Amar has
pointed out that "Slave Power posed a threat to Freedom—of all
kinds." He establishes, for example, that the realization that slavery
"could support itself only through suppression of opposition speech"
led abolitionists to conclude that "freedom of speech for all men and
women went hand in hand with freedom of bodily liberty for slaves."[24]
Slavery also—and more fundamentally—required that men, women,
and children be bound more surely by ties of ownership than by ties
of kinship. Slave Power supported itself by annulment of marital, parental, and paternal rights. Drafters and advocates of the Fourteenth
Amendment had vivid impressions of what it meant to be denied family rights, for that denial was a hallmark of slavery in the United

States. The people who struggled for abolition and reconstruction regarded denial of family liberty as a vice of slavery that inverted concepts of human dignity, citizenship, and natural law. And they regarded the Fourteenth Amendment as an instrument to reenshrine family rights as inalienable aspects of national citizenship and natural law. Their stories must be told because they illuminate the meaning of constitutional liberty.

NEGLECTED STORIES AND PUBLIC POLITICAL DISCOURSE

These stories are relevant beyond the realm of constitutional adjudication. They are also relevant to the public discourse by which we define ourselves as a social and political community and negotiate the meaning of family values. Doctrinal Stories contained in the opinions of our courts, and the Motivating Stories that shape and support them, influence—and are influenced by—the ways in which we negotiate our civic and social identities.

The United States is now embroiled—as it often has been—in struggle between those who valorize individual autonomy and those who valorize community. An ethic of self-reliance and competitive excellence is set against an ethic of care and connectedness. This ethical divide sets the pattern for political discourse: Some of us believe that social welfare programs undermine self-reliance and dampen initiative, others that they nurture potential and lay circuits of civic responsibility; some of us believe that taxation for public works saps earned wealth, others that it is an expression of community and civic pride; some of us want the public sector lean and unintrusive, others want it generous in its protection and support. Family matters are central and telling features of public discourse that swirls around these ideas of autonomy and of community. The family sits strategically between government and the individual. It is thought to have a duty and a special ability to socialize and govern the young. It is also thought to be a uniquely good site for the development and perpetuation of values. Many of us believe that the cure for a multitude of social ills is to strengthen families and family values. But ideological stances shift interestingly when we speak of the family.

We disagree in surprising ways about how family values should be strengthened. Those of us who are inclined to oppose government interventions find ourselves arguing that government should promote, and at times enforce, the "family" values of a perceived majority. Those of us who are inclined to favor government interventions in response to social ills find ourselves arguing that *family* values cannot be imposed—that in a democratic society the function of value formation must be served by families who are at liberty to make their own important value choices. Some of us believe that government intervention in family life has weakened family values—yet find ourselves sympathetic to the idea of state involvement in particular activities like family planning or setting adolescent curfews. Some of us believe that government support is needed if families are to be strong enough to nurture positive values and healthy citizens—yet worry that government support facilitates excessive regulation of family life. Many of us waver among these positions as discussion shifts from abortion and contraception to juvenile crime, to school prayers, to teen pregnancy, to school instruction in sexual hygiene, to child abuse prevention, to school instruction in languages other than English. From one side of the political spectrum, opposition to the idea of family liberty intensifies when it is used to urge tolerance or acceptance of practices that some members of the political community believe immoral, like abortion and homosexual expression. From the other side of the political spectrum, opposition to the idea of family liberty intensifies when it is used to urge restraint in initiatives to educate children in our public schools against the risks of sexually transmitted diseases or to teach principles of tolerance. Whether or not we identify as liberals, we find it hard to be consistently libertarian; whether or not we identify as conservatives, we find that we are conflicted about authoritarian measures. We lack a theoretical framework—a story of the relationships among individuals, families, and the state—that makes sense of our conflicting beliefs about families and family values.

The Supreme Court has read the Fourteenth Amendment and the

Bill of Rights as embodying the competing principles of self-reliance and community that enliven and complicate our public discourse. The Court has found in those provisions a right to be left alone—rugged and individual—but it has also found in them requirements that government avoid systematic subordination, and authority for government to restrict liberty in the name of equity and social welfare. As we shall see, principles both of self-reliance and of community have influenced family rights jurisprudence, which, in turn, has influenced public discourse.

Tension between the principles of self-reliance and mutual care is inevitable, in both civil discourse and constitutional theory. It makes no sense to declare one of these principles victorious. No culture can survive if its people are excessively dependent or controlled; but no culture can survive without systems of mutual protection and support. The best we can do is to develop a sense of history, tradition, and public principles that will inform our efforts to mediate the need for autonomy and the need for community. In other words, we must strive for a deeper understanding of why we prize liberty, why we prize community, and what relationship they should have to each other. That understanding, I will argue, can be found in stories that feature families—families that are, like the trunks of a banyan tree, both independent and connected.

These stories of family bring to constitutional and public discourse the perspectives of those who struggled, in what they regarded as furtherance of the ideals of the Declaration of Independence, to produce the Fourteenth Amendment's charter of national citizenship. The voices in that struggle were heard both within and beyond the halls of Congress. The voices heard outside the halls of Congress came from every sector of our society. They are exemplified by Henry Bibb, an American slave who wrote in 1850: "I presume there are no class of people in the United States who so highly appreciate the legality of marriage as those persons who have been held and treated as property."[25] So, too, for appreciation of the rights to marry, to establish a home, and to create and maintain a family—in a context of community support, but in liberty measured with respect for autonomous human expression.

HOW THE STORIES WILL BE TOLD

Themes in Several Voices

The first four chapters of this book are framed around the Doctrinal Stories that the Supreme Court has told to justify or to strike down restrictions upon liberty with respect to work, marriage, parenting, and procreation. The Doctrinal Story of work grounds my analysis in an examination of the constitutional legitimacy, after Reconstruction, of the most basic and obvious of slavery's deprivations—the right to choose one's work and to pursue it in the marketplace. It also sets out the terms within which the Supreme Court first read the constitutional provisions that abolished slavery and defined freedom for the reunited states. Defining moments in family rights jurisprudence are described as the unfolding, case by case, of Doctrinal Stories told in response to claims of right from litigants seeking to live, to work, to marry, to love, and to parent as they chose. The Fourteenth Amendment serves both as justification for the litigants' claims and as the primary text from which the Doctrinal Stories are drawn.

I have juxtaposed these Doctrinal Stories with Motivating Stories told and lived by those whose struggles produced the Fourteenth Amendment. They are not offered to answer the unanswerable question of "original intent" that has so bedeviled constitutional scholarship, and they do not settle the unsettleable question of how the scope of the Fourteenth Amendment's guarantees was originally imagined. But they do place the amendment in a context of social struggle, and they do reflect the values and aspirations of those who inspired the Fourteenth Amendment's conception and won its promulgation. Hence they are appropriate, albeit neglected, guides to an interpretation that is faithful to history and to tradition.

The Supreme Court and the nation continue to face, and worry over, questions about the range of liberty that people should enjoy with respect to family matters and about the scope of the Court's authority to protect that liberty. These questions may be resolved by repudiating the doctrine of family autonomy, leaving the family subject to any government regulation for which a rational justification, and a legislative majority, can be found. But there is an alternative to repudiation. The questions may also be resolved by new doctrinal and political formulations—formulations that carry more satisfying assurances that the People are wise, and the Court is justified, in defending a substantial measure of family liberty. The final part of this book searches the Motivating Stories for themes from which these new and more satisfying judicial and political stories might be woven.

CHICAGO LEGAL NEWS.

Lex vincit.

MYRA BRADWELL, Editor.

Published EVERY SATURDAY by the
CHICAGO LEGAL NEWS COMPANY
NO. 87 CLARK STREET.

TERMS:

TWO DOLLARS AND TWENTY CENTS per annum, in
advance. Single Copies, TEN CENTS.

CHICAGO, SEPTEMBER 10, 1887.

☞ The Chicago Legal News Office
has been removed to No. 87 CLARK St.,
directly opposite the court house.

Illinois Laws Passed in 1887.

All the laws passed by the Legislature
at its recent session, may be had at the
CHICAGO LEGAL NEWS office, in law sheep
for $2.00; in pamphlet for $1.50.

1

"A WIDE FIELD FOR AMBITION"

● ⬅═══➡ ●

Stories about Work

In preparation for our exploration of the antislavery origins of personal and family autonomy rights, we must consider briefly the
effect the Civil War Amendments had upon the right that is most
conspicuously extinguished by enslavement: the right to control one's
labor. This is necessary for two reasons: First, since Fourteenth Amend-

ABOVE: Masthead of the *Chicago Legal News*, published by Myra Blackwell

ment doctrine was profoundly influenced by early Supreme Court cases concerning the right to work, understanding those cases is necessary to understanding how the Fourteenth Amendment shapes any category of civil rights, including family rights. Second, neglected stories about the right to work are closely related to, and provide an illuminating context for considering, the rights of family that are the central focus of this book.

AT THE DOOR OF AN "HONORABLE PROFESSION"

A Doctrinal Story about the Absence of a Right

In 1872, Myra Bradwell, an aspiring attorney, was denied admission to the bar of the state of Illinois. The reason given for the denial was that Myra Bradwell was a woman, and the state of Illinois regarded law as a man's profession. She took the matter to the Supreme Court of the United States, arguing that inasmuch as she was fully qualified to practice law, her right to do so was a privilege of United States citizenship protected by the Fourteenth Amendment, which, she said, "open[ed] to every citizen of the United States, male or female, black or white, married or single, the honorable professions as well as the servile employments of life."[1] She was relying on the second sentence of Section 1 of the amendment: "No State shall make or enforce any law which shall abridge the privileges or immunities of citizens of the United States; nor shall any State deprive any person of life, liberty, or property, without due process of law; nor deny to any person within its jurisdiction the equal protection of the laws." A majority of the Justices dismissed Bradwell's claim without much discussion. This was understandable, not only because the Justices agreed with their professional brothers in Illinois that only men should have the privilege of practicing law, but also because, just days before, the same majority had ruled, in *The Slaughter-House Cases*, that the Fourteenth Amendment affords no protection against state infringement of the right to pursue a lawful occupation.

The *Slaughter-House* plaintiffs had objected to the establishment of a government-sponsored facility as the only legally authorized site in or around New Orleans for the slaughter of cattle. Claiming that the New Orleans slaughterhouse monopoly was a bargain struck between corrupt Louisiana Reconstruction legislators and a favored set of butchers, they had argued that it unconstitutionally denied them the right to practice their profession.* From the state's perspective, the slaughterhouse monopoly was a successful public health and economic development initiative (begun by the Union general Benjamin Franklin Butler and continued by Reconstruction's multiracial Louisiana political coalition) that ended annual yellow fever epidemics caused by unregulated dumping of slaughterhouse waste, revitalized the local economy, and provided unrestricted access and the basis of viable employment for large numbers of people. On this view it was disadvantageous only to the large wholesale butchers who, in an effort to continue their domination of the industry, became the plaintiffs in *The Slaughter-House Cases*.

The Court gave victory to the state, but it did so on grounds that made it unnecessary for the justices to consider the justifications for centralizing slaughterhouse activity in the Mississippi Delta. Given the public benefits the government-run slaughtering facility promised, the Court might easily have decided that Louisiana had acted appropriately, restricting the liberty of the plaintiffs in relatively insignificant ways in order to advance compelling state interests.† Instead, it denied that the Fourteenth Amendment protected the right to work. The Doctrinal

---

*For many years the conventional wisdom among legal scholars was that the plaintiffs' claim of corruption was justified. Thanks to the nuanced scholarship of Herbert Hovenkamp, among others, we now see that the conventional wisdom of the past was one of the unfortunate consequences of an unjustifiably negative interpretation of Reconstruction generated by Columbia University historian William A. Dunning and his protégés and influenced by what Hovenkamp characterizes as racist reactions to Reconstruction's unprecedented and subsequently unrivaled display of black political power (a power that was most successfully exercised in Louisiana, making it a prime target of criticism). Public control of New Orleans's slaughtering facilities has not been associated by reliable evidence with official corruption. To the contrary, it was, in Hovenkamp's view, "a work of great genius." Herbert Hovenkamp, *Enterprise and American Law: 1836–1937*, 116–124 (1991).

†The public health rationales for the measure should, standing alone, have been sufficient to justify it. New Orleans had suffered yellow fever epidemics in every year between 1812 and 1861, in each of which more than 1,000 people died; as many as 9,000 may have died in 1853. After 1863, when Butler centralized butchering facilities, "only one or two cases of yellow fever were reported annually." *Hovenkamp* at 119.

Story focused on the words "privileges and immunities of citizens" and decided that they referred only to rights uniquely associated with *federal* citizenship. It went like this: The power to define and to guarantee individual civil liberties, such as the liberty to pursue a chosen calling, is a power of state governments. When the colonies united, they did so with the understanding that their independence and powers would be preserved in the new federal system. Recognition of federal authority to challenge state action in the name of individual liberty would "radically [change] the whole theory of the relations of the state and Federal Governments to each other and of both these governments to the people." True, the Civil War and the Reconstruction Amendments somewhat altered the balance of federal and state power, but it is inconceivable that the Reconstruction Congress intended the radical step of conferring upon the federal government authority to challenge, in the name of a right to work or of any other civil liberty, actions of a "sovereign" state, except where those actions affected a right essential to *national* citizenship, like the right to petition the federal government.[2]*

"AND MY DADDY SAY NO"

Motivating Stories of Struggle for the Right to Work

The Doctrinal Story told in *The Slaughter-House Cases* would have been a disappointing surprise to the man, known to us only as Henry, whose life after the Civil War was described in these words by his son:

---

*This Doctrinal Story related to the claim that the right to pursue a calling was a privilege of citizenship guaranteed by the Privileges and Immunities Clause of the Fourteenth Amendment. It was upon this claim that Bradwell relied. The *Slaughter-House* plaintiffs also relied on the amendment's due process and equal protection guarantees. With respect to the claim that the *Slaughter-House* plaintiffs were deprived of life, liberty, or property without due process of law, the Court simply said that exclusion from a calling did not constitute a deprivation of property. With respect to the equal protection guarantee, the Court said that the provision was designed to be applied only (or almost only) against racial distinctions. As we shall see, the narrow construction given to the Privileges and Immunities Clause in *Slaughter-House* subsequently caused the Court to attach to the Due Process and Equal Protection clauses meaning that may have been more easily carried by the Privileges and Immunities Clause.

After the War ended and Tom Williams had come home, he called everybody together and tell them they was free, but that he want to hire them till Christmas—that was in May—to help lay the crop by. He said he'd pay good wages, too. Everybody stayed, but the next spring my daddy say he gonna leave.

Now, I guess he was one of the biggest niggers anywhere around, and he was right smart, too. He could run a gin, and was a right pert carpenter.

Tom Williams wanted him to stay, but my daddy didn't have much use for him, and so he say he gonna leave, anyhow. Then, Tom Williams got mad, and grabbed my daddy's hands, and tied them over his head to a branch on a oak tree, and holler to me, "By the Lord God who made Moses, go get my whip, you Frank!" He took the whip, what was made outen a gin belt, and lashed my daddy till the blood come. He say, "Now you change your mind and give up?" And my daddy say no.

He left him there three or four days, but all the time he made me stay with him and bring him water and bread. Then, he thought he might die, so he say, "Henry, I's gonna let you down and give you a nice soft bed on the porch, till you makes up your mind." But before he unties his hands, he put a chain on his legs.

Then, he carries him over to the porch and chains him to one of the posts. He say, "Henry, I'm gonna let you have one of Mrs. Martha's soft beds, and I'm gonna feed you fried chicken. Now, is you gonna stay?" He kept him there for about a week, but my daddy never did say he would stay.

So, finally, Tom Williams go out and tell everybody for miles around that my daddy is a bad nigger and that he wouldn't work, and for none of them to hire him. Then, he come home and tell Daddy what he done, and turn him loose, and say, "Now go get a job, iffing you can." He thought all the time my daddy would have to come back to him, so's his family wouldn't starve to death.

We set out and come to Aberdeen, and all of us worked hard at first one thing and then another. I was a houseboy in two or three places, and my daddy worked a little farm and

made horse collars to sell. We finally saved up enough to buy
that little farm.[3]*

The man called Henry—the former slave who said "no" to subordination and de facto reenslavement—embodies a version of the
right-to-work ideology of antislavery and Reconstruction. Antislavery
advocates and Reconstruction legislators who struggled to secure, in
the Fourteenth Amendment, a national charter of citizen rights worked
from the premise that each person must have the freedom to work as
s/he chose. They began with acknowledgment of the stark realities of
slavery. Frederick Douglass, the abolitionist activist who spoke of
bondage in the United States with unexcelled authority and effect,
described those realities as follows:

> I will state, as well as I can, the legal and social relation of
> master and slave. A master is one . . . who claims and exercises
> a right of property in the person of a fellow man. . . . The slave
> is a human being, divested of all rights—reduced to the level
> of a brute—a mere "chattel" in the eye of the law. . . . He can
> own nothing, possess nothing, acquire nothing, but what must
> belong to another. To eat the fruit of his own toil, to clothe
> his person with the work of his own hands, is considered steal-
> ing. He toils that another may reap the fruit; he is industrious
> that another may live in idleness . . . and to this condition he
> is bound down as by an arm of iron.[4]

Working from this understanding of slavery, antislavery advocates argued that people in the United States should be free to own, possess,
and acquire what they might by the work of their hands and the fruit
of their toil.

The rhetoric of abolition had consistently defined the right to

---

*This passage has been "translated" from a phonetic representation intended to re-
produce the accent of the speaker, a survivor of slavery interviewed in the 1930s as
part of a WPA writers' project. I shall continue the practice of "translating" these
phonetic reproductions of African-American speech whenever I cite such sources. This
is appropriate to avoid exacerbating the marginalization that is both expressed and
furthered by selective uses of phonetic reproductions of accented English.

work for oneself to preclude limitations based upon caste. Abolitionists understood human fulfillment to require "a wide field of employment for . . . ambition, and learning and abilities."[5] Driven to
disprove the myth of racial inferiority that supported black slavery,
and influenced, no doubt, by the peculiar American delusion of universal upward mobility, black abolitionists were most explicit in insisting on liberty in the choice of callings. They thought the pursuit
of happiness and respect would be impossible "in a land where the
laws and prejudices of society [had the effect of] retarding . . . advancement to the summit of civil and religious improvement." They
sought "the opportunity to reap the reward due to industry and per-
severance,"[6] and they insisted upon "the right to engage in any legitimate business" as part of the right to be "recognized as *men*" with
"no obstructions placed in our way."[7]

In 1865, legislators in Congress echoed this antislavery rhetoric
and—in language that seems to anticipate challenges of the sort posed
by the Doctrinal Story in *The Slaughter-House Cases*—expressed confidence that the federal union had power to gird the right to work with
the force of law. One senator put it this way:

> [O]ur powers are full, ample, complete, to bring back . . . [the
> rebel] States, and restore them, and preserve, also, the rights
> and liberties there of all that breathe God's air. I do not want
> to degrade a single man in the rebel States. [But] I do not want
> them to degrade others, and I do not mean that they shall do
> it. . . .
>
> [W]e must see to it that the man made free by the Consti-
> tution of the United States, sanctioned by the voice of the
> American people, is a freeman indeed; that he can go where he
> pleases, work when and for whom he pleases; that he can sue
> and be sued; that he can lease and buy and sell and own prop-
> erty, real and personal; that he can go into the schools and
> educate himself and his children; that the rights and guarantees
> of the good old common law are his, and that he walks the
> earth, proud and erect in the conscious dignity of a free man,
> who knows that his cabin, however humble, is protected by the
> just and equal laws of his country.[8]

REASON, JUSTICE, AND THE
SOCIAL COMPACT

A Competing Doctrinal Story about the Rights of Men

When a majority of the Supreme Court decided, in *The Slaughter-House Cases*, that the states were not bound by federal law to respect a citizen's right to work, four Justices dissented, arguing that the Reconstruction Congress had considered and forthrightly taken the admittedly radical step of establishing federal power to guarantee basic civil rights. One of these, Justice Swayne, told the story of the Civil War and Reconstruction this way: "These Amendments are all consequences of the late civil war. The prejudices and apprehension as to the central government which prevailed when the Constitution was adopted were dispelled by the light of experience. The public mind became satisfied that there was less danger of tyranny in the head than of anarchy and tyranny in the members. It is objected," he continued, "that the power conferred [by the Fourteenth Amendment] is novel and large. The answer is that the novelty was known and the measure deliberately adopted" in order to guarantee to every person within the jurisdiction of the United States "rights and privileges . . . which, according to the plainest considerations of reason and justice and the fundamental principles of the social compact, all are entitled to enjoy."[9] Another of the dissenters, Justice Field, expressed views about marketplace liberty that were so strong as to preclude labor regulations on the ground that they violated workers' freedom to agree to substandard conditions.[10]

Three of the Justices who dissented in *The Slaughter-House Cases* had a difficult time with Myra Bradwell's claim of a right to work in her chosen profession. They did not want to deny that the Fourteenth Amendment protected the right to engage in a lawful occupation, yet they could not envision the right as encompassing a *woman's* choice to enter what they regarded as a distinctly manly profession. As we have seen, the appeal for universal civil rights had been expressed as a right to be "recognized as *men*." Justice Bradley, joined by Justices Swayne and Field, was true to this rhetoric in his opinion concurring in the denial of Bradwell's claim. The right to work existed, he said, but his words made clear that he imagined it only as a right of men;

when it was imagined as a right of women, justifications for overriding
it leapt to mind:

> The Constitution of the Family organization, which is founded
> in the divine ordinance, as well as in the nature of things, in-
> dicates the domestic sphere as that which properly belongs to
> the domain and functions of woman-hood. The harmony . . . of
> interests and views which belong . . . to the Family institution
> is repugnant to the idea of a woman adopting a distinct and
> independent career from that of her husband.[11]

Only Chief Justice Chase dissented from the Court's ruling that the
state of Illinois could exclude Myra Bradwell from the bar.

Bradwell went on to become publisher of the *Chicago Legal News*,
a remarkably successful weekly that was an officially recognized source
for, among other things, newly enacted statutes. In 1890 the Illinois
Supreme Court reversed itself and made her a member of the bar.

"I RISE BECAUSE I AM NOT A SLAVE"

Motivating Stories of Women and Work

As abolitionists struggled in the mid-nineteenth century for the emancipation of enslaved people, the subordination of women was reinforced by the ideology of "True Womanhood." Prototypical United
States residents no longer centered their work lives on farming or other
home-based production. Work sites were increasingly independent of
the homestead, and the True Woman came to be seen as the guardian
of the hearth, of the family, and of a refined moral sensibility that
might not (or, perhaps, could not) survive in the worlds of politics and
work. The True Woman could not be self-reliant or poor, for need
might drive a self-reliant or poor woman to the workplace. She could
have no public political voice. She was not to be heard, or even found,
in the public or commercial sphere. This ideology undoubtedly reinforced Justice Bradley's commitment to the notion of separate spheres
of masculine and feminine functioning.

There is no simple answer to the question whether the ideology of

True Womanhood was (or was once thought to be) consistent with the goals and ideals of those who inspired, conceptualized, and won the civil rights guarantees of the Fourteenth Amendment. In a society under the sway of the vision of True Womanhood, abolitionists seemed at times to struggle as bitterly to define women's place in the movement as they did to end slavery. Some of them accepted the vision of True Womanhood: responding in 1840 to efforts to include women in the deliberations of the Connecticut Anti-Slavery Society, the chair shouted, "NEVER! I will not sit in a meeting where the sorcery of a woman's tongue is thrown around my heart. I will not submit to PET-TICOAT GOVERNMENT. No woman shall ever lord it over me. *I am Major-Domo in my own house.*"[12] Black abolitionists who embraced the cult of True Womanhood expressed a somewhat different motivation. They seemed to want to relieve black women of the drudgery of manual labor outside their homes and "elevate" them. At the same time, they believed that true, or respected, *manhood* consisted in providing means to protect women from the pressures and vicissitudes of labor and public life. Martin Delany announced in 1855, "Until colored men attain to a position above permitting their mothers, sisters, wives and daughters to do the drudgery of . . . other men's wives and daughters, it is useless, it is nonsense . . . to talk about equality and elevation in society."[13]

Other abolitionists thought the cult of True Womanhood a version of enslavement. Abby Kelley, the extraordinarily successful abolitionist who was the principal irritant at that 1840 meeting of the Connecticut Anti-Slavery Society, earlier that year had defended her right to participate in the deliberations of the American Anti-Slavery Society. Noting that the slave had no voice in Congress, she announced, "I rise because I am not a slave."[14] Some abolitionists worried that progressive women taking a public role in the movement would divide it and narrow its appeal. Frederick Douglass, a staunch supporter of women's rights, nonetheless looked back regretfully on the deep rift caused in the antislavery movement by Abby Kelley: "How beautiful would it have been for that woman, how nobly would her name have come down to us in history, had she said: 'All things are lawful for me, but all are not expedient! While I see no objection to my occupying a place on your committee, I can for the slave's sake forego the privilege.' The battle of Woman's Rights should be fought on its own ground; the slave's cause [is] already too heavily laden."[15] Over years of struggle, most abolitionists learned, however, to accept that women were indispensable and capable champions of freedom. With talents ranging from the shrewd eloquence of Sojourner Truth to the bottomless courage of Harriet Tubman, to the tireless passion and moral clarity of Abby Kelley, to the cold diplomacy of Maria Chapman, to the poetic appeal and analytic focus of Frances Watkins Harper, women raised funds, directed strategy, and stirred consciences to keep the abolitionist movement alive.

From the perspective of the dissenting Justices in the *Bradwell* case, the cult of True Womanhood had survived abolition, civil war, and constitutional change. The Fifteenth Amendment, after all, comported with tradition in granting suffrage regardless of color but only to men. Why should the Fourteenth Amendment be read differently? But from the perspective of women at the vanguard of the antislavery movement, the activism and success of female abolitionists had delegitimated Victorian myths that confined women to the domestic sphere. As Abby Kelley put it in 1851: "[M]y life has been my speech. For fourteen years I have advocated this cause [of women's rights] in my daily life. Bloody feet, sisters, have worn smooth the path by which you have come hither."[16]

Some abolitionists challenged the cult of True Womanhood directly. Abby Kelley argued that women had both the right and the duty to labor in the political and commercial spheres and harshly criticized those who sat "like dolls in the parlor" or worked "for a pittance" when they knew they were "fitted for something better."[17] Henry Blackwell wrote in 1853 to Lucy Stone, his companion in abolitionist and women's rights struggles (and later his wife), to protest against the possibility that an able woman would "stay at home to rock the baby when she ought to be off addressing a meeting or organizing a society."[18] Inspired by the example of his sister, the first woman in the United States to qualify as a physician, [19] Blackwell carefully investigated the possibility that a woman might practice law in the Ohio community where he lived, concluded that "the *study* of law would be a most admirable & desirable one for women—the admission to the Bar a feasible thing & the *practice* of law a *possible* one," and offered to assist if Stone wanted to study law in his state.[20] Sojourner Truth's challenge of the cult of True Womanhood expanded the frame of feminist political rhetoric to include women for whom sitting "like dolls in the parlor" was never an option. As another former slave once put it, black women on plantations "worked, in a manner of speaking, from can to can't, from the time they could see until the time they couldn't."[21] The sensibility of these women was expressed by Truth when she spoke at an 1851 women's rights convention and presented her famous juxtaposition of the image of the True Woman and the image of her own life as a slave:

> That man over there says women need to be helped into carriages and lifted over ditches, and to have the best place everywhere. Nobody ever helps me into carriages, or over mud-puddles, or gives me any best place! And ain't I a woman? Look at me! Look at my arm! I have ploughed, and planted, and gathered into barns, and no man could head me! And ain't I a woman? I could work as much and eat as much as a man—when I could get it—and bear the lash as well! And ain't I a woman?[22]

This was not, of course, a plea to be placed among the ranks of True Women. As Truth later said more clearly, her goal was not a release from work but equal pay for equal work: "[W]e do as much, we eat as much, we want as much."[23]

Women's rights advocates gathered in Worcester, Massachusetts, in 1850 asserted their right to enter "manly" professions and called for an extension of that right to enslaved women:

> Abby Price . . . talked of the injustice of excluding women from trades and professions, followed by Dr. Harriet Hunt, who spoke on medical education for women and read letters of rejection she had received from Harvard Medical School. After Sojourner Truth spoke, the gathering unanimously passed a resolution stating that slave women were "the most grossly wronged of all" and called on convention delegates to raise "the

trampled womanhood of the plantation to a share in the rights we call for ourselves."[24]

From the perspective of the antislavery feminist, slavery was a violation of rights to which all human beings are entitled; a human entitlement to basic, natural rights was the ideological link between the antislavery struggle and the struggle to extend civil rights—including the right to work as one wished—to women. American women embraced this underlying human rights commitment in abolitionism and then refashioned it to do the work of women's liberation.[25]

The Supreme Court has traveled a great distance since the *Slaughter-House* and *Bradwell* cases, and it has fully recognized the intention of the Reconstruction Congress to protect civil rights against state infringement.[26] A state that denied a right to practice law on no better basis than citation of the applicant's gender would have no defense under a contemporary understanding of the Fourteenth Amendment's Equal Protection Clause. It is also likely that its action would be deemed a denial of due process for its arbitrary deprivation of both liberty and property. Nevertheless, the Court's stories about the right to work expose a continuing difficulty. As we shall see, the abolitionist sensibility that informed the Fourteenth Amendment has been largely overlooked even as the Court has recognized rights the amendment was designed to protect, and there is much to be said for renewing our appreciation of that sensibility as we continue to interpret Reconstruction's promise of civil freedom. Yet, to interpret the Fourteenth Amendment in terms of the sensibilities of its proponents is to court the danger of also incorporating Victorian patriarchal assumptions into a jurisprudence addressed to protecting fundamental rights. Our review of history and doctrine continues, then, with sensitivity to the lessons of abolitionist stories matched with wariness of contradictions tolerated as a human rights agenda was advanced in a hierarchical social context.

2

"A THING OF COMMON RIGHT"

• ⇐══⇒ •

Stories about Marriage

We now turn from judicial and antislavery stories about the right
to work to begin our study of rights of family. Stories about
marriage serve well to introduce basic themes of human will and governance that must be addressed in any thoughtful analysis of the family
and its place in a social and political order. The right to marry has a

---

ABOVE: African-American Union soldiers greeting their loved ones

special place both in family rights doctrine and in the history of antislavery thought. In the courts, it was recognized earlier, more straightforwardly, and more confidently than any other family right, although this recognition required the Court to think closely and carefully about fundamental matters of democratic theory. Indeed, it was in cases concerning the right to marry that the Supreme Court first struggled with one of democracy's greatest dilemmas: how to reconcile government's legitimate interest in safeguarding public welfare with a democratic people's interest in personal and family liberty. In antislavery struggle, arguments about the right to marry were central to the critique of legalized bondage. And marriage—together with desertion of the plantation system and armed struggle against Confederate slaveholders—was the most dramatic and powerful means by which former slaves laid claim to citizenship.

WILLIAM MOWRY AND "THE DAUGHTER OF THE INDIAN PERO"

A Doctrinal Story of Common Right

In 1877, the Supreme Court faced its first matter of family law in a case that directly concerned title to certain real estate in and around Pittsburgh. The right to possess this land turned on the validity of a marriage between one William Mowry and a woman referred to by the Court as "the daughter of the Indian Pero,"[1] but otherwise known as Mary Mowry. The Mowrys lived as husband and wife for seven or eight years before William's death; they had one child, a daughter named Elizabeth. One contestant in the suit said he had acquired the land from Mary and Elizabeth Mowry after William died without a will; the other claimed to have gotten it from William's mother. The trial court ruled the marriage invalid because it had not been performed by a magistrate or a member of the clergy, as state law required. This ruling was odd, for common law precedents clearly pointed the way to validating the union, either by treating it as a common law marriage or by excusing the failure of form. Perhaps the trial judge felt and responded to an atmosphere of illegitimacy that had more to do with the races of the Mowrys than with the absence of clergy. The Supreme

Court, on the other hand, was drawn to the common law precedents and saw behind them a cognizable right to marry as one chooses. It therefore wove a Doctrinal Story of presumptive right and ruled that the Mowry marriage was entitled to recognition regardless of the presence or absence of the requisite official.

The claim concerning the property transferred by Mary and Elizabeth Mowry was not presented as a matter of Fourteenth Amendment right, nor was the case (*Meister v. Moore*) decided as such. Yet, in validating the marriage, the Supreme Court treated matrimony as a civil right that took precedence over matters of form and procedure. Consistent with principles underlying both the common law and the Fourteenth Amendment, it interpreted the rule requiring marriage by magistrate or clergy as "directory" only—designed to instruct officials performing or registering marriages, but not intended to result in the extreme sanction of invalidating a relationship understood and lived by the partners as a marriage. This interpretation was based, in part, on the fact that matrimony is a "civil contract," entered, not by leave of state legislation,[2] but by virtue of the fact that "marriage is a thing of common right."[3]

"FOR GOD'S SAKE, HAVE YOU BOUGHT MY WIFE?"

Motivating Stories of Common Right

Scholars of slavery recognize denial of family bonds as a hallmark of slave status: "[T]he slave was always a deracinated outsider—an outsider first in the sense that he originated from outside the society into which he was introduced as a slave, second in the sense that *he was denied the most elementary of social bonds, kinship.*"[4] Slavery in the United States was not exceptional in this respect. Enslaved people were not only outsiders in the sense that they had come from another continent and a set of cultures unfamiliar to the slaveholding class. In law, and often in fact, they were denied the bonds of kinship. The laws of every slaveholding state made it impossible for a slave to enter a legally binding marriage, and they permitted the separation, by sale or otherwise, of slaves who considered themselves husband and wife. Thomas R. R. Cobb, a defender of slavery and author of a comprehensive treatise on its laws, who confessed a bias "by . . . birth and education in [the] slaveholding State [of Georgia]," described the impossibility of legal marriage between slaves and assessed the security of de facto unions between slaves which lawyers characterized as "the contubernial relation":[5]

> The inability of the slave to contract extends to the marriage contract, and hence there is no recognized marriage relation in law between slaves.[6]
> The contract of marriage not being recognized among slaves, of course none of its consequences follow from the contubernial state existing between them. The issue, though emancipated, have no inheritable blood.
> . . . How far this contubernial relation between slaves may be recognized and protected by law, is a question of exceeding nicety and difficulty. The unnecessary and wanton separation of persons standing in the relation of husband and wife, though it may rarely, if ever, occur in actual practice, is an event which, if possible, should be guarded against by the law. And yet, on the other hand, to fasten upon a master of a female slave, a vicious, corrupting negro, sowing discord, and dissatisfaction among all his slaves; or else a thief, or a cutthroat, and to provide no relief against such a nuisance would be to make the holding of slaves a curse to the master.[7]

The abolitionist legal scholar William Goodell read the letter of the law no differently, although he would undoubtedly have quarreled with Cobb concerning the frequency with which slave couples were separated by force of their masters' will or by failure of their masters' enterprises. Goodell reported that "a slave cannot even contract matrimony; the association which takes place among slaves, and is *called* marriage, being properly designated by the word *contubernium*, a relation which has no sanctity, and to which no civil rights are attached."[8]

The human practice of forming life partnerships was not, of course, obliterated for want of legal sanction. Enslaved people celebrated matrimony and lived marriages as best they could. The American slave Henry Bibb described the process by which he and his "wife" were married: "Clasping each other by the hand, pledging our sacred honor that we would be true, we called on high heaven to witness the rectitude of our purpose. There was nothing that could be more binding upon us as slaves than this; for marriage among American slaves, is disregarded by the laws of this country." A former slave interviewed in the 1930s described the process more simply: "When they got married on the places, mostly they just jumped over a broom and that made 'em married. Sometimes one of the white folks read a little out of the Scriptures to 'em, and they felt more married."[9]

Bibb's marriage was disrupted when he was sold to a distant master, and it ended years later when he learned that his wife was the mistress of a slave owner and mother of several of the slave owner's children. By Bibb's account, the marriage ended, not with legal annulment but with the surrender of his resolve, for, in his terms: "The relation once subsisting between us, to which I clung, hoping against hope, for years, after we were torn asunder, not having been sanctioned by any loyal power, [could not] be cancelled by a legal process."[10]

Stories like that of Henry Bibb were common and notorious in the mid-nineteenth century. Gutman's comprehensive analysis of the slave family probes "[t]he best available evidence—that reported by [9,000] Mississippi and northern Louisiana ex-slaves" to Union Army clergy registering marriages "to establish that about one in six (or seven) slave marriages were ended by force or sale."[11] In response to this fact of slave life, the bondsman J. W. Loguen said, when asked whether he was "married": "I determined long ago never to marry until I was free. Slavery shall never own a wife or child of mine."[12] His comment expresses both the shame engendered in a nineteenth-century man who could not guard himself against the abuse or seduction of his wife and the slave's ever-present fear that what Frederick Douglass called the "unnatural power" of slave law would, with one "word of the appraisers, against all preferences and prayers, . . . sunder all the ties of friendship and affection, even to separating husbands and wives, parents and children."[13]

The historian Gerda Lerner reports that "Moses Grandy, suspecting nothing, was standing in the street when the slave coffle passed with his wife in chains."[14] Grandy's biography tells the rest of the story:

> Mr. Rogerson was with them on his horse, armed with pistols. I said to him, "For God's sake, have you bought my wife?" He said he had; when I asked him what she had done, he said she had done nothing, but that her master wanted money. He drew out a pistol and said that if I went near the wagon on which she was, he would shoot me. I asked for leave to shake hands with her which he refused, but said I might stand at a distance and talk with her. My heart was so full that I could say very little. . . . I have never seen or heard from her from that day to this. I loved her as I love my life.[15]

Frederick Douglass described the sale of a husband in these terms: "His going . . . was like a living man going into a tomb, who, with open eyes, sees himself buried out of sight and hearing of wife, children and friends of kindred tie." Some couples preferred literal death to this kind of separation. A former slave reported that her grandmother killed herself when she discovered that her husband had been sold.[16] A 1746 edition of the Boston *Evening-Post* told of a couple that made a suicide pact upon learning that the woman was to be sold "into the Country":

> they resolved to put an End to their lives, rather than be parted; and accordingly, at seven o'clock . . . they went up Stairs into the Garret, where the Fellow, as is supposed, cut out the Wench's Throat with a Razor, and then shot himself with a Gun prepared for the Purpose. They were both found lying upon the Bed, she with her Head cut almost off, and he with his Head shot all to pieces.[17]

The narrative of a slave named Betty reveals another kind of private resolution of the contradiction between slave authority on the one hand and the demands of familial allegiance on the other. Betty's husband, Jerry, had been sold to a slave trader named White. Betty described what happened in the hours before White departed with his purchases for the Deep South:

> Arrangements were made to start Friday morning; and on Thursday afternoon, chained together, the gang were taken across the stream, and encamped on its banks. White then went to Jerry, and, taking the handcuffs from his wrists, told him to go and stay the night with his wife, and see if he could persuade her to go with him. If he could, he would buy her, and so they need not be separated. He would pass that way in the morning, and see. Of course, Jerry was only too glad to come; and, at first, I thought I would go with him. Then came the consciousness that this inducement was only a sham, and that, once exposed for sale in a Southern market, the bidder with the largest sum of money would be our purchaser singly quite as surely as together; and, if separated, what would I do in a strange land? No: I would not go. It was far better for me to stay where, for miles and miles, I knew every one, and every one knew me. Then came the wish to secrete ourselves together in the mountains, or elsewhere, till White should be gone; but, to do this, detection was sure. Then we remembered that White had trusted us, in letting him come to me, and we felt ashamed, for a moment, as if we had tried to cheat; but what *right* had White to carry him away, or even to own him at all? Our poor, ignorant reasoning found it hard to understand his rights or our own; and we at last decided that, as soon as it was light, Jerry should take to the mountains, and, when White was surely gone, either I would join him there, and we would make for the North together, or he would come back, go to White's mother, who lived a few miles distant, and tell her he would work for her and obey her, but he would never go South to be worked to death in the rice-swamps or cotton-fields.
>
> We talked late into the night; and at last, in the silence and dread, worn out with sorrow and fear, my head on his shoulder, we both dropped asleep.
>
> Daylight was upon us when we waked. The sad conscious-

ness of our condition, and our utter helplessness, overpowered us. I opened the door, and there was my mistress, with pail in hand, going to the spring for water. "Oh, what shall I do? Where shall I go?" cried Jerry, as he saw her. "Have no fear," I said. "Go right along. I know mistress will never betray you." And, with a bound, he was over the fence, into the fields, and off to the mountains.[18]

"WE SHALL BE ESTABLISHED AS A PEOPLE"

Marriage as Political Act and Human Right

When the institution of slavery began to crumble, former slaves seized the right to marry enthusiastically not only for its private but also for its social meaning. By formalizing family relationships, African-Americans consciously claimed the status and responsibilities of spouse, of parent, *and* of citizen. The formation of legally recognized marriage bonds signified treatment as a human being rather than as chattel—acceptance as people and as members of the political community.

The rush to take a place in the American political community by forming marriages under American law began as soon as the bonds of ownership were escaped. For many, it began on Civil War battlefields. In what W. E. B. Du Bois described as a labor strike against the slave system, blacks abandoned Confederate plantations and swarmed to Union camps.[19] Many of these would-be soldiers traveled with their families, for, if they did not, the family members left behind were at risk of retaliatory abuse and eviction.[20] After some consternation, the Union Army put the labor of these people to the service of the Union cause, on the theory that they were "contraband." Fifteen months after the start of the war, black enlistment was finally permitted, and black regiments were created, consisting both of escaped slaves and of free blacks, who enlisted in large numbers.[21] As "contrabands" and free blacks became soldiers, they moved to claim rights of family. A black soldier in Tennessee wrote to the division commander to complain that men in his regiment were being kept in handcuffs and denied the right to see their wives:

mens wifes comes here to see them and he will not allow them to come in to they lines uur the men to go out to see them after the comg over hundred miles but evver offiscer here that has a wife is got her here in camps & one mans wif feel jest as near to him as anurther a colard man think jest as much of his wife as a white man dus of his . . . we volenterd and come in to the servest to portec this govverment and also to be portected our selves at the same time but the way colonel luster is treating us it dont seem like to me that he thinks we are human.[22]

When military chaplains were authorized to solemnize marriages between African-Americans, they were inundated with requests. A Freedmen's Bureau agent, who reported legalizing seventy-nine marriages in a single day, described the scene as the opportunity was announced and quoted the response of a black soldier whose character was such "that every word had power":

> Fellow Soldiers:—
> *I praise God for this day!* I have long been praying for it. The Marriage Covenant is at the foundation of all our rights. In slavery we could not have *legalised* marriage: *now* we have it. Let us conduct ourselves worthy of such a blessing—and all the people will respect us—God will bless us, and we shall be established as a people.[23]

The chaplain of a Mississippi black regiment reported the legalization of forty-three marriages, saying, "I think I witness a very decided improvement in the social and domestic feelings of those married by the authority and protection of Law. It causes them to feel that they are beginning to be regarded and treated as human beings."[24] The chaplain of an Arkansas black regiment reported twenty-five marriages registered during January 1865, "mostly, those, who have families; & have been living together for years." He added, "The Colored People here, generally consider, this war not only; their *exodus*, from bondage; but the road, to Responsibility; Competency; and honorable Citizenship."

Enslaved people's commitment to family as a foundation of honorable citizenship did not spring full-blown on the eve of war. The effect of slavery upon the family and the aspirations of African-Americans for family integrity had long been apparent. Goodell's treatise, published by the American and Foreign Anti-Slavery Society to "test the moral character of American slaveholding" by exhibiting the American Slave Code,[25] made the provisions of that code vivid with anecdotal accounts of slave families separated by sale and distanced by the demands of servitude. Accounts of family separations were buttressed by advertisements from Southern newspapers offering rewards for the capture or killing of slaves reported to have run away in order to join family members.[26] Harriet Beecher Stowe had written in 1853 that "[t]he worst abuse of the system of slavery is its outrage upon the family and . . . it is one which is more notorious and undeniable than any other."[27] An 1837 essay on the family in The Liberator declared that "the most appalling feature of our slave system is, the annihilation of the family institution."[28] Samuel Ward, antislavery activist and former slave, embedded a condemnation of the slave system's treatment of the fundamental human right to marry in a bitterly ironic account of the flogging of his father and the response, and subsequent punishment, of his mother. His story captures nicely how denial of family was central to the subordination of human will that slavery required:

> [My father] received a severe flogging, which left his back in . . . [a] wretched . . . state. . . . This sort of treatment of her husband not being relished by my mother, who felt about the maltreatment of her husband as any Christian woman ought to feel, she put forth her sentiments, in pretty strong language. This was insolent. Insolence in a negress could not be endured—it would breed more and greater mischief of a like kind; then what would become of wholesome discipline? Besides, if so trifling a thing as the *mere marriage relation* were to interfere with the supreme proprietor's right of a master over his slave, next we should hear that slavery must give way before marriage! Moreover, if a negress may be allowed free speech, touching the flogging of a negro, simply because that negro happened to be her husband, how long would it be before some such claim would be urged in behalf of some other member of a negro family, in unpleasant circumstances? Would this be endurable,

in a republican civilized community, A.D. 1819? By no means. It would sap the very foundation of slavery—it would be like "the letting out of water": for let the principle be once established that the negress Anne Ward may speak as she pleases about the flagellation of her husband, the negro William Ward, as a matter of right, and like some alarming and death-dealing infection it would spread from plantation to plantation, until property in husbands and wives would not be worth the having. No, no: marriage must succumb to slavery, slavery must reign supreme over every right and every institution however venerable or sacred; *ergo*, this free-speaking Anne Ward must be made to feel the greater rigours of the domestic institution. Should she be flogged? that was questionable. . . . Well, then, . . . they could sell her, and sell her they would.[29]

As we shall see more clearly in discussions of the parental right, the antislavery critique was more than a sentimental reaction to the drama of frustrated love and family separation. It was grounded in an analysis of the human condition as a moral quest for affiliation and self-assertion, an analysis that led to the conclusion that slavery was wrong because it unacceptably frustrated moral and affiliational behavior. Abolitionists undergirded their position with the natural law argument that rights of marriage and family were necessary to the fulfillment of religious and moral duty and therefore inalienable. To be recognized as human was to be recognized as morally autonomous, and moral as well as religious autonomy required *family* autonomy. Antislavery rhetoric reflected as much, demanding human rights and recognition of marriage in the same breath: "The slaves must be immediately recognized as human beings by the laws, their persons and their rights must be protected. Provisions must be made to establish marriage between them."[30]

The widespread commitment among antislavery Americans to protect rights to marry and to form and maintain families was sufficiently deep and appropriately placed to affect the meaning of the Reconstruction Amendments. Indeed it was expressed in Congress as a motivating factor in crafting the Thirteenth and Fourteenth amendments. Many of those expressions touched specifically upon the right to marry. The inability of slaves to form and maintain marital bonds and the inalien-

ability of their right to do so were recurring topics in the debates of
the Reconstruction Congress. Speaker after speaker pronounced marriage rights fundamental and resolved that freedom in the United
States would entail the right to marry:

> The slave could sustain none of those relations which give life
> all its charms. He could not say my wife, my child, my body. It
> is for God to say whether he could say my soul. The law pro-
> nounced him a chattel, and these are not the rights or attributes
> of chattels.[31]

> [I]n none of the slave States . . . is . . . [the marriage] relation
> tolerated in opposition to the will of the slave-owner; and . . .
> in many of them . . . it . . . [is] prohibited absolutely by their
> statute laws. This, I take it then, is the matured, ripened opinion
> of the people of those States. In their opinion the prohibition
> of the conjugal relation is a necessary incident of slavery . . .
> The existence of this institution therefore requires the existence
> of a law that annuls the law of God establishing the relation of
> man and wife, which is taught by the churches to be a sacrament
> as holy in its nature and its designs as the eucharist itself.[32]

> What vested rights [are] so high or so sacred as a man's right to
> himself, to his wife and children, to his liberty, and to the fruits
> of his own industry? Did not our fathers declare that those rights
> were inalienable? And if a man cannot himself alienate those
> rights, how can another man alienate them without being him-
> self a robber of the vested rights of his brother-man?[33]

> Slavery cannot know a home. Where the wife is the property
> of the husband's master, and may be used at will; . . . where man
> and woman, after twenty years of faithful service from the time
> when the priest with the owner's sanction by mock ceremonies
> pretended to unite them, are parted and sold at that owner's
> will, there can be no such thing as home. Sir, no act of ours
> can fitly enforce their freedom that does not contemplate for
> them the security of home.[34]

[W]hen this [Thirteenth] amendment to the Constitution shall be consummated . . . the sharp cry of the agonizing hearts of severed families will cease to vex the weary ear of the nation. . . . Then the sacred rights of human nature, the hallowed family relations of husband and wife, parent and child, will be protected by the guardian spirit of that law which makes sacred alike the proud homes and lowly cabins of freedom.[35]

"THE WILL OF THE SOVEREIGN"

A Doctrinal Story of State Authority

Ten years after announcing, in *Meister v. Moore*, that marriage is a thing of common right, the Supreme Court gave absolute and uncritical deference to the state's power to choose when, how, and whether to sever a marriage bond. Once again, the context was a land claim that turned on the validity of a marriage. The claim was brought by a woman whose husband had acquired property as a homesteader. When the wife sought a share of the land, she learned that her husband had obtained a legislative divorce,[36] without notice to her and, as she alleged, without grounds. In this case, *Maynard v. Hill*, the Court ruled that the wife was powerless to contest the divorce. In language cited to this day in support of the principle of state authority over family matters, it explained that while marriage is a civil contract entered only by consent of the parties, its terms, duration, and continued existence are matters of absolute state control. According to this doctrine, marriage is a construction of the state rather than a right of the celebrants.

It is extreme—both on its face and in the context of related constitutional doctrine—to suggest, as the Court did in the *Maynard* case, that state control of marriage should be absolute. Whether we regard the right to marry as a matter deserving special constitutional protection or simply as an ordinary individual interest, the principles of due process bar the state from compromising that interest in arbitrary ways or by procedurally unfair means. A more careful analysis should have led the Court to question whether the state had a rational basis for dissolving marriages without regard to the existence of cause, and whether the wife could reasonably be denied notice and a right to be heard. But although the Court was rather careless of the rights of the wife, it was right to be mindful of the principles that support reserving to states a generous measure of control over the institution of marriage. As the Justices pointed out, marriage is an institution in which the government has legitimate and important interests, for it deeply influences a community's moral and physical well-being and must therefore be subject, at least in some respects, to "the will of the sovereign."[37]

In the *Maynard* decision, the Justices did not allude to the sense of common law right which they associated with marriage in their *Meister* decision. Nor did they allude to the tension between the idea of common right and the idea that government control of marriage is essential to protecting the moral and physical well-being of the political community. *Meister* and *Maynard* stand, respectively, for inevitable and inconsistent forces with which the Justices must contend. The *Meister* principle of marriage as a "thing of common right" represents judicial recognition of the human need for liberty and autonomy in choosing life's partners and projects, while the *Maynard* principle of marriage as an exercise of sovereign authority represents judicial recognition of government's impetus to protect traditional values and its obligation to assure that family privacy is not a shield for familial abuse. It is in the name of the *Maynard* principle that government is permitted, through matrimonial laws, to do such things as define society as monogamous or heterosexual, prohibit or define divorce terms, intervene against spousal abuse, require spousal support, or prohibit interracial marriage. Most of us applaud government initiatives to protect family members against abuse or exploitation, yet, as the examples in the preceding sentence suggest, protecting traditional values can mean protecting traditions and practices that warrant challenge. History has often shown that well-intentioned government initiatives can be too cavalier with human freedom, and even praiseworthy officials can compromise liberty with an "overbearing concern for efficiency and efficacy."[38] The motivating stories that follow address both dangers. They concern laws that were well-intentioned in the context of certain presumptions about the roles and capacities of men and women. But these laws were resisted, as slavery was resisted, because the presumptions were called into question, and because the laws were thought to constrain too much the freedom that democratic people believe they should have to make personal and moral choices.

"THE FIRST STEP FROM SLAVERY"

Stories of Marriage in Defiance of Sovereign Authority

At the intersection of the feminist and abolitionist movements, a courageous, influential initiative challenged the principles upon which *Maynard* would subsequently rest. In a deep sense, the initiative grew out of the abolitionist idea that human beings must have a significant measure of freedom in making life-defining choices. But it responded most directly and conspicuously to the abolitionist and feminist idea that human beings should not be subordinated on the basis of race or gender. It was an initiative taken in reaction against the character of nineteenth-century marriage laws, and it consisted of a conspicuous set of marriages in defiance of state-regulated norms.

In 1832, the son and imminent daughter-in-law of Robert Owen, founder of the utopian community of New Harmony, were married in a service that included a denunciation of marriage laws of the day which, by giving men control of most of the couple's property, authority as their wives' legal representatives, freedom to discipline their wives, and a variety of similar forms of control, enforced the vision of the family set out by Justice Bradley in Myra Bradwell's case.[39] Six years later, the practice of beginning a marriage while expressly rejecting many of the legal definitions of marriage was given prominence as Angelina Grimké and Theodore Weld took vows in a ceremony witnessed by many of the nation's most outstanding antislavery activists. Grimké, an indefatigable antislavery and feminist organizer, writer, and lecturer, was among the best-known women in America. Weld was also a well-known activist. He believed strongly in women's rights, but he thought the causes of abolition and women's rights secondary to and derivative of a commitment to "the grand principle for which we struggle . . . HUMAN RIGHTS."[40] Both Grimké and Weld were "identified with powerful moral movements: abolition, temperance, woman's rights, the whole great battle with 'factitious life.' "[41] Keenly aware of the ridicule and hostility with which activist women were regarded, the couple determined to set an example by proving that strong and independent minds could find harmony in marriage. The abolitionist community was thrilled by the prospect, and the Philadelphia wedding was timed to fall between the annual convention of the American Anti-Slavery Society and the annual convention of Anti-Slavery Women.[42] It was an orthodox abolitionist gathering with an integrated guest list including antislavery leaders William Lloyd Garrison, Maria Weston Chapman, Abby Kelley, Henry C. Wright, Henry B. Stanton, and Gerrit Smith; a wedding cake was baked "by a colored baker who used nothing but 'free sugar' "; and black and white clergy offered prayers.[43] In a letter to a friend, Maria Chapman described the occasion as "an abolitionist wedding."[44] The couple rejected traditional vows, uttering "such [words] as the Lord gave them at the moment."[45] Weld gave voice to his commitment to human rights as well as to his love of Grimké as he condemned the "unrighteous power vested in a husband by the laws of the United States [and] abjured all authority save the influence which love would give to them over each other." Grimké promised to love and honor her spouse, carefully omitting the word "obey."[46]

"Abolitionist weddings" proliferated. When Abby Kelley and Stephen S. Foster married in 1845, they followed Quaker tradition and drew up their own wedding certificate, documenting "a matrimonial connection in accordance with the divine law of Marriage" and omitting any reference to the laws of the state (Massachusetts) in which they were wed.[47] To the fifty guests, Foster "gave . . . his views relating to marriage" and Kelley spoke, not of a duty of obedience and domestic concern, but "of her anti-slavery life—its toil and sacrifice."[48] Harriet Taylor, who followed developments in the American women's movement,[49] and John Stuart Mill, who worked with her in formulating *The Subjugation of Women*, included a denunciation of governing marriage laws when they married in England in 1851.[50] And it is likely that abolitionist activists Lizzy Hitchcock and Ben Jones, who attended the Kelley-Foster wedding, gave recognition at their own wedding shortly thereafter to the dedicated and egalitarian life they intended to lead.[51]

But the most detailed surviving account of these partnerships in defiance of sovereign authority is that of the courtship and marriage of Henry Blackwell and Lucy Stone. When their courtship began in 1853,

Stone was a thirty-four-year-old feminist and antislavery activist, the
first Massachusetts woman to have received a bachelor of arts degree.[52]
Although she regarded single life as "unnatural," she had vowed "not
to be married ever." "I have not yet seen the person whom I have the
slightest wish to marry," she wrote to a friend, "and if I had, it will
take longer than my lifetime for the obstacles to be removed which
are in the way of a married woman having any being of her own."[53]
Blackwell was an entrepreneur in his late twenties, ideologically committed to feminist and abolitionist causes but principally, although
somewhat ambivalently, engaged in a quest for financial security.
Stone's doubts about marrying Blackwell were overcome between the
spring of 1853 and the spring of 1855, largely through the couple's
correspondence, for she, based in Massachusetts, traveled so much as
an antislavery lecturer that Blackwell imagined she was "born a loco-
motive,"[54] and he, based in Ohio, also traveled often, both for antislavery causes and in connection with land speculation and other
business ventures. Blackwell's very first letter to Stone refuted her
stance against marriage:

> I think if the pursuit of any human profession disqualified me
> for marriage or any other relation necessary to the highest de-
> velopment of the soul, I, as a man, should spurn the profession
> and prefer eternal exile from the paths of men, to falsehood to
> Nature & Destiny. But herein I think is the legitimate function
> of Reason, to so organize and construct our circumstances that
> we may reconcile the conflict of circumstances & duties and be
> true to our *whole nature* & live a symmetrical, rational life true
> to all our faculties.[55]

Although Stone consistently discouraged talk of marriage, Blackwell
regularly returned to the subject in his letters. He set forth his ideals
and aspirations:

> My idea of the relation involves no sacrifice of individuality but
> its perfection—no limitation of the career of one, or both but
> its extension. . . . Perfect *equality* in this relationship . . . I
> would have—but it should be the equality of Progress, of De-

velopment, not of Decay. If both parties cannot study more, think more, feel more, talk more & work more than they could alone, I will remain an old bachelor & adopt a Newfoundland dog or a terrier as an object of affection.[56]

He announced himself liberated from prevailing sexist opinions:

> [A male friend and I] often talk on this question of marriage— he differs from me. He thinks it is dangerous for two persons of strong mind to marry. . . . He laughs at me for my too high ideal [of equality in marriage]. . . . Now I have felt for years the most imperious necessity for marriage. . . . But when it comes to the point, I find that I *cannot* forgo my ideal. Equality with me is a passion. I dislike equally to assume, or to endure authority.[57]

Blackwell then proposed a defiant stance against the laws and customs that enforced female subordination in marriage. Tellingly, his proposal was couched as a stance against *slavery*. He believed that no person should yield—to a master or to a government—a sovereignty that precludes autonomous moral functioning or inhibits life's central affiliative choices. He therefore equated the slave system, under which life partnerships were subject to the will and economic interests of masters, and patriarchal marriage laws, under which life partnerships were constrained to take traditional, but morally unacceptable, forms. People must form families, he argued, in defiance of both. Stone resisted forming a marriage in accordance with patriarchal laws, but Blackwell wrote:

> Give me a *free* man—he can never be made a slave. Give me a free woman—she never can be made one either. Surely you enormously exaggerate the scope & force of *external* laws at the expense of *internal* power when you lay such frightful & hopeless stress upon a few paltry enactments. The great evil I think, in our institutions lies *here*—that they so crush the spirit out of people that they do *not make themselves free.* . . . The first step from slavery is to seek freedom for *ourselves* . . . the next is to seek it for others & for all.[58]

I do believe that certain temperaments, tastes, & dispositions naturally attract, or repel, each other & that we are so constituted that we *need* to form an alliance the most pure & intimate possible, with one individual of the opposite sex. . . . To conceive oneself precluded from assuming it, because the existing laws of Society do not square with exact justice, is to subject oneself to a more abject *slavery* than ever actually existed. Will you permit the injustice of the world to enforce upon you a life of celibacy? The true mode of protest is to assume the natural relation & to reject the unnatural dependence.[59]

And he promised a life of mutual encouragement in noble causes:

I do not want you to forego *one sentiment* of independence, nor one attribute of *personality*. I want only to help you, as best I can, in achieving a really noble & *symmetrical* Life. I want you also to *help me* to do the same. We *can help* each other I am sure not merely as friends—not as lovers, but as husband & wife.[60]

Nonetheless, Stone reported that she experienced pain "at the idea of being placed in the *legal* position of wife."[61] So Blackwell persisted, making specific proposals to circumvent laws by which the husband controlled marital property and family domicile, had no obligation to seek consent for sexual intimacy, and was the presumptive custodian of the children:

As to your property dear—it will be necessary . . . to settle all your *personal* property on yourself. . . . [T]he best way will be to put it into the hands of trustees for your benefit. . . . Then we will engage to *share earnings* on both sides—you to get half of mine & I half of yours, so long as we live together. If we ever separate—each to relinquish all claim to the others subsequent earnings & each to take half the children you having the choice. If separation is from wrong conduct—the right to control children to be decided by arbitrators—one each selected by you & me & one more selected by them. In case of death either party may will his or her property to whomsoever he pleases unless there are children—in which case enough to support & educate them, shall be reserved. . . .

In case of death after separation, unless gross misconduct on either part has been the cause—the survivor takes the children previously held by the other partner & becomes their guardian—otherwise—the deceased partner shall have a guardian nominated by him or her in the will. Neither partner shall be liable for any debts contracted & liabilities incurred by the other partner previous to marriage—nor (except for maintenance if necessary) shall have any claim to property acquired by the other partner previous to marriage—nor shall the private property of either partner be liable for debts of the other. You shall choose when, where & how often you shall become a mother. Neither partner shall attempt to fix the residence, employment or habits of the other—nor shall either partner feel bound to live together any longer than is agreeable to both. All earnings *subsequent* to marriage during its harmonious continuance to be liable for family expenses equally, but all *surplus* of joint earnings to be annually divided & placed to the credit of each.[62]

When Stone eventually agreed to marry, the couple negotiated the terms of the "protest" that they would announce at their wedding. She admitted, "I shall rejoice as much as you, dearest, when we can fully share our life," but insisted that "[t]he promise to love, honor &c &c, I shall never make. Those things are dependent upon the qualities that can inspire them, and if they cease[,] all promises are vain."[63]

The wedding was intended as a public political act. It featured a protest, conceived as a statement that the couple would not "endorse the present unjust laws, but by making our public & outside *contract*, enter a practical & efficient protest against them—the only protest which can be understood & *imitated*."[64] They drafted their words with care and in consultation with abolitionist colleagues,[65] and published them in *The Worcester Spy* and *The Liberator*.[66] This is what Blackwell read as the couple stood together before taking their vows:

While acknowledging our mutual affection by publicly assuming the relationship of husband and wife, yet in justice to ourselves and a great principle, we deem it a duty to declare that this act on our part implies no sanction of, nor promise of voluntary obedience to such of the present laws of marriage, as refuse to recognize the wife as an independent, rational being, while they confer upon the husband an injurious and unnatural superiority, investing him with legal powers which no honorable man would exercise, and which no man should possess. We protest especially against the laws which give to the husband:

1. The custody of the wife's person.
2. The exclusive control and guardianship of their children.
3. The sole ownership of her personal property, and use of her real estate, unless previously settled upon her, or placed in the hands of trustees as in the case of minors, lunatics, and idiots.
4. The absolute right to the product of her industry.
5. Also against laws which give to the widower so much larger and more permanent an interest in the property of his deceased wife, than they give to the widow in that of the deceased husband.
6. Finally, against the whole system by which "the legal existence of the wife is suspended during marriage," so that in most States, she neither has a legal part in the choice of her residence, nor can she make a will, nor sue or be sued in her own name, nor inherit property.

We believe that personal independence and equal human rights can never be forfeited, except for crime; that marriage should be an equal and permanent partnership, and so recognized by law; that until it is so recognized, married partners should provide against the radical injustice of present laws, by every means within their power.

We believe that where domestic difficulties arise, no appeal should be made to legal tribunals under existing laws, but that all difficulties should be submitted to the equitable adjustment of arbitrators mutually chosen.

Thus reverencing law, we enter our protest against rules and customs which are unworthy of the name, since they violate justice, the essence of law.

The Stone-Blackwell protest was, as they had hoped, a model for antislavery couples;[67] so was Stone's decision to retain her name: for years after the marriage, women who retained their surnames after marriage were known as "Lucy Stoners."[68] Each "abolitionist" marriage reinforced commitment to principles of equality and fundamental human freedom that marked the entitlement of all people and transcended the inconsistent enactments or pronouncements of states.

"A FEATURE OF THE LIFE OF ASIATIC AND AFRICAN PEOPLE"

A Doctrinal Story about Marriage Forms

Abolitionist marriages challenged state authority in the name of a cause that state and local governments have come, albeit partially and slowly, to support. Though truly equalitarian marriages remain somewhat rare, twentieth-century reforms eased the tension between legal norms and the equalitarian ideal. Married women are no longer without legal identity. Obligations of spousal support are now mutual. Laws governing marital property try to allow for shared control and equitable distribution in the event of divorce. Private marriage contracts are increasingly recognized.

But laws that forbid polygamy, and the Doctrinal Stories the Supreme Court has woven in support of those laws, have admitted of no such compromises. The doctrine was articulated in 1878, one year after the *Meister* Court proclaimed marriage "a thing of common right." The case, *Reynolds v. United States*,[69] involved the practice of polygyny in Mormon communities.* Like many family rights cases, this one arose out of a conflict between a family's moral or religious convictions and

---

*Polygyny is the taking of multiple wives, polyandry the taking of multiple husbands— the two forms of polygamy. Although the Mormon practice was polygyny, not polyandry, bigamy laws extend to both forms of polygamy, and the Court consistently discussed the issue in terms of the more general concept.

the requirements of secular law. But unlike most family rights cases, *Reynolds* was a complaint, under the Bill of Rights, against a law of Congress, rather than a Fourteenth Amendment claim against the law of a state. What was for Reynolds adherence to a divine command to take as many wives as his circumstances permitted was for Congress, legislating with respect to the territory of Utah, a criminal offense. Reynolds had been convicted of bigamy and sentenced to a term of imprisonment.

When his conviction and sentence were appealed to the Supreme Court, both the plaintiff and the Justices addressed the constitutional question exclusively in terms of freedom of religion. They did not consider whether the right to follow religious choice in one's family organization had special constitutional status because the choice implicated both the First Amendment's guarantee of freedom of religion, and broader rights of personal and family autonomy.[70] This narrowing of the issue before the Court was understandable, but not inevitable. The right of *religious* autonomy is rather explicitly assured by the First Amendment, one clause of which provides that "Congress shall make no law . . . prohibiting the free exercise [of religion]." By contrast, a constitutional guarantee of *family* autonomy is based on implicit, rather than direct, provisions in the amendments, and in 1878 the jurisprudence of family autonomy was undeveloped. So the litigants and the Court turned to the explicit and tested doctrines of religious liberty.

But they might have done otherwise. As the Reconstruction debates showed, students of American law had long believed that natural family rights were inalienable and implicit in any legitimate relationship between subject and state. In discussing the Civil Rights Act of 1866, Senator Lyman Trumbull had, for example, described civil liberty as liberty that could only be restrained when restraint was necessary to public well-being. This was "the liberty to which every citizen is entitled . . . the liberty which was intended to be secured by the Declaration of Independence and the Constitution of the United States originally."[71] On the following day, speaking to the same subject and particularizing the claims of inalienable civil liberty, Senator Howard prominently included family rights.

Could rights of family be thought to encompass the right to choose

a plural marriage form? Should they be? The constitutionality of enforced monogamy might have been debated in this context. In subsequent cases, the Supreme Court recognized a constitutional duty to
accommodate, *on the combined grounds of religious freedom and family
autonomy*, other family religious practices that are outside the mainstream, albeit less shocking to it than polygamy. But, in *Reynolds* and
in subsequent polygamy cases, the debate was kept within the context
of First Amendment doctrine narrowly conceived.

In determining that Reynolds's conviction did not violate the First
Amendment, the Court had to distinguish between religious belief and
religious practice. It was undisputed that Reynolds's religion required
him to take as many wives as he was able to support. If Reynolds could
not legally follow this requirement of nineteenth-century Mormonism,
then what rights could he claim under the First Amendment? The
Court resolved this puzzle by theorizing that the constitutional right
of free religious exercise encompasses the entertainment of ideas, but
not the taking of action. It said that the Free Exercise Clause protected
Reynolds's right to *believe* that it was his religious duty to take more
than one wife, but did not give him the right to take more than one
wife. This belief-action dichotomy, announced by the Court for the
first time in *Reynolds*, is controversial, and it has been used only sporadically in subsequent cases. Of course, it raises as many questions as
it answers: Don't the words "free *exercise*" in the First Amendment text
justify the protection of action as well as belief? Is it possible to forbid
communal religious worship, or the taking of wine in a ceremony like
Christianity's Holy Communion, or fasting, so long as freedom of belief
remains?[72]

Perhaps because it anticipated these questions, the *Reynolds* Court
did not rely exclusively upon the belief-action distinction but also drew
upon the more coherent, though equally troublesome, notion that one
can test the constitutional legitimacy of a law by asking whether it
was, or would have been, tolerable to the Constitution's framers.[73] Like
the belief-action dichotomy, the test of initial tolerability has been
controversial. It has two premises: that the framers did not intend to
invalidate laws they tolerated, and that their intention, thus understood, is controlling. If a law is said to violate the First Amendment,
the test requires that the Court consider whether the law was tolerated

by those who framed the First Amendment. If a practice is said to violate the Thirteenth Amendment, the test requires that the Court consider whether the practice was tolerated by those who framed the Thirteenth Amendment. Since the Fourteenth Amendment has been understood to incorporate concepts embodied in the first eight amendments, the test may require that cases concerning it be analyzed in terms of the intentions of the framers of the first eight amendments as well as those of the framers of the Fourteenth Amendment.

Writing from a conventional Eurocentric perspective, the Supreme Court described polygamy as "a feature of the life of Asiatic and African people" that was consistently outlawed in Western European cultures and condemned within them (by all sectors save the Mormon Church) as an "odious" practice leading to patriarchy and despotism.[74] In the terms of the test of initial tolerability, proof that the framers considered polygamy odious was enough to establish that its prohibition was consistent with the First Amendment. The First Amendment was not intended, the Court reasoned, to protect conduct that the framers themselves saw fit to outlaw, and if antipolygamy laws were enacted, approved, or enforced by the framers, that would be enough to establish the validity of subsequent similar laws.

More recent First Amendment jurisprudence has often—but not always—incorporated a more demanding standard than the Justices imposed in Reynolds, requiring the government to justify infringements upon religious liberty by reference to legitimate and important public interests. Moreover, since *Reynolds* the Supreme Court has recognized that some constitutional concepts have a broader meaning than the test of initial tolerability can capture. More developed constitutional measures would put states defending polygamy prohibitions to the task of demonstrating that they were justifiable in nonreligious, public welfare terms. The *Reynolds* Court alluded to justifications of this sort, for in the process of establishing that the framers chose not to tolerate polygamy, the Court discussed the public interests that motivated their choice. Thus began the inquiry that should be central to a contemporary analysis: does the government have a good enough reason, beyond a history of intolerance, to impose, in particular instances or in particular ways, upon the autonomous functioning of a family?

As we have seen, the Supreme Court explained the Western European view that multiple marriage was "odious" and prohibitable by pointing out that polygamy encouraged a patriarchal principle leading to despotism. This suggests that the Justices imagined only polygyny and found it oppressive to women and corrupting of men. But the reference might nonetheless be puzzling. Since American society in the 1870s was nothing if not patriarchal, one might wonder why the Court was moved to condemn polygamy as an enshrinement of the patriarchal principle. The opinion suggests that it imagined polygyny as a practice that led to an *excess* of patriarchy—to patriarchy written larger than the family—and imagined despotism as the logical result of that excess. Patriarchy was condemned not as a principle of family governance, but as a principle that corrupts when applied on a larger scale. The Court conceded that under wise leadership polygamy might continue, at least for a time, without "disturb[ing] the social condition." But the risk of social corruption was presumed to be sufficiently great that governments had good cause to forbid polygamous marriage.

Like so many aspects of nineteenth-century American political and social thought, this social corruption hypothesis is better understood when considered with reference to slavery, the social condition by which the society's ideas were often tested. The scholars Akhil Reed Amar and Daniel Widawsky have pointed out that antislavery advocates thought of slavery and polygamy as related evils, both leading to patriarchal excess; the Republican platform in 1856 declared it "both right and the imperative duty of Congress to prohibit in the Territories those twin relics of barbarism—Polygamy, and Slavery."[75] Charles Sumner proclaimed on the floor of the Senate in 1860, "By license of Polygamy, one man may have many wives, all bound to him by marriage-tie, and in other respects protected by law. By license of Slavery, a whole race is delivered over to prostitution and concubinage, without the protection of any law. Surely, Sir, is not Slavery barbarous?"[76]

The portrayal of slavery and polygamy as comparable routes to the corruption of male power was too vivid to have been lost to the *Reynolds* Court in 1878. Post-emancipation inquiries had produced evidence of widespread sexual exploitation by slave owners. A free man of color had, for example, reported that between one-tenth and one-fourth of the slaves on southern Louisiana plantations were of mixed race. He later testified:

> [B]etween the wife and favorite women of the planter there was often the greatest jealousy; the planters were generally in the habit of cohabiting with their slave women; in consequence wives often made false statements against these favorites and had them whipped; for fear they would not be punished, wives often had them whipped in their presence; the slave relation was often the source of great domestic difficulty; the fact of cohabitation was well known to both parents and children.[77]

A white man who had worked on a Mississippi plantation was asked about the "comparative virility of the blacks and mulattoes." His response confirmed that he had lived and worked with men who bred slaves and at times sired their stock:

> I think the blacks are much superior. The mulattoes cease almost altogether to produce in the third generation. I think the cross between a yellow woman and a white man is better than the cross with a black man. It is very difficult to form an opinion, because it is very seldom they go back. You scarcely ever see a cross between a full-blooded negro and a yellow woman; it is more uncommon than the cross between a white woman and a black man—because that is not uncommon. . . . It is true that owners and overseers cohabit with the negroes, but they always regret it.[78]

Post-emancipation reports of this kind revived antislavery's emphatic pre-emancipation charges of slave breeding. William Goodell's *American Slave Code* had reported that in every slave state, by express law or by practice, "the *child* follows the condition [of servitude] of *the mother*, whoever the *father* may be!" He made clear the economic function of this hereditary pattern: "under its sanction, the slave 'owner' very frequently holds and sells his own children as 'property,' though sometimes as white as himself." Antislavery tracts "emphasized in graphic—almost lurid—terms, [that] slavery gave white masters free sexual access to a virtual harem of black women slaves."[79] Samuel Ward was vehement in his critique of chattel slavery as allowing for barbaric and mercenary domestic practices:

> [T]here are persons here [in Canada] who have escaped from their own parents—some of them as white as the whitest Europeans; others who ran away from the men by whom they were treated, in some respects, as wives—escaping with the children which were the fruits of those connections. . . . Their appearance and demeanor but too plainly show, that the system from which they escaped includes some of the most debasing immoralities in the whites, quite equal to what it forces upon the blacks. What a sunken community must that be, in which men belonging to the Church can beget children contrary to the seventh commandment, without needing to blush! What a religion must that be, which declares that the system, of which these deeds are part, is ordained, sanctioned, owned and blest, of God! And, apart from all moral and religious considerations, how wretchedly depraved, how unnatural in his feelings, how near the level of the lowest heathen—not to say, of the brutes that perish—must be that man who complacently sells the children of his own body! Ah! the slaveholders are publishing, as in so many legibly written volumes, in the faces of their mulatto offspring, the sad, sickening evidences of their abominable immoralities.[80]

In Syracuse, New York, Ward reported the case of "[a] poor Mulatto man, named Jerry, [who] at the suit of his own father had been arrested under the Fugitive [Slave] Law: What a sight! and what sounds! A slave, in a free Northern city chained as no felon would be chained, with the blood of Anglo-Saxons in his veins. Still, a slave; the son of a wealthy planter in Tennessee, and still a slave; arrested by a United States officer and several assistants, who were sworn to support the glorious Federal Constitution."[81]

So vivid was the image of slavery as an opportunity for sexual exploitation, motivated both by lust and by greed, that Amar and Widawsky quite plausibly attribute the notorious and bloody caning of

Sumner on the floor of the Senate in 1856 to the double entendre in his description of slavery as the "mistress" of Southern men in general and of Senator Andrew Butler (the cousin of Sumner's assailant) in particular—a description carrying the clear "implication that Senator Butler was sleeping with slaves."[82]

Antislavery advocates took every opportunity to marshal majoritarian aversion to polygamy in the service of abolitionism, arguing that both polygamy and slavery were domestic evils no government was required to condone. As Sumner argued in the course of the Kansas-Nebraska debates:

> The relation of master and slave is sometimes classed with the domestic relations. Now, while it is unquestionably among the powers of any State, within its own jurisdiction, to change the existing relation of husband and wife, and to establish polygamy, I presume no person would contend that a polygamous husband, resident in one of the States, would be entitled to enter the national Territory with his harem—his property if you please—and there claim immunity. Clearly, when he passes the bounds of that local jurisdiction, which sanctions polygamy, the peculiar domestic relation would cease; *and it is precisely the same with slavery.*[83]

The abolitionist political strategy linking slavery and polygamy as "barbarous" practices suggested that one could not confidently expect appropriate limits to be kept upon male social and sexual prerogatives. The strategy was successful not only because it played upon anti-Mormon prejudice but also because it coincided with the current preoccupation with the family as "the head, the heart, the fountain of society." Ronald Walters, writing of social thought in the antebellum period, has argued that "feminists and anti-feminists, abolitionists and anti-abolitionists, reformers and anti-reformers all directed their attention to the same institution. Rather than being a mere sentimental convention, concern for the family was bound up with the most serious social and cultural debates in ante-bellum America." For abolitionists, "[d]estruction of the home"—both the home of the slave and the home of the slavemaster—"fit with slavery's symbolic function as the exemplar of what could go wrong with society."[84] The delegitimization and recurrent disruptions of the slave family were thought to undermine the slave's morality. And the plural, interracial sexual unions that were slavery's consequence undermined the image of the white family as the head, heart, and fountain of a monogamous, Christian society, leaving in its stead a moral equivalent of polygamy—an image of patriarchy taken to excess. A white woman of the antebellum South put it this way: "[l]ike the patriarchs of old, our men live all in one house with their wives and their concubines."[85] Linda Brent, who escaped slavery and the unwanted attention of a "master," exposed the heart of the issue when she described her own sexual exploitation and her master's constant reminders that she was his property and "must be subject to his will in all things."[86]

However strongly the members of the *Reynolds* Court might have been influenced by a social consensus that polygamy was barbarous, akin to slavery, and anathema to social order, their convictions could not have resonated within the Mormon community. According to some accounts, Mormon women of the time saw themselves as oppressed not by polygyny but by the hostile efforts of non-Mormons to dictate matters of religious and family choice. Mormon women were the first in the nation to be explicitly granted the right to vote; women's suffrage was officially supported by the Mormon Church; Mormon women were encouraged to develop their talents in vocations such as politics and medicine; and Mormon women repeatedly petitioned against laws that disrupted their lifestyle.[87]

Reynolds had argued that polygamous marriage was his religious duty, to be shirked upon pain of damnation in the life to come, and that polygamy was deemed by a majority within the territory of Utah to be consistent with Christian law.[88] In the context of the belief-action dichotomy, this argument had no relevance. He was entitled to believe but, the Court said, the First Amendment afforded no protection for his bigamous actions. In the context of the test of initial tolerability, Reynolds's arguments equally had no effect. The framers, all of them non-Mormon men of European descent, tolerated antipolygamy laws, and would not have thought them inconsistent with basic civil rights.

From the Mormon perspective, the belief-action dichotomy and

the test of initial tolerability were tricks of sophistry that subverted
First Amendment freedom and gave rein to intolerance. The Church
of the Latter-day Saints wrote the history of George Reynolds, "private
secretary of President [Brigham] Young, and a man of honor and integrity," and his indictment in 1874 for the crime of bigamy in this
way:

> This was to be a test case. The "Mormon" people felt confident
> that the law was unconstitutional as it restricted them in the
> exercise of their religion and plural marriage had been com-
> manded by the Lord. Elder Reynolds hearing of his indictment
> voluntarily appeared in court, and gave himself up for trial.
>   . . . [T]rial was held . . . before Alexander White, chief jus-
> tice of Utah. Judge White manifested a determination to be
> severe, and when a verdict of guilty was rendered, he sentenced
> Elder Reynolds to pay a fine of five hundred dollars and serve
> a term of two years in the penitentiary at hard labor. The su-
> preme court of Utah confirmed the decree, and an appeal was
> taken to Washington.
>   . . . [On] January 6, 1879, . . . [the Supreme Court] handed
> down a decision unanimously confirming the sentence of the
> courts of Utah, and also declaring the anti-bigamy law of 1862
> to be constitutional. This decision was of the utmost concern
> to the Latter-day Saints, who were confident that the supreme
> court, in justice, could not give confirmation to a law which
> they sincerely believed to be an infringement of their religion.
>   . . . President John Taylor, convinced that this decision was
> an assault on the exercise of religion guaranteed by the Con-
> stitution, stated . . .
>   When the Constitution of the United States was framed
> and adopted, those high contracting parties did positively agree
> that they would not interfere with religious affairs. Now, if our
> marital relations are not religious, what is? This ordinance of
> marriage was a direct revelation to us through Joseph Smith,
> the Prophet. You may not know it, but I know that this is a
> revelation from God and a command to his people, and
> therefore it is my religion. I do not believe that the Supreme

Court of the United States has any right to interfere with my religious views, and in doing it they are violating their most sacred obligations. . . .

We acknowledge our children; we acknowledge our wives. [W]e have no mistresses. We had no prostitution until it was introduced by monogamy, and I am told that . . . other diabolical deeds are following in its train. The courts have protected these people in their wicked practices. We repudiate all such things, and hence I consider that a system that will enable a man to carry out his professions, and that will enable him to acknowledge his wife or wives and acknowledge and provide for his children and wives, is much more honorable than that principle which violates its marital relations and, whilst hypocritically professing to be true to its pledges, recklessly violates the same and tramples upon every principle of honor, which sits down coolly and deliberately decides how many children shall be murdered and how many shall live.

. . . A petition from over thirty thousand citizens of the territory, asking for the pardon of the defendant was forwarded to President Rutherford B. Hayes, who ignored it.[89]

Over the next half century, the Supreme Court repeatedly considered and rejected the claims of Mormons inhibited by state or federal law in their practice of polygyny.[90] It continued to discuss the claims of polygynous Mormons in terms of the explicit First Amendment right of free exercise of religion rather than in terms of the more implicit right of family autonomy. Some Justices, however, came to see the matter in less parochial terms: in a 1946 case involving prosecution under the Mann Act, Justice Francis Murphy observed that polygamy is a basic form of marriage, more common in history than any other form, and described it as "a cultural institution rooted deeply in the religious beliefs and social mores of those societies in which appears."[91]

The Church of Jesus Christ of the Latter-day Saints officially repudiated polygyny in 1890, but small communities of more traditional Mormons continue the practice in isolated regions of Utah, Arizona, Idaho, and California. These communities periodically inspire prose-

cutions for bigamy, or proceedings designed to "rescue" children from
the "immoral" influence of their plural families.[92] It seems inevitable
that one of these controversies will reach the Supreme Court. When
it does, there will be new doctrinal stories against which to review the
immensely difficult questions that will be raised on both sides about
governmental restrictions against plural marriage. Litigants arguing in
support of polygamous families will be able to draw upon First Amendment doctrine that requires a more critical look at the state's justifications for limiting either belief or action. They will also be able to
draw upon a jurisprudence of family autonomy that offers developed
alternatives to the religious liberty claim. Litigants arguing on behalf
of the government will be able to take advantage of recent revivals of
theories of initial tolerability and of the belief-action dichotomy. They
will be able to draw on theories, recently legitimized by the Court when
it considered prohibitions of homosexual intimacy, that a majoritarian
judgment of odiousness is its own justification for prohibitive laws. And
they will be able to draw upon evolved principles of equality that may
be disserved by approval of polygyny in a larger cultural context of
female subordination. It is safe to predict that the Court would require
the government to justify its decision to dictate marriage form, but
how it would assess the possible justifications is more difficult to predict, especially in a culture committed to moral autonomy but troubled
by an apparent erosion of moral values. The argument that authorizing
polyandry reinforces gender-based subordination raises a fascinating set
of difficult issues. Would judges informed by late-twentieth-century
feminism, like eighteenth-century antislavery advocates, consider polygamy to be an excess of patriarchy, or would they switch fields and
challenge patriarchy altogether, arguing for egalitarian relationships
without regard to the number and genders of the partners? Would they
consider the practice of polygamy to be a repudiated and dying form
or a matter of living tradition? And how would they deal with the
knowledge that it is inappropriate in a multicultural polity to rely, as
the *Reynolds* Court did, upon the argument that polygamy is "a feature
of the life of Asiatic and African people" condemned as "odious" in
Western European cultures?

A FIRST AMENDMENT MOTIVATING STORY

Officially sanctioned religious persecution drove many settlers to migrate to the Americas from Europe, and it continued to plague many Americans during the colonial period. Experiences of persecution taught these settlers the human cost of religious constraint and motivated them to guarantee religious freedom that was more thoroughgoing than mere tolerance of unorthodox belief. Expressing a commitment deepened by national memories of religious persecution, James Madison, who, with Thomas Jefferson, embodied the Founders' ideas about church and state, argued that "the duty we owe to our Creator and the Manner of discharging it, can be directed only by reason and conviction, not by force or violence."[93] His assertion, like the antislavery declarations about civil liberty, was born of a vivid consciousness of what it was like to live without moral autonomy, and expresses an especially informed commitment to having the Constitution give maximum rein to the human capacity for moral choice.

The nexus between constitutional commitment and national history has often been recognized by United States' judges, and that recognition has caused them to give religious freedom a grander scope than did the Justices who decided *Reynolds*. The highest court of Virginia described the nexus as follows:

> Is it not known . . . that even in the dawn of our struggle against Britain, for *civil* liberty, many meek and pious teachers of the gospel were imprisoned, persecuted, and treated as criminals?
>
> The only crime of these men, was, their worshipping God according to the dictates of their own consciences! There is not a gentleman old enough to know the fact, who has not seen ministers of the gospel of Christ, teaching their doctrines through the grated windows of a prison![94]

In the federal courts, First Amendment interpretation has often turned on fine distinctions among the historic evils of religious persecution,[95] but there has been little disagreement over the years that history motivated a commitment to thoroughgoing protection of religious freedom.

What result should we expect if a religious objection to enforced monogamy is argued to a Supreme Court that is mindful of the historic motivations for deferring to individual moral choice and can regard traditions that sanction multiple marriage with respect rather than horror?

A RELEVANT, IF NOT MOTIVATING, STORY

In the context of this book, Motivating Stories have been defined as stories that directly or indirectly inspired the Reconstruction Congress as it worked to reconceptualize and safeguard the basic rights of citizenship. The marriage rights that were highlighted by the experience of slavery were rights of recognition, integrity, and autonomy, rather than rights of choice with respect to family form. The slave family had faced illegitimacy (regardless of family form), the constant threat of disruption, and both great and subtle frustrations in the fulfillment of parental and spousal roles, but the slave was not seen as having been victimized by the imposition of an unwanted marriage form. By the mid-nineteenth century, African-Americans were decidedly monogamous and explicitly sought no more than legitimation and authority to function fully in monogamous family roles.

But it might have been otherwise. Herbert Gutman, one of the most thoughtful and careful historians of the African-American family, has written: "West African beliefs and practices were not entirely discarded during the harsh middle passage [to North America and slavery, or] during the initial phases of mainland enslavement. Those experiences narrowed choice but did not quickly transform diverse African social and cultural beliefs. . . . Some Africans and first-generation Afro-Americans sought to establish modified West African polygamous domestic arrangements."[96] Had slaves persevered in preserving this aspect of African heritage, those who inspired and framed the Fourteenth Amendment would, perhaps, have had to confront more explicitly the contradiction exposed by George Reynolds: that between the autonomy of private subcultures and the majoritarian impulse to enforce a common vision of morality and social form.

A PERFECT EQUALITY

A Doctrinal Story of Social Caste

Thus far, we have regarded slavery in the United States as a system that undermined human autonomy and choice so radically, and in such fundamental ways, that it came to be seen as inconsistent with basic principles of human rights. A system that compromised the right to use one's labor to chosen ends or to establish and maintain a marriage did violence to an ideal of personhood. By its radical deprivations of civil rights, slavery imposed a civil death, such that the enslaved person was unable to go about the characteristically human projects of applying energy to chosen ends, establishing and honoring affiliations, and making moral choices.

The slaveholding class was at pains to justify this system in a polity that professed to hold as self-evident principles of human equality and inalienable human rights. The contradiction between national principle and slaveholding practice was resolved by a color-caste ideology that justified the denial of slaves' rights of personhood and autonomy in terms of racial hierarchy. Civil rights and moral autonomy were conceived as necessary only by virtue of the moral and intellectual condition of the white race. Slavery was said to be appropriate because the enslaved, being persons of color, were inadequate to the demands of civil participation and moral personhood. In light of their moral and intellectual inferiority, slaves were segregated—geographically and conceptually—from the political and social mainstream. In heart, mind, and body, an enslaved race was properly held, and properly held itself, apart and subordinated to the will of a master race.

Many slaveholders responded to the abolition of slavery and the constitutional reconstruction wrought by the Thirteenth, Fourteenth, and Fifteenth amendments with a determination to continue by other means the color-caste segregation and subordination that had formerly been enforced by slavery. The "Jim Crow" system of official race segregation was central to that scheme, and in 1896 the Supreme Court considered its constitutionality. In *Plessy v. Ferguson*, the Justices decided that the Fourteenth Amendment's guarantee of equal protection of the laws was not violated by official race segregation so long as segregated facilities were "equal."[97] The color-caste lines erected by Southern state legislatures to continue racial subordination after the abolition of slavery were thus made immune from constitutional attack. Official segregation became a common feature of systems of public accommodations in the Southern states, including buses, drinking fountains, bathrooms, parks, and schools.

The *Plessy* holding was entirely consistent with the literal meaning of the Fourteenth Amendment guarantee that "no State shall . . . deny to any person within its jurisdiction the equal protection of the laws," and it was not repudiated until 1954, in *Brown v. Board of Education*.[98] Of course, the contrary result in *Brown v. Board of Education* was also entirely consistent with the literal meaning of the Equal Protection guarantee. The phrase "equal protection of the laws" can plausibly be read either to permit or to condemn the principle of separate but equal. The difference in interpretation turns largely upon whether one regards the separation as natural and benign or as unfairly presumptive of racial hierarchy and predictably subordinating.

The Justices who voted with the majority in *Plessy* thought racial segregation natural and benign, and the entire Court presumed white supremacy. The majority wrote that social (as opposed to civil and political) inferiority, racial "instincts," and social prejudices were beyond legal remedy; a dissent by the first Justice Harlan argued, in terms that have been disturbingly persuasive to contemporary Justices, for official "color blindness" despite, or perhaps in gracious accommodation for, a dominance by the "white race" that should "continue for all time." The majority denied that segregation had a subordinating intent or a necessarily subordinating effect, arguing that "enforced separation" does not constitute "a badge of inferiority," but is neutral—except, perhaps, in the "construction" put upon it by the subordinated group—and they justified racial separation as a matter of natural inclination and affinity.[99]

The racialist assumptions expressed in *Plessy* were not strictly necessary to its result, for the decision was also buttressed by the principle of initial tolerability—the argument that even acts the Court knows to be malign are constitutionally valid so long as they appeared benign to those who crafted the constitutional provision at issue. Many supporters of the Fourteenth Amendment surely tolerated racial segregation. Even apparently fervent opponents of slavery were unable at times to overcome the conceptual and social barriers against comfortable interracial contact. As Charlotte Coleman sat in the white section of a Boston hall for a meeting of the Boston Female Anti-Slavery Society, she got a note from a white member remarking that "colored people were very well in their place." On another occasion, a white antislavery advocate expressed astonishment "at the impudence of the colored people in going to [meetings] and taking their places anywhere."[100] Many whites who fought against the South in the Civil War did so with ambivalence about the multiracial society that emancipation might bring about. And many who struggled against slavery also struggled against a strong internalized racialism. Antislavery champion Charles Sumner wrote this to his family after his first encounter with slaves: "My worst preconception of their appearance and ignorance did not fall as low as their actual stupidity. They appear to be nothing more than moving masses of flesh, unendowed with any thing of intelligence above the brutes." Years later, he predicted that emancipated blacks would remain in the South as "a dependent and amiable peasantry." As Frederick Douglass told him in an 1855 letter, Sumner was unable, despite his stalwart abolitionism, to recognize "the entire manhood and social equality of the colored people."[101] Relying on the Fourteenth Amendment framers' sometimes ambivalent and often unquestioning toleration of segregation, the majority Justices were able to rationalize the *Plessy* result even to those who did not share their assumptions that racial segregation is the natural order of human existence.

Brown v. Board of Education's holding that official school segregation is unconstitutional required that the Court jettison the concept of initial tolerability (for purposes of deciding the school segregation cases, if not for all time), and look behind *Plessy*'s presumption that official separation of the races in the aftermath of slavery was benign. The progression from *Plessy* to *Brown* is therefore a crucial feature of American constitutional theory. Despite its consistency with the practices of Reconstruction legislators, the doctrine announced in *Plessy* was inadequate in confronting the fundamental contradiction between segregation and the ideal of free and equal citizenship. This inadequacy demonstrated the poverty of the test of initial toleration. In rejecting *Plessy*, the *Brown* Court put a democratic ideal over literalism and nineteenth-century practice, and it freed constitutional jurisprudence of the prejudices, though not the egalitarian principles, of the Reconstruction era. Thus free to offer a meaningful analysis of practices challenged under the Fourteenth Amendment, the Court could candidly assess the effect white supremacy had on the design and enforcement of segregation laws. What it found was that enforced racial separation had a demoralizing and hurtful *effect* upon black schoolchildren. What it must have known was that the Jim Crow system was subordinating *in its design as well as in its effect*. This deeper critique of segregation became explicit only later, and in the context of family rights jurisprudence.

Although lawyers and laypeople alike associate the principle of "separate but equal" with cases about public accommodations, the principle began in Supreme Court jurisprudence as a rationalization for antimiscegenation laws. And it had a harder, longer, and more decisive history in that context than in the context of railway cars, public parks, swimming pools, bathrooms, drinking fountains, or schools. The explanation for this difference is undoubtedly that the family is our most contested, and most emotionally charged, social sphere. But, as is often the case, contest and emotion concealed economic and social interests: Antimiscegenation laws lived longer and died harder because they were so crucial to the preservation of the color-caste system.

Intermarriage across social groups inevitably implies mobility across social groups. Whereas a class system admits of vertical mobility and a certain proportion of intermarriage, a caste system proscribes marriage, as well as any other form of upward or downward social movement, between higher- and lower-status groups.[102] When racial segregation replaced slavery as a method of economic and social subordination, it delimited a caste system. Slavery's de-legitimation of family ties among African-Americans was replaced by inviolable legal barriers between African-American and European-American family lines. Hence the antimiscegenation laws.[103] The Reconstruction Amendments ensured that former slaves would not be deracinated outsiders, completely without civic life or recognized family ties, but the antimiscegenation laws relegated them to an inescapably separate social and civic sphere.

Despite all the emotional, economic, and social baggage carried by proscriptions against intermarriage, the Supreme Court eventually applied the principle of *Brown* to miscegenation laws, repeating in family rights jurisprudence *Brown*'s progression from naiveté to social analysis, and from literalism to idealism. But the Court's initial complicity in maintaining legal barriers against sexual contact and marriage across caste lines was deep and long-standing.

After *Reynolds v. United States*, and its decision that freedom of religion could not encompass a right of multiple marriage, the next step in the development of family rights doctrine was the creation of a doctrinal antecedent to *Plessy*: a principle of separate but equal regulation of sexual practices. Tony Pace, a black man—his "race" determined under Alabama law by the *"presence"* of "African" blood— had been convicted in an Alabama court of cohabitation with a white woman—her "race" determined by the *"absence"* of "African" blood. The couple could not have married lawfully in Alabama.[104] Alabama's marriage laws, as well as its criminal proscriptions of out-of-wedlock cohabitation, erected a barrier between those who were of "pure" (white) blood and those who were not.*

Pace was sentenced to two years of imprisonment, a harsher sentence than would have been possible had he and his partner been of similarly "pure" or "impure" blood. Like George Reynolds, Tony Pace argued from an explicit, often recognized provision of the Constitution rather than from an implicit right of family autonomy. He argued that when the state increased punishment on grounds of race, it violated the Equal Protection Clause.

The Supreme Court rejected Pace's claim summarily. In the unanimous opinion of the Justices, the challenged Alabama law equally protected whites and blacks. Although unmarried cohabitation with a

---

*This method of dividing the "races" is not neutral or inevitable. The choices embedded in it are apparent if we make the effort to imagine alternatives—for example, a legal scheme in which marriages, and other forms of social and sexual intercourse, are forbidden between people who are of "pure" black blood and people who are not.

person of the same race carried lesser penalties, the races were similarly vulnerable for similar offenses. All were punishable for out-of-wedlock cohabitation with a person of the same race, and all were vulnerable to greater punishment for cohabitation with a person of a different race. They noted that the Equal Protection Clause explicitly forbids racial discrimination in the imposition of criminal penalties: no person "shall . . . be subjected, for the same offense, to any greater or different punishment" on the basis of race or class.[105] But, said the Court, the Equal Protection Clause does not forbid discrimination among offenses simply because that discrimination is based upon the race of the participants. As Justice Field put it, "[w]hatever discrimination is made in the punishment prescribed . . . [for interracial and intraracial cohabitation] is directed against the offense designated and not against the person of any particular color or race."[106] The perfect equality of the scheme was demonstrated by the case at bar: Pace's white partner had been sentenced to an equal term of imprisonment.[107]

Because the doctrine of initial tolerability permits the Court to rationalize giving constitutional approval to a law that seems to violate evolving notions of equal protection (or some other constitutional imperative), there is always a possibility of discrepancy in a doctrinal story of initial tolerability between the Justices' and the framers' conceptions of equality. In *Pace*, the Justices did not refer to the possibility that antimiscegenation laws might violate a developed sense of equality, nor was there talk of initial toleration. By the Court's account, the underlying decisions—to define the two races in terms of the purity of one, to differentiate interracial from intraracial cohabitation, and to regard the former as the more serious offense—seemed natural and innocent.

The holding of *Pace* was not squarely overruled until 1967.

A QUESTION LEFT FOR POSTERITY

Mixed Motivating Stories of Caste and Choice

Abolitionists and antislavery activists spoke differently on the subjects of miscegenation and the right to marry, and their words provide both

support and challenge for the Court's conclusions in *Pace*. Some held
the separatist views attributed to them by the *Plessy* Court, supporting
the argument that, under the principle of initial tolerability, antimiscegenation laws were constitutionally permissible. Others were able
to contemplate a right of marriage across racial lines.

Lydia Maria Child, a white abolitionist and popular novelist,[108]
thought that antimiscegenation laws violated freedom of conscience:

> An unjust law exists in this Commonwealth [Massachusetts],
> by which marriages between persons of different color are pro-
> nounced illegal. I am perfectly aware of the gross ridicule to
> which I may subject myself by alluding to this particular; but I
> have lived too long, and observed too much, to be disturbed by
> the world's mockery. . . . [T]he government ought not to be in-
> vested with power to control the affections, any more than the
> consciences of citizens. A man has at least as good a right to
> choose his wife, as he has to choose his religion. His taste may
> not suit his neighbors; but so long as his deportment is correct,
> they have no right to interfere with his concerns.

Yet Child's commitment to freedom of conscience and choice in the
selection of marriage partners did not shield her from the social pressures that constrained that choice: "[T]his law is a useless disgrace to
Massachusetts. Under existing circumstances, none but those whose
condition in life is too low to be much affected by public opinion, will
form such alliances; and they, when they choose to do so, will make
such marriages, in spite of the law."

Despite her belief that intermarriage could occur only at the fringes
of a social order dominated by an ideology of white racial purity,
Child's feminist and social reformist stance led her to support legal
recognition of interracial unions:

> I know two or three instances where women of the laboring
> class have been united to reputable, industrious colored men.
> These husbands regularly bring home their wages, and are kind
> to their families. If by some of the odd chances, which not

unfrequently occur in the world, their wives should become heirs to any property, the children may be wronged out of it, because the law pronounces them illegitimate.[109]

David Ruggles, black abolitionist, author, editor, and bookseller, opposed antimiscegenation laws on different grounds. Perhaps because of political expediency, or racial pride, he was loath to advocate interracial unions. But he understood that the prohibition of "amalgamation," in the context of United States culture of the time, implied racial hierarchy and marked his people as inferior; social equality and antimiscegenation laws were incompatible concepts. These competing sentiments led Ruggles to oppose antimiscegenation laws in guarded terms. Like Child, he bowed to the social consensus against miscegenation, but whereas Child found her opposition to antimiscegenation laws in arguments of liberty and social welfare, Ruggles reacted to the laws' affront to the human dignity of African-Americans:

> Abolitionists do not wish "amalgamation." I do not wish it, nor does any colored man or woman of my acquaintance, nor can instances be adduced where a desire was manifested by any colored person; but I deny that "intermarriages" between the "whites and blacks are unnatural." . . .
>
> Why is it argued that our elevation "to an equality" with other "Americans is incongruous and unnatural"? Simply because public opinion is against it. Now we don't wish to alter public opinion respecting intermarriages, but we do respecting our "equality."[110]

Samuel Ward, who, like Frederick Douglass, was a fugitive slave when he wrote and spoke in the abolitionist cause, addressed the question of miscegenation with a rare and admirable understanding of the conceptual limitations of his era. Ward first described the miscegenist practices of escaped slaves in Canada. Like Ruggles, he took care to mark and to condemn the suggestion that miscegenation represents a pollution of white bloodlines. He was optimistic about the physical and intellectual properties of mulatto children, but, on the central questions of moral advancement and social acceptance, he reserved judgment. His words are a powerful argument against the principle of initial tolerability:

> Fugitives coming to Canada are, the majority of them, young, single men. Many more young than old, many more male than female, come. Then, these look about them for wives. Coloured young women are comparatively scarce; and, in spite of the prevalent prejudice, they marry among this very lower class of whose Negro-hate I have said so much. Hence, while you get so much evidence of the aversion betwixt these classes, you see it to be no strange thing, but a very common thing, for a black labourer to have a white wife, of a like class. In other circumstances, one would not wonder at it; but considering the bitter feeling of the whites, it is, to say the least of it, an anomaly, that blacks should propose on the one hand, and that whites should accept on the other. However, the history of poor human nature and its actions is full of these anomalies. It is certainly without pain that I add, these matches, so far as I know, are happy ones. How far this anomaly may tend in future to correct the prejudice, I cannot tell. How powerful, how wide-spread, how speedy, will be its operation, are matters upon which I do not even venture to speculate. That it is a condescension on the part of the white, that it at all elevates the individual Negro, I of course deny. That the progeny of such marriages will be physical and intellectual improvements upon the parental stock of both sides, admits of no doubt: whether a corresponding moral advantage will result, is quite another thing. That is a question *of* posterity; and *for* posterity, and *to* posterity, I beg to leave it.[111]

William Jay, a white antislavery advocate and the son of John Jay, first Chief Justice of the Supreme Court, took an entirely different stance. Miscegenation itself was unthinkable to Jay; he approached the issue as one of antislavery politics. Approval of miscegenation was, he believed, a position wrongly and absurdly attributed to antislavery advocates in order to discredit their cause:

One of the designs falsely imputed to . . . [abolitionists] is that
of bringing about an amalgamation of colors by intermarriages.
In vain have they again and again denied any such design; in
vain have their writings been searched for any recommendation
of such amalgamation. No Abolitionist is known to have married a negro, or to have given his child to a negro; yet has the
charge of amalgamation been repeated, and repeated, till many
have, no doubt, honestly believed it.

During the very height of the New-York riots, and as if to
excite the mob to still greater atrocities, the editor of the Commercial Advertiser asserted, that the Abolitionists had "sought
to degrade" the identity of their fellow citizens, as a "nation of
white men, by reducing it to the condition of MON-
GRELS." . . .

No one, in the possession of his reasoning faculties, can
believe it to be the duty of white men to select black wives;
and Abolitionists have given every proof the nature of the case
will admit, that they countenance no such absurdity.[112]

In Congress, the question of miscegenation arose when it was proposed that basic civil rights be extended to former slaves. It was understood that the right to marry was a fundamental civil right and
feared that its extension to blacks would provide them a license to
intermarry. The response of House and Senate civil rights proponents
was in the style of William Jay—the response of pragmatic politicians,
conspicuously and perhaps quite honestly outraged at the suggestion
that abolition entailed contemplation of interracial marriage. The following exchanges occurred during an 1866 Senate debate on the Freedmen's Bureau Bill:*

SENATOR HENDRICKS: If the law of Indiana, as it does, pro-
hibits under heavy penalty the marriage of a negro with a
white woman, may it be said a civil right is denied him

---

*The Freedmen's Bureau Bill, a precursor of the Fourteenth Amendment, provided in
relevant part that "the right to make and enforce contracts . . . and to have full and
equal benefit of all laws and proceedings concerning personal liberty . . . shall be secured to and enjoyed by all the citizens" of the secessionist states.

which is enjoyed by all white men, to marry according to their choice . . . ?

SENATOR TRUMBULL: How does this law interfere with the law of Indiana preventing marriages between whites and blacks: Are not both races treated alike by the law of Indiana? Does not the law make it just as much a crime for a white man to marry a black woman as for a black woman to marry a white man, and vice versa? I presume there is no discrimination in this respect, and therefore your law forbidding marriages between whites and blacks operates alike on both races. This bill does not interfere with it.[113]

SENATOR DAVIS: The previous section provides that the freedman shall be entitled to all the civil rights and privileges that a white person is entitled to. Now let me give you an example. It has been made a crime in Kentucky—and I hope it always will be; it shall never cease to be with my consent, at least— for any negro to intermarry with a white person. . . . Suppose that under this famous bill a negro applies to the county court clerk of Bourbon county for a marriage license to intermarry with a white woman, and the clerk refuses because the law does not permit such an alliance—it denounces it as a crime, and it punishes all persons who assist in the perpetration of that crime. . . . What does the negro do? He goes and makes complaint to this bureau; this bureau sends its corporal's guard with fixed bayonets to the clerk's office and commands the clerk to issue this license against the highest penal sanctions of our law. . . .

SENATOR TRUMBULL: The Senator says the laws of Kentucky forbid a white man or woman marrying a negro, and that these laws of Kentucky are to exist forever; that severe penalties are imposed in the State of Kentucky against amalgamation between the white and black races. Well, sir, I am sorry that in noble Kentucky there is such a disposition to amalgamation that nothing but penalties and punishments can prevent it. But, sir, it is a misrepresentation of this bill to say that it interferes with those laws.[114]

The sentiments of civil rights advocates in the House of Representatives were similar. The following comment, made during a discussion of the civil rights of blacks in the District of Columbia, again combines disdain for miscegenation with the antislavery charge that sexual exploitation and plural interracial sexual unions were emblematic of slaveholders' moral corruption:

> REPRESENTATIVE FARNSWORTH: [T]he gentleman from New Jersey [Mr. Rogers] refers to another bugbear with which to scare ignorant people, that of amalgamation. He recites the statutes of various States against the intermarriage of blacks and whites. Well, sir, while I regard that as altogether a matter of taste, and neither myself nor my friends require any restraining laws to prevent us from committing any error in that direction, still, if my friend from New Jersey and his friends are fearful that they will be betrayed into forming any connection of that sort, I will very cheerfully join with him in voting the restraining influence of a penal statute. I will vote to punish it by confinement in the State prison, or, if he pleases, by hanging— anything rather than they should be betrayed into or induced to form any such unnatural relations. As for my own side of the House, we have no fears of that kind. Amalgamation is an outgrowth of slavery. It is where slavery has existed that you find it, not where the negro is free and has the right of self-protection.[115]

If the *Reynolds* test of initial tolerability were all, then these uncontradicted words of Trumbull and Farnsworth would go far to support the *Pace* result. On the other hand, Ward's agnosticism and his openness to the possibility of social and moral advancement suggest that we would do well to leave ourselves open to interpretations of the framers' principles that the framers themselves could not have accepted. To perceive this is to settle the most profound constitutional question of our time: whether the principles of our constitutional democracy are larger than the imaginations of the men who framed them.

A RIGHT "ESSENTIAL TO THE ORDERLY PURSUIT OF HAPPINESS"

A Doctrinal Story of Marriage Choice

As we have seen, the Court rejected *Plessy*'s doctrine of separate but equal when it decided, in 1954, that segregated schools functioned as a badge of inferiority for black children, even if they had equal facilities and resources. Immediately after *Brown*, the Court invalidated segregated facilities of every description, and it did so with no more explanation than citation to *Brown*. With the demise of the *Plessy* doctrine of separate but equal, the Court's decision in *Pace* seemed destined to be overruled, and laws against intermarriage were expected to fall. The miscegenation issue was presented to the Court in 1955, but the Justices avoided decision, not wishing further to inflame Southern states that were already up in arms over *Brown*'s order to desegregate elementary and secondary schools.[116] In 1966, the miscegenation issue was again raised, in *Loving v. Virginia*,[117] and now the Court was prepared to face it.

In *Loving*, as in *Brown*, the proponents of racial separation sought to apply the test of initial toleration, presenting evidence that those who debated and voted on the Fourteenth Amendment opposed integration and abided laws that enforced segregation. In *Loving*, as in *Brown*, the Court found the historical evidence inconclusive and looked behind the framers' conscious intent to evaluate the reasonableness of the segregating law. The *Brown* Court had accepted social science evidence that segregation was in fact harmful to black schoolchildren, but it had been silent on the question whether this harm was the predictable result of a system designed to preserve racial hierarchy. Analysts who were critical of the *Brown* decision but supportive of its result offered the argument, lacking in the *Brown* opinion, that school segregation was unconstitutional because its *purpose* was to subordinate and stigmatize the black race. Charles Black made this argument most eloquently:

> [I]f a whole race of people finds itself confined within a system which is set up and continued for the very purpose of keeping

it in an inferior station, and if the question is then solemnly
propounded whether such a race is being treated "equally," I
think we ought to exercise one of the sovereign prerogatives of
philosophers—that of laughter. The only question remaining
(after we get our laughter under control) is whether the segregation system answers to this description.

Here I must confess to a tendency to start laughing all over
again. I was raised in the South, in a Texas city where the
pattern of segregation was firmly fixed. I am sure it never occurred to anyone, white or colored, to question its meaning. . . .
The fiction of "equality" is just about on a level with the fiction
of "finding" in the action of trover. I think few candid southerners deny this. Northern people may be misled by the entirely
sincere protestations of many southerners that segregation is
"better" for the Negroes, is not intended to hurt them. But I
think a little probing would demonstrate that what is meant is
that it is better for the Negroes to accept a position of inferiority, at least for the indefinite future.[118]

The *Loving* Court avoided the Doctrinal Stories of actual harm that
critics of *Brown* had assailed. It accepted the thesis that Virginia's antimiscegenation statute had white supremacist origins and a racially subordinating purpose, and ruled for that reason that its prohibition of
interracial marriage was a denial of equal protection.

The matter might have been closed at this juncture, for the Equal
Protection Clause of the Fourteenth Amendment was adequate to void
the challenged statute. But the opinion went further. The Court had
not recognized in *Brown* (and has not since recognized) a right to
education, but had justified its ruling solely in terms of the government's obligation to give its citizens equal treatment. *Loving* was different. The Court cited not only a theory of equal protection as refined
by the post-*Brown* controversy but also the independent constitutional
status of the right to marry. Chief Justice Warren, writing, as he had
in *Brown*, without dissent, included a Part II that told a Doctrinal Story
independent of the Equal Protection claim. It began with these words:
"These statutes also deprive the Lovings of liberty without due process
of law in violation of the Due Process Clause of the Fourteenth

Amendment. The freedom to marry has long been recognized as one of the vital personal rights essential to the orderly pursuit of happiness by free men."[119] Part II was reportedly "toned down" at the request of Justice Black, who "didn't want any sort of natural law notion creeping into the opinion,"[120] and it provided nothing beyond these two sentences to link the right to marry to the language or history of the Fourteenth Amendment. Nevertheless, a nearly unanimous Court clearly affirmed the special constitutional status of this right of family.*

THE DOCTRINAL STORY EVOLVES

The privileged constitutional status for the right to marry that *Meister* anticipated and *Loving* acknowledged has been reaffirmed in subsequent cases. It was the basis of the Supreme Court's decision, in the 1978 case of *Zablocki v. Redhail*,[121] invalidating a novel assertion of state power to decide which of its citizens were sufficiently responsible or wealthy to take spouses.

States have traditionally defined the marriage relation as a union of competent adults (or older children), involving mutual responsibilities to each other and to any children they bear or adopt. Except for the now invalidated requirement that marriage partners be of the same race, and the requirements, as yet untested in the Supreme Court, that they be of different genders and from sufficiently different bloodlines, states have not often tried to screen marriage partners fitting the traditional definition. Marriage has been regarded as a state for which all of a certain age are qualified. But in the 1970s, the state of Wisconsin deviated from this libertarian pattern to try to do something about the socially devastating problem of noncustodial parents' neglect of child-support obligations. Wisconsin passed a law requiring that noncustodial parents under court order to provide child support must obtain

---

Brown was decided in a single opinion that each of the Court's nine members signed. In *Loving*, eight Justices joined (but did not sign) the Chief Justice's opinion. Justice Stewart filed a two-sentence concurrence, apparently taking the Fourteenth Amendment to require "color blindness" rather than to prohibit subordination and saying that in his view the criminality of an act simply could not depend upon the race of the actor.

judicial approval to receive a license to marry. Although the law was appropriately gender-neutral, it targeted "Deadbeat Dads," without whose support so many women and children lived in poverty. The legislature reasoned that they should demonstrate their ability and willingness to meet old family obligations before taking on new ones. According to the unfortunately sweeping terms of the new law, a marriage would be precluded for any parents delinquent in making support payments or unable to demonstrate that their children were not, and were not likely to become, public charges.

The plaintiff in *Zablocki* argued that the law was an unjustifiable limitation of the fundamental right to marry and that it also discriminated against those whose children need public support, not because of an absence of parental responsibility, but because of parental poverty. A majority of eight Justices agreed that marriage is a fundamental or specially protected right and that the statute was unconstitutional.

But agreement on a constitutional standard was more difficult. The Justices struggled to identify a test, or set of principles, against which the Wisconsin statute could be measured. The Fourteenth Amendment charter of civil freedom explicitly confers federal protection on the right to enjoy the "privileges and immunities of citizenship," the right to "due process of law" in face of governmental threats to "life, liberty or property," and the right to enjoy "equal protection of the laws." These three great clauses—the Privileges and Immunities Clause, the Due Process Clause, and the Equal Protection Clause—are the direct textual support for civil rights protection against state action. For reasons that are not altogether clear or satisfactory, the Supreme Court has not repudiated its ahistorical pronouncement in the *Slaughter-House* case of 1873 that the Privileges and Immunities Clause protects only rights pertaining specially to *federal* citizenship. The clause has therefore been dormant for a century. Reliance upon the Due Process Clause also presents difficulties, the first being with the word "process," which suggests that deprivations of life, liberty, and property are constitutionally permissible so long as achieved with procedural regularity—with "due process" in the most literal sense. From time to time, and often in family rights cases, the Supreme Court has concluded that particular invasions of liberty violate the Due Process Clause, not because of their procedural flaws but because they are simply unjustifiable. This course has been taken when the state's action compromised rights that the Supreme Court thought fundamental, or especially important, to constitutional conceptions of liberty and citizenship. There is, then, a list of *substantive* due process rights about which the Court has been especially solicitous, giving them more protection than *procedural* fairness can afford. However, as we shall see presently, the history of the Court has been such that since the late 1930s many Justices have been reluctant to rely upon substantive Due Process jurisprudence. This leaves the Equal Protection Clause, with its command that the law not discriminate unreasonably among classes of people. When laws have compromised important or fundamental rights of some classes of people but not of others, the Court has often relied on the Equal Protection Clause, and given especially strict attention to the reasonableness of the *discrimination* in light of the importance of the affected right.

Justice Marshall, writing for five members of the Court in *Zablocki*, took the Equal Protection course. Because the Wisconsin statute substantially interfered with the right to marry, "critical examination" was required to assure that the denial of marriage rights to the affected class was "supported by sufficiently important state interests and . . . closely tailored to effectuate only those interests."[122] The majority granted that Wisconsin's interests were substantial, but found its means crudely tailored and almost gratuitously destructive of a fundamental right. Justice Stewart, though he agreed, admonished his colleagues for hiding behind the mechanical-sounding rules of Equal Protection analysis and denying the enormous power the Supreme Court wields when it invalidates laws in the name of individual liberty. He argued that the Court's decision depended, and should be acknowledged as depending, on recognizing that the right to marry, which each of the Justices in the majority thought fundamental, is specially guarded for reasons that are *substantive* and matter regardless of concerns about procedure or discrimination.[123]

The constitutional significance of the right to marry was again affirmed in 1987 when the Supreme Court voted unanimously in *Turner v. Safley* to invalidate restrictions on the marriage of prison inmates. Justice O'Connor's opinion for the Court gave texture and emphasis to the marriage right, articulating emotional, religious, economic, and parental interests that remained to inmates and were entitled to constitutional protection even though sexual relationships were precluded or limited by their incarceration. She recognized that under our laws marriage is a precondition for government benefits and a variety of other property rights. Looking from economic matters to affiliational ones, she observed that marriage can also be a precondition for the "legitimation" of children. Looking deeper, she described marriage as an expression "of emotional support and public commitment" that carried "spiritual significance," often constituting "an exercise of religious faith as well as an expression of personal dedication."[124]

3

"THE CHILD IS NOT THE CREATURE OF THE STATE"

• ⇐⇒ •

Stories about Parenting

Most adults leave or extend their families of origin to take partners and form new families. People do this for a variety of
reasons. Many find life's possibilities enhanced by the mutual support
and intimacy of a life partnership. As Justice O'Connor observed in
Turner v. Safley, the commitment that we associate with marriage has

---

ABOVE: An emancipated family

important psychological, social, economic, and spiritual meanings. For some, the central purpose and satisfaction of a family commitment is to produce and nurture children. Child rearing is, for most of us, a singular joy and a uniquely challenging responsibility. And nearly all of us participate—if not as parents, then as extended family, teachers, neighbors, or friends—in guiding the next generations. It is in these interactions with children that we most explicitly articulate, develop, and teach what we think of as family values.

But we also express our concern for children in less personal ways. Our communities create systems that support and supplement the care that nuclear and extended families give their children. We pass laws about and enforce minimum standards for the care and support that children receive from their parents. We assume responsibility for children who do not receive enough care within their families. We provide public education that supplements—and sometimes contradicts—the teaching a child gets at home. And we provide, albeit in grossly limited ways, public health services and economic support for families that lack the money to give their children basic care and shelter.

The legal boundaries between public and private responsibility for children are indistinct. It is not altogether clear what child-rearing practices or medical treatments, or educational programs, or other child-directed measures the government may require or forbid. Moreover, it is not always clear which bonds between children and adults are recognized as family bonds. The answers to these questions have depended not only on the letter of state laws regulating family life but also on principles enshrined in the Fourteenth Amendment; these establish rights, subject to some conditions, to maintain a parental relationship, to have a measure of liberty in child rearing, and, some would argue, to expect a measure of public responsibility for children.

Constitutional principles that affect the parental relation, like those that affect the marital relation, have been developed without attention to the Reconstruction era's concern with family liberty. Yet the Fourteenth Amendment's guarantee of civil freedom was the achievement of people who were deeply influenced not only by slavery's effect upon the marital relation but also by its arguably more far-reaching effect upon the parental relation. In what follows, Doctrinal Stories will trace once again the articulation of constitutional principles; Motivating Stories will trace unexplored legacies of slavery and of antislavery thought and struggle.

A DOCTRINAL STORY "TOUCHING THE RELATION BETWEEN INDIVIDUAL AND STATE"

In the second decade of the twentieth century, the Supreme Court confronted a set of direct conflicts between state authority to educate and indoctrinate the young and the authority of families to guide the development of their children in ways the state might not approve. The participants displayed all the uncertainties about libertarian and authoritarian governance that characterize contemporary debates about family values. Political majorities—conspicuously inspired by wartime patriotic fervor and hostility against immigrant groups, but claiming as well a desire to unite and uplift a diverse citizenry—were set against political minorities inspired by the wish to uphold and transmit the traditions of their forebears in other lands. In each case, the majority invoked the power of the state to assure that children were trained in patriotism and prepared for citizenship. In each case, parents and teachers protested that the socialization of young minds was a matter that democracy left to private discretion.

Meyer v. Nebraska and its companion cases[1] were challenges to state laws that prohibited foreign-language instruction in public schools before the eighth grade. The laws had been enacted, and approved by state courts, to reduce what their proponents described as "the baneful effects of permitting foreigners, who had taken residence in this country, to rear and educate their children in the language of their native land."[2] They were challenged as infringements of the liberty of teachers to teach and the liberty of parents to choose instruction for their children.

The teachers who were plaintiffs in *Meyer* argued that the Fourteenth Amendment gave federal courts power to prevent state violations of their civil right to pursue a calling and to work as they chose to work. This is exactly the argument that the Court had rejected when Louisiana butchers brought *The Slaughter-House Cases* and when Myra Bradwell claimed the right to practice law in Illinois: in 1873, the

Court had ruled, in the contexts of deciding the butchers' right to work and Myra Bradwell's right to practice law, that the mission of the Fourteenth Amendment was not bold enough to encompass an assertion of federal power to discipline the states for violations of civil rights. But fortunately for the *Meyer* plaintiffs, the Court had rather quickly abandoned the broad Doctrinal Story it told in *Slaughter-House* and *Bradwell*. Although the meaningfulness of the Privileges and Immunities Clause—the clause upon which the butchers and Ms. Bradwell had principally and quite reasonably relied—was not recaptured, in the years following *Bradwell* and *Slaughter-House*, the Court had quickly found in the Due Process Clause authority to protect against infringements of property rights, whether or not those rights had a uniquely federal character. Rejecting the argument that the requirement of "due process" is fairly applied only to address procedural deficiencies, the Court read the Fourteenth Amendment's assurance against government-imposed deprivations of life, liberty, or property without due process of law as requiring not only that the *procedures* by which government acts be fair and reasonable but also that the deprivations be justifiable as a matter of *substance*. Government actions came to be regarded as violations of due process if they lacked adequate procedural safeguards *or* if they lacked reasonable justification. Indeed, in the years between 1897 and 1937,[3] the Supreme Court, at least in cases touching economic rights of property and contract, generously protected substantive due process rights and liberties (including, surprisingly to some, those of corporate entities).

The expansiveness and confidence of the Court's post-*Slaughter-House* decisions protecting individual and corporate property rights spilled over as the Justices considered the *Meyer* plaintiffs' claim to more personal rights. Justice James McReynolds's opinion for the majority followed the pattern of a previous string of cases invalidating labor and consumer protection laws in the name of economic liberty, causing Justice Holmes, among others, to worry that his colleagues were extending a misguidedly libertarian practice of invalidating reasonable public welfare measures.[4] The Court began its opinion with a broad pronouncement of inalienable entitlement. The Justices in the majority described the liberty protected by the Fourteenth Amendment as including, "[w]ithout doubt," rights of autonomy and self-definition:

"the rights to contract; to engage in the common occupations of life; to acquire useful knowledge; to marry; to establish a home and bring up children; to worship according to the dictates of individual conscience; and to enjoy other privileges recognized at common law as essential to the orderly pursuit of happiness in a state of freedom."[5] They announced forthrightly that the Fourteenth Amendment protected these rights against state action that was arbitrary or unreasonable in relation to the government's purpose. And they affirmed federal power to scrutinize restrictive state laws by a measure that took into account the importance of the compromised freedom and the importance and legitimacy of the state's goals. In the cases before it, the Court found that despite the states' legitimate interest in promoting national loyalty and a sense of citizenship, its interference with the autonomous choices of parents and teachers to instruct children in different languages was not justified.

The Supreme Court explained its decision to invalidate English-language schooling requirements in terms of two distinct aspects of the "privileges . . . essential to the orderly pursuit of happiness in a state of freedom." First, in an ironic echo of *Slaughter-House* and *Bradwell*, it said that the requirement violated the teachers' Fourteenth Amendment right to pursue their calling. Second, and more important to the development of family rights jurisprudence, it said that the requirement violated the right of parents to control the socialization of their children. In a stroke, the teacher's "right . . . to teach [as s/he reasonably saw fit] and the right of parents to engage [the teacher] so to instruct their children" were held to be "within the liberty of the [Fourteenth] Amendment."

The Court based its definition of the "right of parents" upon choices made by the people of the United States concerning the structure of their government and the relationship between it and the citizen. The choices were explained by reference to paths conceptualized in ancient Greece but not followed in the English or American context. American people, said the Court, had rejected the values underlying the Platonic model of mandatory communal marriage and child rearing and the Spartan practice of consigning young males to the custody of official guardians for education and training. These measures, although approved by "men of great genius" as appropriate to the development of ideal citizens, were antithetical to principles "touching the relation between individual and State" upon which United States institutions rested.[6] Although the Court appreciated the appeal of measures designed to "foster a homogeneous [and loyal] people,"[7] it found the prohibition of foreign-language instruction more Spartan and Platonic than American and without a basis that was reasonable in the United States' political context.[8]

Justices Holmes and Sutherland, taking a narrower view of the requirements of due process, joined the majority with respect to an Ohio law concerning the teaching of German but dissented with respect to the more general requirement in Iowa and Nebraska that all elementary school instruction be in English, finding its reasonableness a subject as to which rational minds might differ.[9] Holmes wrote for both Justices, emphasizing his consistent belief that the initiatives of representative government are constitutional so long as they have a rational basis. But he did not directly challenge the majority's Doctrinal Story of family liberty, and the Court's central holding—that a substantive right of family autonomy protects parents' liberty to make choices about how their children will be reared and educated—became the law of the land with little fanfare or debate.

Two years later, the Court considered a broader state effort to control the education of its youth. In *Pierce v. Society of Sisters*,[10] a Catholic school sought to enjoin the enforcement of a Nebraska law requiring that all children attend public schools until they completed the eighth grade or reached the age of sixteen. The Court did not rely upon the right of freedom of religion or the right of schoolteachers to speak, teach, or earn a living, but justified its decision by invoking the parental right it had first acknowledged in Meyer. Although it had, in Meyer, weighed state interests in fostering loyalty and patriotism against parents' rights to autonomy, the Court did not even discuss the social benefits of universal public education. It simply said that the public school requirement unconstitutionally interfered with the liberty of parents and guardians to direct the upbringing and education of their children.[11] And, in a passage that lawyers have used consistently in succeeding years, it rearticulated the rationale for including parental rights among the liberties specially protected by the Due Process Clause:

The fundamental theory of liberty upon which all governments in this Union repose excludes any general power of the State to standardize its children by forcing them to accept instruction from public teachers only. The child is not the mere creature of the State; those who nurture him and direct his destiny have the right, coupled with the high duty, to recognize and prepare him for additional obligations.[12]

The decision was without dissent.

Meyer and Pierce are great mysteries of Supreme Court jurisprudence. The laws they invalidated were undoubtedly motivated in large part by a mix of intolerance and paternalism with respect to foreign-born people. The laws struck in Meyer were typical of prohibitions of foreign-language instruction enacted in a large majority of the United States in the years immediately following the Great War. Even sympathetic students of those laws acknowledge that they were motivated in important part by anti-German bias of the war years and a nativist distrust of anything foreign.[13] The Oregon private school prohibition that Pierce invalidated was passed as a result of a national campaign initiated by the Ku Klux Klan and more respectable organizations, like the Scottish Rite Masons, believed to have been used by the Klan as fronts. The Scottish Rite Masons' commitment to public schools was a component of their opposition to "an alleged effort of Catholics to sap the strength of the common school and against the specter of 'Bolshevist' instruction in private schools." Their goal was to teach all children in the United States "along standardized lines, which will enable them to acquire a uniform outlook on all national and patriotic questions." The campaign for the Oregon law has been described in a careful analysis as "anti-immigrant, anti-Catholic, anti-Bolshevist, [and] anti-elite." Still, in the minds of mandatory public school adherents these sentiments appear to have rested with surprising comfort alongside paternalistic ambitions to foster feelings of national pride and mutual concern that would transcend ethnic, racial, and class lines.[14] The irony is that James McReynolds, the author of the opinions invalidating the English language requirements as expressions of intolerance, is a strong contender for the distinction of being the most intolerant of the Court's members across the years. Indeed, accounts

of the Justice mirror the most pejorative accounts of the factions behind the legislation his opinions condemned. He has been described
as "the most bigoted, vitriolic, and intolerant individual ever to have
sat on the Supreme Court . . . 'crotchety,' 'overbearing,' 'rude' and 'sav-
age.' He openly despised most everyone from Jews to women lawyers
to legislators to African-Americans. His antisemitism was legendary,
even in those intolerant times. He was unspeakably rude to his Jewish
colleagues, Brandeis and Cardozo, refusing to shake hands, turning his
back on them in conference, disdaining their writings, and explaining
'that for four thousand years the Lord tried to make something out of
Hebrews, then gave it up as impossible and turned them out to prey
on mankind in general.' "[15] In *Berger v. United States*, when the Court
overturned the criminal conviction of German defendants because of
the trial judge's explicitly anti-German remarks, McReynolds dissented, referring to "malevolents from Germany, a country . . . engaged
[at the time of the trial] in hunnish warfare and notoriously encouraged
by many of its natives who, unhappily, had obtained citizenship here,"
and expressing sympathy with the trial judge's "detestation for all persons of German extraction who were at that time wickedly abusing
privileges granted by our indulgent laws."[16]

What would cause such a person to conclude with unqualified confidence that the Klan-sponsored school laws were unconstitutional?
One might suppose that Justice McReynolds was a constitutional and
ideological libertarian who believed that even groups he detested were
entitled to be safe from government constraints. But McReynolds was
not consistently libertarian even with respect to market controls; he
made his political reputation as a trustbuster, believing that government regulation was preferable to private monopoly control of the
marketplace. The more likely explanation is that challengers of the
school laws waved the issues of communism and socialism to keep a
conservative Court distracted from the direct beneficiaries of the laws
and on the libertarian path carved in cases challenging labor and consumer protection laws. Legal scholar Barbara Bennett Woodhouse argues in a calculatedly provocative retelling of the story of the *Meyer*
and *Pierce* litigation that the most influential advocate in both cases
was William Dameron Guthrie, an ultraconservative Columbia University law professor who represented the Society of Sisters in *Pierce*

and filed a strategic friend-of-the-court brief in *Meyer*.[17] Guthrie was a vocal opponent of social welfare legislation. He defended the now infamous *Lochner* decision invalidating a maximum sixty-hour workweek for bakers by complaining that Lochner ran a clean bakery and there was no reason to make him a criminal, and he opposed child labor laws as "communistic."[18] His briefs are the apparent source of Justice McReynolds's Platonic analogy, but Plato is not the central villain in Guthrie's account; he refers to *The Republic* in the course of suggesting that the school laws would produce "state-bred monsters" and were "in consonance only with the communistic and bolshevistic ideals . . . obtaining in Russia." Although Guthrie was a devout Catholic, he seemed pointedly to avoid focusing on Catholic schools as the target of the laws; he emphasized that the laws threatened all religions and facilitated tyranny. Counsel for the plaintiffs in *Meyer* also invoked anticommunist opposition to universal public schooling, noting that the Nebraska foreign-language prohibition was a compromise enacted in order to block passage of a bill prohibiting private schooling, and making pointed references to Soviet Russian laws forbidding religious and minority language instruction.[19]

The *Meyer* and *Pierce* decisions have had a checkered reputation. When they were announced, they were widely regarded as commendable vindications of the principle of tolerance. Nonetheless, many commentators worried that the Court's principle of due process liberty was dangerously broad. It was in response to these cases that Felix Frankfurter argued in the pages of *The New Republic* that the Supreme Court could not guarantee toleration and was on treacherous ground as it tried to do so. But later, when the Court ceased its automatic invalidations of social welfare legislation that inconvenienced businesspeople, criticism of *Meyer* and *Pierce* lost its bite, and over the years the cases were consistently reaffirmed as emblems of constitutional liberty. It was more than fifty years after the end of the *Lochner* era that Professor Woodhouse, whose family law scholarship is rich and sophisticated, retold the *Meyer* and *Pierce* litigation and stimulated a new critique. Her retelling suggested that the principles announced in the McReynolds opinions reinforced a conception of children as the property of their parents and that those who saw the opinions only as emblems of liberty ignored the healthy child welfare reformist motives that mixed with nativism and bigotry as the school laws were crafted. She is right; and there is more. On second look we see that although McReynolds's sunlit words express a sense of human entitlement that is widely shared in our culture, they suffer the limitations of being inspired by hostility to socialist methods rather than by either an affirmative account of the value of family liberty or a conscientious effort to define that liberty so that it does not preclude respectful expressions of collective responsibility.

"MY MOTHER'S NAME WAS ELIZABETH"

*Motivating Stories Touching the Relation
Between Parent and Child*

Recognition of a constitutional right to be a parent, and to function in that role with a generous measure of autonomy, has ample, but heretofore unacknowledged, support in the history of antislavery and Reconstruction. Slavery began, of course, with family separation, as men, women, and children were purchased or kidnapped from families and communities and transported among strangers to America and slavery. The first-generation American slave carried memories of lost families. Most of those memories survived only in the oral traditions of enslaved people, but some were recorded. After the successful mutiny by the slave cargo of the *Amistad*, for example, interviews with the men and women who had seized their freedom documented familial losses: Singgbe had been taken from a father, a wife, and three children; Gilabaru from a wife; Burna from a wife, child, father, three sisters, and a brother; Sessi from three brothers, two sisters, a wife, and three children; Ndamma, from a mother, brother, and sister; Kinna from his parents, grandparents, four brothers, and a sister; Ngahoni, from a wife and child; Fakinna from a father, wife, and two children; another Burna from a mother, four sisters, and two brothers; and Kagne from her parents, four brothers, and four sisters.[20]

The violation of family was repeated on American soil in each succeeding generation of slaves. We have seen that enslaved people in the United States could not form legally recognized marriages and that partnerships between them were disrupted by sale, hiring out, and apprenticeship. But as a tool of subordination and a disavowal of common humanity, denial of the right to marry was secondary to the denial of parental ties, which touched each enslaved person at the moment of birth, imposing a social construction by which s/he would be defined as a commodity rather than as the child of a family, community, and nation. The *Narrative of the Life of William W. Brown* opens with a description of that process: "I was born in Lexington, Ky. The man who stole me as soon as I was born, recorded the births of all the infants which he claimed to be born his property, in a book which he kept for that purpose. My mother's name was Elizabeth."[21] Because Elizabeth Brown was his slave, the man who "stole" William Brown was entitled under the law to claim each of her children as his property. A more detached observer, the Treasury Department Special Agent for the South Carolina Sea Islands, made the point less dramatically in a report to the Secretary of the Treasury: "The children have been regarded as belonging to the plantation rather than to a family, and the parents . . . in their condition can never have but a feeble hold on their off-spring."[22] When an infant was designated slave, it was—to borrow Brown's term and his sense of natural right—stolen from parental care and claimed, like its mother and, perhaps, like its father,* as a commodity. In parental care and control, the child is dependent on the discretion and goodwill of one, two, or several adults with whom it has bonds of biology or of chosen familial commitment and, in all but the most extraordinary cases, bonds of affection. As commodity, the child is subject at every stage to disruption of those bonds. It was this legal and social construction of the slave as commodity rather than as the child of parents, community, and nation that the historian Moses Finley referred to when, quoting Plautus's *Captivi*, he examined the slave's profound social isolation. At a time when the father was the head and emblem of the family, Finley asked, "What father, when he is a slave?"[23]

As the history of slavery has been retold and reinterpreted, we have been cautioned against exaggerating the impact of slaveholders' own-

---

*As we have seen, slave status was legally derived from the mother. The father was often a slave and often not. In the case of William Brown, the father was "a relative of . . . [the] master, and connected with some of the first families of Kentucky." *Brown* at 1.

ership and treatment of enslaved children. Analyses of American slavery that focus on economic incentive argue that the slaveholders, motivated to protect their property interest, saw to it that the health of slave children was safeguarded. These arguments are plausible and helpful to a balanced understanding of slavery, but nonetheless—for reasons no doubt having to do with the human capacity to behave irrationally and with qualitative differences between parental and institutional care—enslaved children clearly suffered from the system's interference with the functioning of their biological and psychological families. Historians of the slave family point out that the physical and emotional effects of these interferences were ameliorated by networks of surrogate caregivers. As a result of what Herbert Gutman describes as "conceptions of quasi-kin and non-kin social obligation," friends and extended family members saw to the needs of biological and fictive kin of tender years.[24] Indeed, these networks continue to function for many families in the United States, and Doctrinal Stories that extend constitutional rights of family to persons outside the nuclear family implicitly acknowledge them. But, as the entire slave community was handicapped by overriding calls to serve the master, the networks of actual and fictive kin could not always protect children against isolation and want of supervision. Notwithstanding the moderating effects of the masters' economic self-interest and of networks of extended care within the slave community, enslaved people and other abolitionists justly and persistently decried the slavemasters' interferences with parenting and the treatment they gave to the children they claimed to own.

The effect of being designated property rather than child was manifest even as an infant felt hunger and the instinct to suck and the mother felt concern and the instinct to nurse. The oral history of Charlotte Brooks describes these moments:

I had a little baby when my second master sold me, and my last old master would make me leave my child before day to go to the canefield; and he would not allow me to come back till ten o'clock in the morning to nurse my child. When I did go I could hear my poor child crying long before I got to it. And la, me! my poor child would be so hungry when I'd get to it! Sometimes

I would have to walk more than a mile to get to my child, and when I did get there I would be so tired I'd fall asleep while my baby was sucking. He did not allow me much time to stay with my baby when I did go to nurse it. Sometimes I would overstay my time with my baby; then I would have to run all the way back to the field.[25]

Aunt Charlotte, what became of your baby? were you blest to raise it?

No; my poor child died when it was two years old. Old master's son was the father of my child.

Did its father help to take care of it?

Why, no; he never noticed my child.

Did you have any more children?

Yes; but they all died.

Why could you not rear any of them?

La, me, child! they died for want of attention. I used to leave them alone half of the time. Sometimes old mistress would have some one to mind them till they got so they could walk, but after that they would have to paddle for themselves. I was glad the Lord took them, for I knowed they were better off with my blessed Jesus than with me.[26]

Henry Bibb reports that on the plantation where he lived and worked mothers who were not permitted to leave the cotton fields carried their infants with them to the fields. He thought the number of slave children raised on these plantations low because "[t]he mothers had no time to take care of them—and they . . . [were] often found dead in the field and in the quarter for want of care of their mothers."[27]

The problem was reported more officially by a New Orleans free man of color testifying before the American Freedmen's Inquiry Commission in 1864:

In relation to child-bearing, the feeling of planters was divergent; some planters desired the negro women to have children, and some did not; some planters worked the women as hard as the men; in some instances they were obliged to labor in every stage of conception [sic]; these statements relate exclusively to the sugar plantations; . . . some [slave women] were kept at work while with child, and others sent to labor one week after confinement; sometimes they were compelled to labor up to the moment of conception [sic]; they usually performed men's labor; to this there were some exceptions; ordinarily, they were given one month to recover; mothers were permitted to nurse children one half hour three times a day; I have heard, but do not know, of women being taken with labor pains in the field; slavery on the plantations had no regard for family relations.[28]

A former slave's autobiographical narrative describes the situation from the child's perspective:

When I was about four years of age, . . . I began to feel another evil of slavery—I mean the want of parental care and attention. My parents were not able to give any attention to their children during the day. I often suffered much from *hunger* and other similar causes. To estimate the sad state of a slave child, you must look at it as a helpless human being thrown upon the world without the benefit of its natural guardians.[29]

As this suggests, slavery's disregard of family relations had consequences for children beyond hunger and the health and safety risks associated with want of supervision. Being "thrown upon the world without benefit of natural guardians" also exposed children to the emotional deprivation and persistent anxiety that isolation from consistent adult attention and frequent and prolonged absences of parent figures inevitably produce.[30]

Enslaved people's capacity to educate and socialize their children was as restricted as their capacity to meet the children's physical and emotional needs. This restriction cut deeply. Most enslaved parents could not send their children to school or choose or reject apprenticeship training for them. Their capacity to give their children home instruction or to supervise and control their daily activities was severely hampered. And these difficulties were compounded by an undermining of parental authority so persistent and insidious that it threatened to negate the good effects of whatever care and attention enslaved parents did manage to provide.

The autobiography of Jacob Stroyer vividly depicts the erosion of parental authority. Stroyer was a slave whose parents had been able, apparently, to instill a basic trust in their capacity and concern in his first years. He describes the incident by which the slave system began to undermine that trust, when he got permission, even though he was "too small to work," to do small chores in a stable:

> It was not long after I had entered my new work before they put me upon the back of a horse which threw me to the ground almost as soon as I had reached his back. It hurt me a little, but that was not the worst of it, for when I got up there was a man standing near with a switch in hand, and he immediately began to beat me. Although I was a very bad boy, this was the first time I had been whipped by any one except father and mother, so I cried out in a tone of voice as if I would say, this is the first and last whipping you will give me when father gets hold of you.
>
> When I had got away from him I ran to father with all my might, but soon found my expectation blasted, as father very coolly said to me, "Go back to your work and be a good boy, for I cannot do anything for you."[31]

When subsequently the boy was ordered to work in the cotton fields against the wishes of his absent mistress, he submitted, for he "had already learned the lesson that father and mother could render me no help."[32] The message was double-edged: the owner and his agents had ultimate power to decide how the child would work and learn, and the parents were helpless in the face of the slaveholder's authority.

The message of parental helplessness was reinforced at moments when the child was present but not directly involved in the encounter with slaveholder power. Years after the fact a former slave recalled:

> My pappy name Jeff and belong to Master Joe Woodward. He live on a plantation across the other side of Wateree Creek. My

mammy name Phoebe. Pappy have to get a pass to come to see Mammy, before the war. Sometime that creek get up over the bank and I, to this day, remembers one time Pappy come in all wet and drenched with water. Him had made the mule swim the creek. Him stayed over his leave that was writ on the pass. Patrollers come ask for the pass. They say: "The time done out, nigger." Pappy try to explain, but they pay no attention to him. Tied him up, pulled down his breeches, and whipped him right before Mammy and us children.[33]

Another former slave remembered a parent who resisted the comparable humiliation of being disciplined by a white *child* for whom she had been a de facto parent. By resisting, the parent affirmed her authority vis-à-vis the offending child and asserted her dignity in the sight of her own child, but in the end she lost her relationship with both.

She didn't work in the field. She worked at a loom. She worked so long and so often that once she went to sleep at the loom. Her master's boy saw her and told his mother. His mother told him to take a whip and wear her out. He took a stick and went out to beat her awake. He beat my mother till she woke up. When she woke up, she took a pole out of the loom and beat him nearly to death with it. He hollered, "Don't beat me no more, and I won't let 'em whip you."

She said, "I'm going to kill you. These black titties sucked you, and then you come out here to beat me." And when she left him, he wasn't able to walk.

And that was the last I seen of her until after freedom. She went out and got on an old cow that she used to milk—Dolly, she called it. She rode away from the plantation, because she knew they would kill her if she stayed.[34]

James Pennington saw himself and his brethren as men who suffered "the deep and corrupting disgrace of having our wives and children owned by other men."[35] He attributed his determination to rebel

against slavery to a moment when he witnessed his father's humiliation. The father had been questioned about the whereabouts of fellow
slaves and replied that he could not say where they were. The following
exchange then ensued:

> "By Eternal, I'll make them know their hour. The fact is, I have
> too many of you; my people are getting to be the most careless,
> lazy, and worthless in the country."
>
> "Master," said my father, "I am always at my post; Monday
> morning never finds me off the plantation."
>
> "Hush, Bazil! I shall have to sell some of you; and then the
> rest will have enough to do; I have not work enough to keep
> you all tightly employed; I have too many of you."
>
> All this was said in an angry, threatening, and exceedingly
> insulting tone. My father was a high-spirited man, and feeling
> deeply the insult, replied to the last expression,—"If I am one
> too many, sir, give me a chance to get a purchaser, and I am
> willing to be sold when it may suit you."
>
> "Bazil, I told you to hush!" and suiting the action to the
> word, he drew forth the "cowhide" from under his arm, fell upon
> him with most savage cruelty, and inflicted fifteen or twenty
> severe stripes with all his strength, over his shoulders and the
> small of his back. As he raised himself upon his toes, and gave
> the last stripe, he said, "By the *** I will make you know that
> I am master of your tongue as well as of your time!"[36]

Pennington, on his way to breakfast, heard this exchange, and saw and
heard the blows inflicted upon his father. He describes his reaction and
that of his family:

> Let me ask any one of Anglo-Saxon blood and spirit, how you
> would expect a *son* to feel at such a sight?
>
> This act created an open rupture with our family—each
> member felt the deep insult that had been inflicted upon our
> head; the spirit of the whole family was roused; we talked of it
> in our nightly gatherings, and showed it in our daily melancholy

aspect. The oppressor saw this, and with the heartlessness that was in perfect keeping with the first insult, commenced a series of tauntings, threatenings, and insinuations, with a view to crush the spirit of the whole family.[37]

These messages of parental vulnerability and subordination were repeatedly burned into the consciousness of slave parents and children, undermining their sense of worth, diminishing the sense of family security and authority, eroding the parents' function as a model of adult agency and independence, and, most importantly for our purposes, kindling a determination that freedom would entail parental prerogatives.

Two years after the Emancipation Proclamation, "[o]n the Bradford plantation in Florida, one untoward incident followed another. First, the family cook told Mrs. Bradford 'if she want any dinner she kin cook it herself.' Then the former slaves went off to a meeting with Northern soldiers to discuss 'our freedom.' Told that she and her daughter could not attend, one woman replied 'they were now free and if she saw fit to take her daughter into that crowd it was nobody's business.' "[38] Eric Foner reports that after emancipation "Georgia freedman James Jeter was beaten for claiming the right of whipping his own child instead of allowing his employer and former master to do so."[39] He also quotes the following complaint, made to the governor by a black North Carolinian in 1869:

I was in my field at my own work and [Dr. A. H.] Jones came by me and drove up to a man's gate that live close by . . . and ordered my child to come there and open that gate for him . . . while there was children in the yard at the same time not more than twenty yards from him and jest because they were white and mine black he wood not call them to open the gate. . . . I spoke gently to him that [the white children] would open the gate. . . . He got out of his buggy . . . and walked nearly hundred yards rite into my field where I was at my own work and double his fist and strick me in the face three times and . . . cursed me [as] a dum old Radical. . . . Now governor I wants you to please rite to me how to bring this man to jestus.[40]

Foner recognizes "political meaning" in this encounter, a meaning expressed both by the emancipated father's refusal "to let a stranger's authority be imposed on his family" and by his decision to bring the matter to a Reconstruction governor as a reversion to de facto slavery and a denial of justice.[41]

The unyielding demands of servitude and the disregard and infantilization of slave parents that so severely compromised the welfare of enslaved children and of their families paled in comparison with a greater and more insidious peril: the ever-present possibility of irremediable physical separation. The oft-told story of parent-child separation resulting from sale or other reallocations of slave resources was, for abolitionists, abundant proof of the depravity of the slave system. For enslaved family members, it was a subtext of panic in every parental script.

At times, the threats to one's ability to be a parent and to the integrity of one's family were realized in rapid succession. The compilers of the Fisk Collection of slave narratives observed that when slave traders transported people from place to place, "it was not uncommon for a mother to have her nursing child taken from her and sold along the roadside."[42] Here is how one survivor of slavery described those losses:

> Often . . . young children [in the slave coffle] grew very noisy, being too young or unsophisticated to understand the gravity of the situation. The driver would complain of a child's crying and warn the mother to stop the noise. If the crying persisted, the driver would take the child away from its mother and give it away to the first home the gang came across. The mother would run up to the driver and fall on her knees begging for him to return her child to her. . . . after one such occurrence, a feeling of horror would shoot through every mother on the coffle, as each would imagine this happening to her.[43]

A former slave told the story from the child's perspective:

> Who I is, how old I is, and where I is born, I don't know. But Master Buford told me how during the war a slave trader name

William Hamilton come to Village Creek, where Master Buford live. That trader was on his way south with my folks and a lot of other slaves, taking them somewheres to sell. He camped by Master Buford's plantation and asks him, "Can I leave this little nigger here till I comes back?" Master Buford say, "Yes," and the trader say he'll be back in about three weeks, soon as he sells all the slaves. He must still be selling them because he never comes back so far, and there I am and my folks am took on, and I is too little to remember them, so I never knows my pappy and mammy. Master Buford says the trader comes from Missouri, but if I is born there I don't know.

The only thing I remembers about all that am there am lots of crying when they tooks me away from my mammy. That something I never forgets.[44]

The threat of parent-child separation was not restricted to the trader's coffle; it was ever-present, continuing even if the family had the fortune to be sold to one master. Slave narratives suggest that, apart from the separations occasioned by the dawn-to-dusk work requirements, young children were often hired or apprenticed out to work for persons other than their, and their parents', owners. Pennington reported that the slaveholders "often hire the children of their slaves out to non-slaveholders, not only because they save themselves the expense of taking care of them, but . . . [to] get among their slaves useful trades." Pennington himself was hired out to a stonemason from an unspecified age until he was eleven, when he was hired out to a blacksmith. The move from stonemason to blacksmith further fragmented Pennington's family, separating him from his brother.[45] Moses Grandy reported that when he "became old enough to be taken away from . . . [his] mother and put to field work" he was "hired out for the year, by auction, at the court house, every January" until he was twenty-one. He described this as "the common practice with respect to slaves belonging to persons who are under age."[46] Henry Bibb reported being "taken away from my mother, and hired out to labor for various persons, eight or ten years in succession." The first time this happened, Bibb was "young and small." All his wages were expended for the education of a white playmate who was also his owner.[47]

The parent-child disruptions associated with being hired out could be mitigated in some instances by visitation, though this had its dangers and costs. Work requirements limited only by slaveholders' grace and a pass system enforced with all the energy generated by fear of rebellion often immobilized enslaved parents and hireling children. The patrollers who pulled down a man's pants and whipped him when he overstayed a visit with his wife and child on a neighboring plantation would be no more lenient in the case of a parent visiting a child hired out to a local tradesperson. Still, when children or parents were hired out there was hope of continued, albeit limited, contact. People whose families were separated by hiring arrangements had still to fear the greater loss of being separated by sale. James L. Smith's autobiography reports the sense of loss as a child, distanced from her mother and brothers by being hired out as a servant, learns that her family has been abruptly sold. Smith, who witnessed the seizure of the mother, ran to inform the daughter:

> She was standing by the fire in the kitchen as I entered—she was the servant girl of John Langsdon, the man who taught me the shoe-maker's trade. As soon as I related to her this sad news she fell to the floor as though she had been shot by a pistol; and, as soon as she had recovered a little from the shock we started for her mother's cabin home, reaching there just in time to see her mother and her two brothers take the vessel for Norfolk, to be sold. This was the last time we ever saw her [mother].[48]

The element of surprise in these separations was apparently not happenstance. James K. Polk wrote his wife on September 26, 1834, that he had decided to purchase land in Mississippi and ship his slaves there. "The negroes have no idea they are going to be sent to the South, and I do not wish them to know it, and therefore it would be best to say nothing about it at home, for it might be carreyed [sic] back to them."[49] The possibility of these unexpected family separations meant that parents and children lived in constant anxiety. Linda Brent reported that as a slave she was "[a]lways . . . in dread that by some accident, or some contrivance, slavery would succeed in snatching my children from me."[50] Henry Bibb wrote that he "could not look upon" his daughter "without being filled with sorrow and fearful apprehensions, of being separated by slaveholders, because she was a slave, regarded as property."[51] Slavery's unceasing threat of sudden family separation was realized for Diana Wagner:

> [H]er mistress said, "Come on, Diana, I want you to go with me down the road a piece." And she went with her, and they got to a place where there was a whole lot of people. They were putting them up on a block and selling them just like cattle. She had a little nursing baby at home, and she broke away from her mistress and them and said, "I can't go off and leave my baby." And they had to get some men and throw her down and hold her to keep her from going back to the house. They sold her away from her baby boy. They didn't let her go back to see him again.[52]

The story of Diana Wagner was probably known to only a few of her acquaintances until it was elicited in the course of the WPA slave narrative project. But there were no slaves, former slaves, or other abolitionists who did not know of comparable violations of the parental bond. The terror of vulnerability to parent-child separations by sudden sale was vivid to black abolitionists, many of whom had endured it themselves. Moses Grandy wrote in 1844 that his mother often hid her children in the woods, keeping them alive with berries, potatoes, raw corn, and strained water puddles, to avoid their being sold. Grandy recalls that the strategy was not always successful:

> After a time, the master would send word to her to come in, promising he would not sell us. But, at length, persons came who agreed to give the prices he set on us. His wife, with much to be done, prevailed on him not to sell me; but he sold my brother, who was a little boy. My mother, frantic with grief, resisted their taking her child away. She was beaten, and held down; she fainted; and, when she came to herself, her boy was gone. She made much outcry, for which the master tied her up to a peach-tree in the yard, and flogged her.[53]

Solomon Northup recalled children who instinctively clung to their
mother's neck at any sign of unusual activity, and remembered mothers
who had lost their children to sale but continued to talk to them in
the cotton fields and cabins as if they were present.[54] Henry Brown
wrote of the loss of his child to a slave coffle:

> These beings were marched with ropes about their necks, and
> staples on their arms, and, although in that respect the scene
> was no very novel one to me, yet the peculiarity of my own
> circumstances made it assume the appearance of unusual horror.
> The train of beings was accompanied by a number of wagons
> loaded with little children of many different families, which as
> they appeared rent the air with their shrieks and cries and vain
> endeavors to resist the separation which was thus forced upon
> them, and the cords with which they were thus bound; but what
> should I now see in the very foremost wagon but a little child
> looking towards me and pitifully calling, father! father![55]

Frederick Douglass wrote that upon the death of a master he was

> immediately sent to be valued and divided with the other prop-
> erty.... No one could tell amongst which pile of chattels I
> might be flung. Thus early, I got a foretaste of that painful
> uncertainty which in one form or another was ever obtruding
> itself in the pathway of the slave. It furnished me a new insight
> into the unnatural power to which I was subjected. Sickness,
> adversity, and death may interfere with the plans and purposes
> of all, but the slave had the added danger of changing homes,
> in the separations unknown to other men.
>   ... One word of the appraisers, against all preferences and
> prayers, could sunder all the ties of friendship and affection,
> even to separating husbands and wives, parents and children.[56]

Like the lovers and de facto spouses I described earlier, parents who
learned they were to be separated from their families by sale often
preferred the risks of escape, with some hope of family reunion in free
territory, to the risks of isolation from family and friends and purchase

by a brutal and distant master. Mattie Jackson's father learned he had been sold to a distant owner, and "previous to his delivery to his new master he made his escape to [Illinois]." The separation was painful, but the family could take solace in the hope that the father would live free and that the wife and children "through the aid of some angel of mercy might be enabled to make their escape also, and . . . [join the father,] to part no more on earth."[57] Ann Ward, consigned to sale for coming to the defense of her husband as he was beaten, agonized over the prospect during a reprieve granted while she nursed an ailing child back to health for the profit of the master. In the words of that son:

> Sometimes pacing the floor half the night with her child in her arms—sometimes kneeling for hours in secret prayer to God for deliverance—sometimes in long earnest consultation with my father as to what must be done in this dreaded emergency—my mother passed days, nights, and weeks of anguish which well-nigh drove her to desperation. But a thought flashed upon her mind: she indulged in it. It was full of danger; it demanded high resolution, great courage, unfailing energy, strong determination; it might fail. But it was only a thought, at most only an indulged thought, perhaps the fruit of her very excited state, and it was not yet a plan; but, for the life of her, she could not shake it off. She kept saying to herself, "supposing I should"—Should What? She scarcely dare say to herself, what. But that thought became familiar, and welcome, and more welcome; it began to take another, a more definite form. Yes; almost ere she knew, it had incorporated itself with her will, and become a resolution, a determination. "William," she said to my father, "we must take this child and run away."[58]

But neither escape nor safe passage to free territory gave security to the black family. Mattie Jackson and her mother survived a difficult journey to Illinois, but advertisements of their escape preceded them, and they were returned to slavery. The Ward family achieved freedom, but, as Samuel Ward reports, "we were all liable at any time to be captured, enslaved, and re-enslaved—first, because we had been robbed of our liberty; then, because our ancestors had been robbed in like manner; and, thirdly and conclusively, in law, because we were black Americans." Indeed, two of Ward's cousins, who had escaped to New York, were recaptured and returned to slavery in 1828. Ward wrote, "I never saw a family thrown into such deep distress by the death of any two of its members, as were our family by the re-enslavement of these two young men. Seven-and-twenty years have past, but we have none of us heard a word concerning them, since their consignment to the living death, the temporal hell, of American slavery."[59]

Indignation against these violations of the parental bond was a central rallying cry of the antislavery movement. Using a common device of antislavery rhetoric, Peter Randolph tried to generate empathy with enslaved people by calling upon universal feelings of family affection:

> Proslavery men and women! for one moment only, in imagination, stand surrounded by *your* loved ones, and behold *them*, one by one, torn from your grasp, or you rudely and forcibly carried from them—how, think you, would you bear it? Would you not rejoice if one voice, even, were raised in your behalf? Were your wife, the partner of your bosom, the mother of your babes, thus ruthlessly snatched from you, were your beloved children stolen before your eyes, would you not think it sufficient cause for a nation's wail? Yea, and a nation's interference![60]

Frances Ellen Watkins Harper, using the sentimental verse popular in her day to great political effect, chose parent-child separation as a central image in her antislavery poetry. "The Slave Mother (A Tale of the Ohio)" captures the persistent dread of the slave parent:

> I have but four, the treasures of my soul,
> They lay like doves around my heart;
> I tremble lest some cruel hand
> Should tear my household wreaths apart.[61]

"Lines," published both in collections of Harper's poetry and in the *National Anti-Slavery Standard*, denounces slavery for its brutal disregard of motherhood:

> *At the Portals of the Future*
> *Full of madness, guilt and gloom*
> *Stood the hateful form of Slavery,*
> *Crying Give, Oh! give me room—*
>
> *Room to smite the earth with cursing*
> *Room to scatter, rend and slay,*
> *From the trembling mother's bosom*
> *Room to tear her child away.*[62]

"Bury Me in a Free Land," published in *The Liberator* in 1864 (and mailed to a man awaiting execution for participation in the Harper's Ferry raid), repeated the theme of mother-child separation:

> *I could not sleep, if I heard the tread*
> *Of a coffle-gang to the shambles led*
> *And the mother's shriek of wild despair*
> *Rise, like a curse on the trembling air.*
>
> *I could not rest, if I saw the lash*
> *Drinking her blood at each fearful gash;*
> *And I saw her babes torn from her breast,*
> *Like trembling doves from their parent nest.*[63]

"Family separation was the greatest perceived sin of American slavery,"[64] and the theme of parental separation was a staple of antislavery oratory. Reports of a speech of Sarah Parker Remond, given in Dublin in 1859, confirm the impression that condemnations of family separations were present in abolitionist rhetoric "not here and there, but in dreary succession":

> Time this evening was too precious to admit of any detail of those sickening and soul-harrowing scenes, which, alas! are too

common in Slave States to command a passing notice. It might
be enough to state that at the beck of a cruel master, husband
and wife are continually separated and sold, never again to meet
in this world; children are torn from their parents, and mothers
bereaved of their beloved little ones.[65]

William Lloyd Garrison's *Declaration of Sentiments of the American Anti-
Slavery Society* decried the fact that "at least one-sixth part of our countrymen . . . are ruthlessly torn asunder—the tender babe from the arms
of its frantic mother—the heart-broken wife from her weeping husband—at the caprice or pleasure of irresponsible tyrants."[66] John
Greenleaf Whittier described slavery as a system "which tears without
scruple the infant from the mother, the wife from the husband, the
parent from the child."[67] An antislavery minister in Ohio wrote to his
slaveholding brother in Virginia: "The flood of grief that rolls over the
sable and woe-worn cheek, when a wife or a child is snatched from the
embraces of the fond husband or parent, speaks the passions of the soul
in a language too strong to be resisted by anything less than implacable
prejudice."[68] Antislavery students at Lane Seminary in Cincinnati,
Ohio, condemned slavery for "its sunderings of kindred."[69] Henry Bibb
wrenched hearts during his antislavery lectures with renditions of "The
Mother's Lament," a song often sung by slaves about to be sold.[70]

Like many white abolitionists, Abby Kelley learned of family separations from those who had suffered them. She was moved by an
interview she conducted early in her career as an abolitionist with
Dolly Harris, a runaway slave, who told her, "When I was separated
from my husband I thought it was a dreadful thing, but when they
came and tore my child from me, it would have been easier for me to
have died than to endure it." In the only surviving example of her
early speeches, Kelley mocked the claim of the United States to be
"the freest nation on earth," saying, "Her sons were free, yes! Free to
snatch the babe from the arms of its father or mother." In explaining
her determination to continue, in defiance of nineteenth-century
norms, to travel the antislavery lecture circuit after her own child's
birth, Kelley said, "We shall see whether I care so much for my baby
as to forget the multitudes of broken hearted mothers."[71] Later, she
said, "when I left my little daughter I [felt] as though I should die. But

I have done it for the sake of the mothers whose babies are sold away from them."[72] Kelley taught her young daughter to understand why her mother sacrificed their time together to work in the antislavery cause by telling the child "about the slave children who were taken from their mothers, explaining that her own mission was to preach to the 'wicked' men responsible for slavery and to 'make them good so that they would let the poor slave mothers go home.' "[73]

Angelina Grimké was thorough in her denunciation not only of physical separations of slave parents and their children but also of the undermining of parental authority:

> Persons who own plantations and yet live in cities, often take children from their parents as soon as they are weaned and send them to the country; because they do not want the time of the mother taken up by attendance upon her own children, it being too valuable to the mistress. As a *favor*, she is, in some cases, permitted to go to see them once a year. . . . Parents are almost never consulted as to the disposition to be made of their children; they have as little control over them, as have domestic animals over the disposal of their young. Every natural and social feeling and affection are violated with indifference; slaves are treated as though they did not possess them.[74]

''WHAT DEFINITION WILL YOU ATTACH TO THE WORD 'FREEMAN' ''?

Rights of Family as Antislavery Ideology and Reconstruction Promise

Although the picture of enforced parent-child separation lends itself to sentimental treatment, protest against the denial of family was not only emotional but also decidedly political. Antislavery people's commitment to family integrity and parental autonomy was, like their parallel commitment to the right to marry, related to a theory of human entitlement and freedom. When an article in an 1836 issue of the *Anti-Slavery Record* denounced slavery as "nothing but a system of tearing asunder family ties," it said those ties were protected by "sacred law which slavery scornfully sets at nought."[75] "The Family," wrote another abolitionist, "is the head, the heart, the fountain of society, and it has not a privilege that slavery does not nullify, a right that it does not counteract, nor a hope that it does not put out in darkness."[76] Anti-slavery advocates considered the rights, privileges, and hopes associated with forming and maintaining families inviolable as a matter of divine, natural, moral—and, for some, constitutional—law.

As early as 1774, enslaved people petitioning the government of Massachusetts grounded their claim to freedom in an argument of a natural right to family integrity and autonomy. They—like William W. Brown, who also lived the experience, and like the scholars Finley and Patterson, who studied systems of slavery across the centuries—described enslavement as a theft of the self from the family: "[W]e were unjustly dragged by the cruel hand of power from our dearest friends and sum of us stolen from the bosoms of our tender Parents and from a Populous Pleasant and plentiful country and Brought hither to be made slaves for Life in a Christian land."[77] These eighteenth-century American slaves then noted the repetition of family abrogation in each new generation:

> [W]e are deprived of every thing that hath a tendency to make life even tolerable, the endearing ties of husband and wife we are strangers to for we are no longer man and wife than our masters or mistresses thinkes proper marred or onmarried. Our children are also taken from us by force and sent maney miles from us wear we seldom or ever see them again there to be made slaves of for Life which sumtimes is vere short by Reson of Being dragged from their mothers Breest.[78]

The petitioners argued that slavery's abrogation of family ties made them unable to fulfill religious and moral obligations of family, for they were "rendered incapable of shewing . . . obedience to Almighty God[. H]ow can a slave perform the duties of a husband to a wife or parent to his child[?]"[79] As Grimké would charge decades later, and as a similar petition had explained the year before, when enslaved people were denied rights of family they were excluded from appropriate human social intercourse and treated as if they were beasts: "[W]e are rendered unable to do, or to possess and enjoy any Thing, no, not even *Life itself*, but in a Manner as the *Beasts that perish*. We have no Property! We have no Wives! No Children! We have no City! No Country!"[80] The 1774 petitioners claimed emancipation and the restoration of family autonomy as a matter of natural and moral right: "[We] have in common with all other men a naturel right to our freedoms without Being depriv'd of them by our fellow men as we are a freeborn Pepel and have never forfeited this Blessing by aney compact of agreement whatever."

Antislavery whites shared with black freedom fighters this belief that family integrity and autonomy were matters of moral and natural right. The 1833 *Declaration of Sentiments of the American Anti-Slavery Society* followed its condemnation of the tyranny of family separations with an assertion of inalienable rights and liberties: "Every man has a right to his own body—to the products of his own labor—to the protection of law—and to the common advantages of society." The society affirmed that slave laws were "before God utterly null and void; being an audacious usurpation of the Divine prerogative, a daring infringement on the law of nature, a base overthrow of the very foundations of the social compact, a complete extinction of all the relations, endearments and obligations of mankind, and a presumptuous transgression of all the holy commandments."[81] At times, antislavery advocates argued that in addition to violating divine law, natural law, and the social contract, slavery violated the Constitution. Angelina Grimké in 1837 made this more sweeping claim. Relying in part upon the Preamble's dedication to justice, general welfare, and the blessings of liberty,[82] she argued that the Constitution embodied natural law principles that forbade slavery. The nation was therefore required, on legal as well as on moral and spiritual grounds:

1. . . . . [T]o reject with indignation, the wild and guilty phantasy that man can hold property in man. 2. To pay the laborer his hire, for he is worthy of it. 3. No longer to deny him the right of marriage, but to let every man have his own wife, and let every woman have her own husband. . . . 4. To let parents have their own children, for they are the gift of the Lord to them,

and no one else has any right to them. 5. No longer to withhold the advantages of education and the privilege of reading the Bible. 6. To put the slave under the protection of equitable laws.[83]

Although antislavery people continued to disagree about whether the Constitution required amendment to prohibit slavery, it became increasingly clear to all of them that a democratic constitution *should* prohibit not only slavery but any denial of rights as fundamental as the rights to marry and to parent. In the late nineteenth century, the demand for "man's natural birthright of freedom"[84] had ripened into what Frederick Douglass conceptualized as a demand for "a new order, a new definition of American nationality,"[85] for an understanding of citizenship "that would include blacks, and [a constitutional scheme under which it would] 'mean as much [to be called a United States citizen] as it did to be called a Roman citizen in the palmiest days of the Roman Empire.' "[86] The call was for

> a free country—a country not saddened by the footprints of a single slave—and nowhere cursed by the presence of a single slaveholder. We want a country which shall not brand the Declaration of Independence a lie. We want a country whose fundamental institutions we can proudly defend before the highest intelligence and civilization of the age . . . a country in which . . . patriotism shall not conflict with fidelity to justice and liberty.[87]

When the Civil War ended and terms of national reconstruction were needed, antislavery people insisted that in the reunited states, freedom, with its guarantee of "life, liberty and the pursuit of happiness," would assure to all members of the national community rights of family affiliation that slavery had trampled. An African-American soldier named Thornton, fighting for freedom in the Civil War, was asked at a celebration of the signing of the Emancipation Proclamation to share his recollections of slavery and his feelings about freedom. He recalled family separations and expressed his expectation that they were ended: "I cried all night. What's the matter, Thornton? Tomorrow my child is to be sold, never more see it till judgment—no more that; no more that! no more that!"[88] Southern slaves, who

> could be sold, disciplined, and moved without recourse, and . . . had no right to marry, educate their children, or provide for their parents . . . expected the destruction of their owners' sovereignty to open a world of new possibilities. If slavery denied them the right to control their persons and progeny, freedom would confer that right. . . . As free people, former slaves expected to be able to organize their lives in accordance with their own sense of propriety, establish their families as independent units, and control productive property as the foundation of their new status.[89]

Across the country, "black men and women shared a passionate commitment to the stability of family life as a badge of freedom."[90]

The Reconstruction Congress directly addressed the abolitionists' insistence that former slaves, and all other citizens, be secure in the parental relation. The debates of the Thirty-eighth and Thirty-ninth Congresses reveal that as these bodies shaped the Thirteenth and Fourteenth amendments, they were deeply affected by the widely publicized accounts of parental separations and fully responsive to the argument that rights of family are inalienable. Moreover, the members of Congress knew that the parental bond was still fragile in the former Confederacy. Carl Schurz, a Republican writer and political figure commissioned to report to Congress on the postwar condition of the South, made it clear that Southern whites still had "an ingrained feeling that the blacks at large belong to the whites at large."[91] As a result, sentiments of the kind expressed by a Mississippi planter to General Fisk were to be expected:

> He had on his plantation a little girl, and wrote me a long letter in relation to it, which closed up by saying: "As to recognizing the rights of freedmen to their children, I will say there is not one man or woman in all the South who believes they are free,

but we consider them as stolen property—stolen by the bayonets of the damnable United States government."[92]

Working with heightened sensitivity to the notorious and continuing
deprivation of family integrity, members of the Thirty-eighth Congress
debating the Thirteenth Amendment repeatedly acknowledged the
fundamental and inalienable character of rights of family. Senator
Clark denounced slavery as having "destroyed the sanctity of marriage,
and sundered and broken the domestic ties."[93] Representative Broomall pronounced it "strange that an appeal should be made to humanity
in favor of an institution which allows the husband to be separated
from the wife, that allows the children to be taken from the mother;
ah! that allows the very children of the deceased slaveholder himself
to be sold to satisfy his merciless creditors." Representative Shannon
spoke out against "tearing from the mother's arms the sucking child,
and selling them to different and distant owners."[94] Representative
Kelly decried the "unnatural separation and sale of husband and
wife from each other and from their children" as a deprivation of
the "common blessings" that slaves, like all human beings, are "by
nature entitled to."[95] Senator Sumner asked that his colleagues imagine an extraterrestrial visitor beholding the spectacle of slavery:
"[A]stonishment . . . would swell to marvel as he learned that in this
republic . . . there were four million human beings in abject bondage,
degraded to be chattels, despoiled of all rights, even the . . . sacred right
of family; so that the relation of husband and wife was impossible and
no parent could claim his own child."[96] Senator Harlan described, and
condemned as contrary to natural law, the "incidents of slavery," the
first two of which were denial of the marriage relation and abrogation
of the parent-child relation. The second was described this way:

> Another incident is the abolition practically of the parental
> relation, robbing the offspring of the care and attention of his
> parents, severing a relation which is universally cited as the
> emblem of the relation sustained by the Creator to the human
> family. And yet, according to the matured judgment of these
> slave States, this guardianship of the parent over his own chil-
> dren must be abrogated to secure the perpetuity of slavery.[97]

Representative Farnsworth declared "a man's right to . . . his . . . children" inalienable,[98] and Congressman Kasson identified

> three great fundamental natural rights of human society which
> you cannot take away without striking a vital blow at the rights
> of white men as well as black. They are the rights of a husband
> to his wife—the marital relation; the right of father to his
> child—the parental relation; and the right of a man to the
> personal liberty with which he was endowed by nature and by
> God, and which the best judicial authorities of England have
> for a hundred years declared he could not alienate even by his
> own consent.[99]

Senator Wilson declared that upon ratification of the Thirteenth
Amendment the law would protect the "hallowed" relations of parent
and child.[100]

In the Thirty-ninth Congress, House and Senate members followed
approval of the Thirteenth Amendment with passage of measures to
implement its principles of liberty. These measures were designed to
contain the effects of laws, known as the Black Codes, which member
states of the former Confederacy passed to define the civil status of
former slaves. The Black Codes were grounded in what Carl Schurz
had described as a sense of entitlement to black service; they sought
to perpetuate white control over black labor as well as to maintain,
through the Jim Crow system, the civil and social subordination
of black people. And, as Congress learned when it investigated
the activities of former Confederate states after the war, the Black
Codes repeated slavery's abrogation of rights of family. Although
the Codes all legitimized slave marriages,[101] the Codes of Mississippi
"compel[led] all freedmen to marry whomsoever they . . . [were then]
living with, and to support the issue of what was in many cases
compulsory cohabitation."[102] In some jurisdictions, slavery was effectively continued through the device of making black children the
wards or apprentices of whites, and the procedure by which this was
done (unlike apprenticeship arrangements involving white children)
did not require parental consent; as Senator Donnelly reported, "[t]he

black code of Tennessee provides that . . . children [of the 'vagrant' Negro] may be bound out against his wish to a master by the county court."[103]

Congress was determined that despite the best efforts of the former Confederacy, slavery's usurpations of family rights would not survive emancipation. As Representative Eliot said in support of a homestead provision of the Freedmen's Bureau Bill, "[N]o act of ours can fitly enforce . . . freedom that does not contemplate . . . the security of the home."[104]

The Civil Rights Act of 1866, formulated to ensure the liberties incident to freedom, and subsequently constitutionalized with the Fourteenth Amendment,[105] was intended to provide the security of home, not by the provision of land or place, but by the guarantee of rights of family. The first version of the act spoke only in terms of discrimination, prohibiting "any inequality of civil rights and immunities among the inhabitants of [former Confederate] States."[106] Senator Sherman proposed that the act be amended to "secure to the freedmen of the southern States certain rights, naming them, defining precisely what they should be, [and including] the right . . . to be protected in their homes and family [as a] . . . natural [right] of free men."[107] Senator Sumner also urged specification of the rights of freedmen, including among them the rights "to contract marriage, and to make any arrangement whatever concerning their family affairs."[108] The act *was* amended to specify rights to which freedmen were entitled; the amended version did not use the terms "parent," "child," "marriage," or "family," but it was understood to encompass familial rights, and it specifically guaranteed the rights

> to make and enforce contracts, to sue, be parties, and give evidence, to inherit, purchase, lease, sell, hold, and convey real and personal property, and to full and equal benefit of all laws and proceedings for the security of person and property, as it is enjoyed by white citizens, and . . . [to] be subject to like punishment, pains, and penalties, and to none other.[109]

In the common understandings of the day, rights of contract, of property, and of equal benefit of law encompassed rights of marriage and family integrity, for the right to marry was understood as a right of contract;* rights of family integrity were understood as male rights to possession or ownership of wives and children;† and the provision of rights equal to those of white citizens was understood to guarantee to former slaves the traditional and common law rights of marriage and parental custody and control.‡

The argument that the Reconstruction Congress secured rights of family to all people in the United States would have been tenuous had the Thirty-ninth Congress rested with passage of the Civil Rights Act. Of course, it did not. After passage of the Civil Rights Act, the Thirty-ninth Congress, acting in part against the possibility that it lacked constitutional authority to grant the rights it enumerated, proposed a Fourteenth Amendment to the Constitution. Covering at least the ground it had sought to cover by passage of the Civil Rights Act, Congress proposed that every person in the United States be assured the privileges and immunities of citizenship, be protected against deprivations of life, liberty, or property without due process of law, and be guaranteed the equal protection of the laws.

The Civil Rights Act and the Fourteenth Amendment did more for former slaves than assure them these broad protections. Each conferred in addition the full rights of citizenship. Rights of family were understood not only as liberty and property interests but also as com-

---

*For example, Senator Hendricks said in opposition to the Civil Rights Act, "[M]arriage is a civil contract, and to marry according to one's choice is a civil right." *Cong. Globe*, 39th Cong., 1st Sess. 318 (1866); Senator Fessenden said in support of the act, "[The black man] has the same right to make a contract of marriage . . . that a white man has." *Cong. Globe*, 39th Cong., 1st Sess. 505 (1866).

†As Representative Wood said in opposition to the Thirteenth Amendment: "The social and domestic relations are equally matters of individual ownership with flocks and herds, houses and lands. The affections of a man's wife and children are among the dearest of his possessions, and as such are under the protection of the law." *Cong. Globe*, 38th Cong., 1st Sess. 2941 (1864).

‡As Congressman Kasson had pointed out, liberty interests in establishing and maintaining the marriage relation and the parental relation were "fundamental natural rights of human society" that "the best judicial authorities of England ha[d] for a hundred years declared that . . . [a person] could not alienate even by his own consent." *Cong. Globe*, 38th Cong., 2d Sess. 2000 (1865).

ponents of the privileges and immunities inherent in citizenship. Senator Trumbull offered the amendment to the Civil Rights Act that conferred citizenship rights upon freedmen.[110] His subsequent remarks describe the intended scope of these rights:

> It is difficult, perhaps, to define accurately what slavery is and what liberty is. Liberty and slavery are opposite terms; one is opposed to the other.
> ... Civil liberty ... is thus defined by Blackstone: "Civil liberty is no other than natural liberty, so far restrained by human laws and no further, as is necessary and expedient for the general advantage of the public." That is the liberty to which every citizen is entitled.[111]

When consideration of the Trumbull amendment resumed on the following day, Senator Howard responded to those who argued that Congress lacked the authority to enforce general citizenship rights in behalf of freedmen. He argued that citizenship rights were the entitlement of free men born on American soil. He spoke specifically of rights of home and family:

> [The slave] had no rights, nor nothing which he could call his own. He had not the right to become a husband or a father in the eye of the law, he had no child, he was not at liberty to indulge the natural affections of the human heart for children, for wife, or even for friend.
> ... Is a free man to be deprived of the right of ... having a family, a wife, children, home? What definition will you attach to the word "freeman" that does not include these ideas? The once slave is no longer a slave; he has become, by means of emancipation, a free man. If such be the case, then in all common sense is he not entitled to those rights which we concede to a man who is free?[112]

FAMILY, GOD, AND COUNTRY

Doctrinal Stories about the Shaping of Young Minds

Although the Supreme Court ignored antislavery and the determination of people like Sumner, Trumbull, and Howard, or Grimké, Kelley, and Garrison, or Douglass, Harper, and Ward when it decided *Meyer* and *Pierce*, it did acknowledge in those cases a Fourteenth Amendment right of parental autonomy. It was soon required to elaborate the limits of that right—to consider when a state's interests in influencing or protecting children would, and would not, justify an unwanted interference with the authority and autonomy of a parent. The Court's consideration of this question has been deeply affected by doctrinal developments concerning liberty of contract and liberty in the use of property. Although these doctrinal developments did not explicitly concern rights of family, they so affected the Court's confidence and its sense of authority to safeguard liberty threatened by state initiatives that one must see them as necessary background to the Court's interpretive work with respect to family liberty.

In the first three and a half decades of the twentieth century, the Supreme Court regularly invalidated state and federal laws designed to check exploitation in the marketplace. These invalidations of social welfare laws were based on the theory that the laws unreasonably restricted people's liberty to control their property and to contract with others as they saw fit. The Court gave a broad reading to the concepts of contractual liberty and liberty of property. And it often gave little constitutional significance to the social welfare rationales that legislators had offered for compromising these liberties.[113] The result was that adherence to a laissez-faire economic policy was read as intrinsic to the Fourteenth Amendment and the Bill of Rights. Setting a minimum wage or requiring minimally safe working conditions was deemed to interfere with the employer's and the employee's right to bargain as s/he saw fit;[114] consumer protection measures were deemed unreasonably restrictive of a free bargaining process between merchants and consumers.[115]

In the mid-1930s, the Court—under a great deal of fire—adopted a much more modest view of its constitutional power to invalidate market controls. In the midst of the Great Depression, it was hard to sustain, or to defend against political attack, the idea that labor and consumer protection laws unreasonably interfered with the liberty of businesses or with the liberty of the workers and consumers they were designed to protect. Court decisions that undermined legislative efforts to regulate wages, prices, working conditions, and the marketing of consumer goods produced a political crisis. The crisis was resolved by reconsidering the compatibility between constitutionally protected liberties and economic controls. Confessing the error of its recent ways, the Court returned to the view that a rational basis was enough in the usual case to justify a challenged law. In its hasty retreat from a now repudiated doctrine, the Court announced that it was willing to presume the constitutionality of most legislative judgments. Duly enacted laws, it said, would be upheld if any known or imaginable state of facts gave the legislative judgment a rational basis. A state or federal law was safe from constitutional attack if, as Justice Frankfurter later explained it, the legislature "could, in reason, have enacted it."

One of the cases establishing this presumption of constitutionality, *United States v. Carolene Products*,[116] concerned a due process attack upon federal legislation prohibiting the sale of "skimmed milk compounded with any fat or oil other than milk fat."[117] In a ruling that rings with irony in a cholesterol-fearing age, the Court applied the presumption to defer to a legislative judgment based on "the great importance to public health of butter fat."[118] The Court then paused briefly to consider whether the presumption of constitutionality that trumped Carolene Products' liberty right to distribute milk without butterfat was appropriate in all cases in which a law was challenged as infringing constitutional rights. In that breath-length pause, the Court suggested, in a footnote penned by Justice Stone, that the presumption may be weaker in three instances: when the state's action appears to be restricted by a specific constitutional provision such as one contained in the Bill of Rights; when it "restricts . . . political processes . . . ordinarily . . . expected to bring about repeal of undesirable legislation"; and when it is directed at "discrete and insular minorities."[119] For more than half a century, this now famous Footnote Four was accepted as a marker of the constitutional liberty that survived the era of a judicially enforced laissez-faire economic policy. Counterbalancing the Court's confession of excessive solicitude for economic liberty, Footnote Four stood for the Court's continuing sense that liberties must be safeguarded against state actions that violate specific constitutional provisions, or distort the political process, or exploit a majoritarian advantage.

The Footnote Four formulation is problematic, of course, for the property rights that the Court was trying to enforce in its laissez-faire era *are* specifically provided for by the Constitution. Judges and scholars understand today what was less clear in the heat of battle for the Court's acceptance of an economic policy that would address severe depression and opportunistic market practices: the error "was not in invoking a value the Constitution did not mark as special; the text evinces the most explicit concern with 'liberty,' 'contract,' and 'property.' The error lay in giving that value a perverse content."[120] It was not wrong of the Court to defer to rights of liberty, contract, and property; it was wrong to interpret those rights in ways that precluded adequate provision for the general welfare. As we shall see, Justices Kennedy, O'Connor, and Souter put this insight brilliantly in a recent opinion: The laissez-faire Court's "interpretation of contractual freedom . . . rested on fundamentally false factual assumptions about the capacity of a relatively unregulated market to satisfy minimal levels of human welfare."[121]

Despite its lack of perfect coherence, Footnote Four did call for continued vigilance in evaluating state actions that limit rights special to our constitutional traditions or disadvantage people who are specially vulnerable in our constitutional system. At the same time, the controversy that surrounded the Court's laissez-faire economic requirements, and the embarrassment of its retreat under fire from those policies, left institutional scars and made the Justices habitually wary of vigorously enforcing the rights of citizens against the will of a popularly elected body.

The effects of the Court's wariness are clear in family rights jurisprudence. Despite the promise of Justice Stone's footnote, the Court ruled in 1940, with only Justice Stone in dissent, that claims in the name of family and religious freedom have no constitutional force against a state determination that all public school children must pay daily obeisance to the flag. The case, *Minersville v. Gobitis*, was brought by a family of Jehovah's Witnesses, for whom the flag salute violated biblical commands. For adhering to their sense of religious duty, the children had been expelled from school. The children and their parents challenged the expulsion, claiming that an exemption should be made for a conscientious religious objection to the practice of saluting the flag. Justice Frankfurter, writing for the majority, referred respectfully to the family rights that were at stake. Although the opinion was couched almost exclusively in terms of the plaintiffs' First Amendment rights of religious freedom, it recognized the effect the flag salute requirement had upon the autonomy of a Jehovah's Witness family, and noted that the state was asserting a "right to awaken in the child's mind considerations as to the significance of the flag contrary to those implanted by the parent."[122] But it was a time of prewar patriotism for the nation and post-laissez-faire sheepishness for the Court. Arguments premised on the constitutional stature of individual and family liberties could not overcome the Court's resistance to thwarting a patriotic, and legislated, social choice. Justice Frankfurter wrote that government interest in achieving national loyalty was "inferior to none in the hierarchy of legal values," and denounced as unwarranted overreaching any judicial effort to question the state's bases for determining that the mandatory flag salute was an effective and acceptable means to instill that loyalty. Justice Stone's dissent protested, with a reference to his *Carolene Products* footnote, that to approve a flag-salute requirement that made no exception for those with earnestly held religious objection was "no less than . . . surrender of the constitutional protection of the liberty of small minorities to the popular will."[123]

Prewar patriotism and judicial sheepishness in the protection of civil rights proved to be a dangerous mix. In the weeks after the *Gobitis* decision, hundreds of attacks upon Jehovah's Witnesses were reported to the Department of Justice. One Witness was burned; another was kidnapped, beaten, and castrated; others were tied together with rope and paraded through the streets. A 1942 Justice Department report linked a two-year uninterrupted record of violence and persecution of the Witnesses to the Court's ruling.[124]

In 1943, the Justices reconsidered flag-salute requirements in public schools. In an unusually swift departure from precedent, the Court reversed itself, with three Justices acknowledging that they had changed their view of the issue. Whereas the Court had decided by a vote of 8–1 to uphold the school flag-salute requirement in *Gobitis*, it decided by a vote of 6–3 to overturn a virtually identical requirement in *West Virginia v. Barnette*.[125] Moreover, the Court made clear that exemptions from statements of obeisance to the flag must be respected with or without religious basis.

The relationship between economic regulation issues and the flag-salute issue was clearly revealed in the *Barnette* opinions. Justice Jackson, writing for the majority, described the Bill of Rights as a document born in the eighteenth century of a philosophy that held the individual to be the center of society and deemed individual liberty incompatible with governmental restraint. He confessed that it was difficult to interpret the Bill of Rights in a twentieth-century context in which laissez-faire had been repudiated in economic affairs and public benefits were sought through social planning and legislated governmental controls. He acknowledged that these difficulties "disturb self-confidence" as judges ponder their duty in the face of a complaint that liberty has been unconstitutionally infringed.[126] But he affirmed, in words that have become well worn in defense of civil liberties, that "[t]he very purpose of a Bill of Rights was to withdraw certain subjects from the vicissitudes of political controversy, to place them beyond the reach of majorities and officials and to establish them as legal principles to be applied by the courts. One's right to life, liberty, and property, to free speech, a free press, freedom of worship and assembly, and other fundamental rights may not be submitted to vote; they depend on the outcome of no elections."[127] Justices Black and Douglas concurred, saying forthrightly that reluctance to interfere with state regulatory power had influenced their decision in *Gobitis* and that long reflection had convinced them that the *Gobitis* decision was wrong.[128] Justice Murphy, also concurring, spoke of a similar original reluctance cured by reflection that convinced him of a paramount duty to "uphold . . . spiritual freedom."[129]

The *Barnette* majority made a point of justifying its decision in terms of the free speech requirements of the First Amendment—rather than in terms of the Fourteenth Amendment. This had not been done in earlier cases when the Court defined family rights and safeguarded them against state authority.[130] The decision to do it in *Barnette* is further evidence of the effects of the laissez-faire controversy the Court had recently weathered. Those who questioned the Court's authority to invalidate state laws had argued that judicial authority required a more concrete basis than the surmised meaning of vague language such as that constituting the Due Process Clause. The Bill of Rights, being somewhat more detailed, was arguably less controversial ground for judicial decision. The Bill of Rights, however, restricts federal, not state authority. Nonetheless, on the theory that the Fourteenth Amendment was intended to protect citizens against state violations of the basic rights and liberties specified in the Bill of Rights, the Supreme Court has held that the Bill of Rights, or parts of it, are "incorporated" by the Due Process Clause of the Fourteenth Amendment and therefore applicable to the states. This theory of incorporation has it that to deprive a citizen of liberty "where the federal government could not" is to deprive that citizen of liberty without due process of law.[131] The theory is reasonable, and it allows for a measure of consistency between constitutional principles that must be followed by the federal government and those that must be followed by the states. As we shall see, however, the theory has the disadvantage of focusing the Court on the language, experiences, and intentions of the Founders and blinding the Court to the language, experiences, and intentions of the architects of Reconstruction. It is therefore not an ideal guide for interpreting the *reconstructed* Constitution.

Applying the theory of incorporation, the *Barnette* Court ruled, in effect, that the flag-salute requirement would have violated the First Amendment had it been imposed by the federal government and that, because a federally imposed flag-salute requirement would violate the First Amendment, a state-imposed flag-salute requirement violates the Due Process Clause of the Fourteenth.

In a long, solitary dissent,[132] Justice Frankfurter disputed the *Barnette* majority's assertion that reference to the Bill of Rights addressed the Court's alleged want of authority to invalidate rational state action. The majority had argued that the First Amendment afforded greater protection to freedoms of speech, press, assembly, and worship than to freedom to function without restriction in the marketplace—that the right of religious freedom was, for example, entitled to more judicial solicitude than the freedom of a public utility to do business as it chose.[133] Frankfurter responded (in words that undoubtedly inspired Robert Bork's equation of the liberty to pollute and the liberty to practice contraception) that "[t]he [Fifth Amendment] right not to have property taken without just compensation—a right arguably implicated by regulation of a public utility—has, so far as the scope of judicial power is concerned, . . . no less claim than freedom of the press or freedom of speech or religious freedom."[134] By this reasoning, state laws—whatever their subject and whatever their effect on individual rights and liberties—were susceptible to no due process objection, so long as "legislators could in reason have enacted [them]."[135] To this day, the Supreme Court and its critics are preoccupied with the question that divided Frankfurter and the *Barnette* majority. To this day, the Supreme Court, chastened by its once overzealous protection of economic rights, struggles to decide whether claims to protection against marketplace controls are constitutionally different from claims to protection against state measures touching more personal liberties.

In 1944, the two claims came to the Court in a single package.[136] Once again, the plaintiff was a Jehovah's Witness. She did not question the state's authority to impose the requirement at issue, but she claimed exemption on grounds of religion and family autonomy. Sarah Prince was an extended-family member acting as guardian of a young child. It was forbidden under Massachusetts law that the child display or sell goods of any kind in any street or public place. Both Prince and the child believed it a religious duty to display and sell religious literature to the public at large. Prince was convicted under Massachusetts child labor laws of permitting and facilitating the child's public display of *Watchtower* and *Consolation* magazines, or, in her words, for leading the child in "exercising her God-given right and her constitutional right to preach the gospel."[137] The Supreme Court considered that conviction in *Prince v. Massachusetts.*

The Court's opinion in *Prince* does not heed the restrictions that kept the *Barnette* Court within the compass of the First Amendment, but goes back to the unqualified assertions of family rights contained in the *Pierce* and *Meyer* opinions. Citing *Pierce*, the Court reaffirmed that family autonomy is a principle fundamental to American democracy: "It is cardinal with us that the custody, care and nurture of the child reside first in the parents, whose primary function and freedom include preparation for obligations the state can neither supply nor hinder."[138] It was in recognition of this principle, said the Court, that its prior decisions had "respected the private realm of family life which the state cannot enter."[139] Yet, despite this libertarian prose, the Court was unable in 1944 to invalidate or qualify a child labor law. After all, invalidation of child labor laws had earned the Court some of its most strident criticism during the economic laissez-faire period.[140] The Court found that the Massachusetts regulation was justifiable in service of the state's efforts to advance child welfare. It therefore affirmed Ms. Prince's conviction.[141]

With the *Prince* decision in 1944, the Court ended a period of broad assertion and irregular protection of parental rights and entered a period of dormancy with respect to the family. As we shall see, the Court next considered family rights when, in the 1960s, it began to face complaints against state regulation of family planning and sexuality. As I shall explain, in the context of these cases, the Court found a way to claim adherence to the text of the Bill of Rights even as it recognized family rights that bore no clear relation to that text: it devised a doctrine of family *privacy*, resting upon "emanations" from the First, Third, Fourth, and Fifth amendments, and the text of the Ninth.

As the doctrine of family privacy was unfolding, the Court confronted a new and unusually complex issue of parental autonomy. In 1972, in *Wisconsin v. Yoder*,[142] Amish parents challenged the requirement that their children attend school until the age of sixteen. These parents believed that public schooling beyond the eighth grade undermined the Old Order Amish commitment to "informal learning-through-doing; a life of 'goodness,' rather than a life of intellect; wisdom, rather than technical knowledge; community welfare, rather than competition; and separation from, rather than integration with, contemporary worldly society."[143] All seven Justices hearing the case were persuaded that the school attendance law interfered impermissibly with free exercise of the Amish religion.

The factual record in *Yoder* was appealing to the Justices. The parents established that they were part of an endangered, two-century-old religious tradition; that their program of learning-by-doing was an educationally sound means of preparing young people for life in an Old Order Amish community; and that those who were socialized in the community became self-sufficient, law-abiding citizens. The record in *Prince* had been lacking in this respect. It did not give the Justices a context for imagining a healthy, well-socialized child living and growing according to an ethic and an order that the law did not contemplate. Moreover, public animosity against the Jehovah's Witness community may have made it harder for the Justices to think it so suitable for nurturing children that it could be permitted to disregard child protective laws. These matters of context and strategy are important, for the rationales of *Prince* and *Yoder* are difficult to reconcile. In each case, the Court paid homage to the right of parents to control the religious upbringing of their children. It is not self-evident that the state has a greater interest in protecting children against the dangers of *Watchtower* sales than in protecting children against missing the ninth grade, yet the claim of the Amish parents succeeded where Prince's claim had failed.

The opinions in *Yoder* broke new constitutional ground and brought new constitutional difficulties to the surface. Chief Justice Burger wrote an opinion for the Court that implicitly renounced the belief-action distinction used in *Reynolds* and its progeny for validating laws against polygamy. He affirmed that the free exercise of religion guaranteed by the Constitution protects not only the right to hold religious views but also the right to act consistently with those views.[144] Relying principally upon the Religion Clauses of the First Amendment, but also upon the "enduring American tradition" of deference to "the primary role of parents in the upbringing of their children,"[145] he held that interference with Amish child-rearing practices was not justified by the state's interest in affording children one or two additional years of classroom education.

The *Yoder* case made the Justices consider more deeply than ever before, or since, the profoundly difficult issues that arise when there is a difference between family and state and the contest is not about the need to protect the child from undeniable harm but is about the child's heart and mind. The children whose education was at issue in *Yoder* were not at risk of physical harm. They were not abused or neglected. They were at risk only of being educated to traditional Amish ways; detached, and perhaps alienated, from the larger community; sheltered from alternative life possibilities. The state wanted to achieve what

Justice Frankfurter's opinion in *Gobitis* had so candidly acknowledged as the purpose of its flag-salute requirements: "to awaken in the child's mind considerations . . . contrary to those implanted by the parent."[146] *Barnette* held that a state could not intervene in this way to instill national loyalty. But, as the Justices realized, the purposes of public schooling are broader. Public schooling is thought to prepare the child to function both as citizen and in other aspects of its life. Public schooling therefore can be seen as something that benefits the child as clearly as it benefits the state that requires it. *Barnette* did not answer the question whether this more generous state purpose justifies state action that is inconsistent with a family's values and religious beliefs.

Different Justices took very different approaches to the issue. Justice Burger, who wrote the opinion of the Court, seemed to rely heavily upon the Amish parents' assurances that their children would become law-abiding and self-supporting citizens. He focused on the benefits that compulsory school laws promised to the larger community: assurances that the children would not become dependent upon the state, or be unlawful, or behave offensively. Working with an eye to the community rather than to the child, it was harder for Justice Burger to accept the state's defense that it was obliged to unseat the preferences of Amish families to assure a broad education for their children. The education the Amish community gave to its children was adequate from the community's perspective: Amish children were law-abiding, did not behave offensively, and did not become public charges.[147]

For other Justices, the issue was more difficult. They saw the school attendance law not only as a means of protecting the community but also as a step toward an egalitarian ideal. A comprehensive education would assure each individual control over his or her destiny,[148] and means to maximize human potential.[149] For these Justices, deference to family governance risked subordinating the rights and interests of individual children. Justices Stewart, Brennan, and White addressed this concern in narrow, carefully worded concurrences; Justice Douglas concurred only with respect to a child who had testified that she held an independent desire to continue her education according to the Amish tradition. In these concurrences, the Justices addressed for the first time an issue that would have continued significance as constitutional family rights doctrine matured: the risk that constitutional recognition of family privacy and autonomy would leave individuals subject to the misjudgments—or even to the tyrannies—of older, or otherwise more powerful, family members.

Justice Douglas introduced a second issue that was also to become significant in the development of family rights. He challenged the Chief Justice's explicit reliance on the Amish people's social acceptability, good citizenship, and deism. For him, the ideal of religious tolerance required that these values be deemed irrelevant to recognizing the freedom to exercise religion in ways that do not harm others. Moreover, he believed that draft resisters' cases had established—appropriately, for a nation with an extraordinary diversity of beliefs and life-defining moral codes—that deism could not be a prerequisite for the enjoyment of religious liberty.[150]

Yoder made the Justices look more deeply than ever before into a "little commonwealth" of home and family life with its own values and its own system of governance. The Yoder families had a measure of cultural independence unusual in a postindustrial age. The Justices thought their system of values and governance commanded constitutional respect and required autonomy for its very survival. But, as Prince shows, the Doctrinal Story of family autonomy will not always vindicate a family's independence and values when the law intervenes to guide and influence its children.

"MY MOTHER'S AND FATHER'S THEOLOGY"

Motivating Stories of Family, God, and Master

Government did not intervene, either to protect or to influence enslaved children. Their families contended instead with private citizens who held sovereign authority over the people they owned. As a Union major general pointed out in a letter to a Tennessee senator, the slaveholding class had constructed a government to protect their own "lives, liberty and property," but

> [t]hey did not embrace the negroes within that system. . . .
> [They] referred the government of that whole class to such individuals of the white race, as accident might select with the

designation of masters. They gave to those masters, with but few limitations, and restrictions, full power over the persons of their subjects, and in turn held them responsible for their health, morals and conduct. The master was Governor to control them, lawgiver to furnish them rules of civil conduct, priest if he chose to be so, to prescribe the faith to be believed, and the code of morals to be observed, Chancellor to dissolve or prohibit marriage, control their domestic relations, and settle all controversies amongst them.[151]

In the priestly capacity, slaveholders assumed, consistently with color-caste ideology, that their wards were intellectually and morally inferior. In the eyes of some masters, this inferiority made the enslaved unsuited for religious training. These slaveholders punished any enslaved person who appeared to engage in religious practice.[152] Religion was inappropriate among them, slaves were told, because "you niggers have no souls, you are just like those cattle, when you die there is an end of you, there is nothing more for you to think about than living. White people only have souls."[153] James Mars remembered hearing this message as an enslaved child: "some of the people said that slaves had no souls, and that they would never go to heaven, let them do ever so well."[154]

Other slaveholders thought religious instruction appropriate for slaves so long as they were instructed in a religious doctrine of obedience to *human* authority:

They wasn't no church for the slaves, but we goes to the white folks' arbor on Sunday evening, and a white man he gets up there to preach to the niggers. He say, "Now I takes my text, which is, Nigger obey your master and your mistress, 'cause what you git from them here in this world am all you ever going to get, 'cause you just like the hogs and the other animals—when you dies you ain't no more, after you been throwed in that hole." I guess we believed that for a while 'cause we didn't have no way finding out different. We didn't see no Bibles.

The instruction given to Lunsford Lane was more subtle:

[O]n the Sabbath there was one sermon preached expressly for the colored people which it was generally my privilege to hear. I became quite familiar with the texts, "Servants be obedient to your masters." — "Not with eye service as men pleasers." — "He that knoweth his master's will and doeth it not, shall be beaten with many stripes," and others of this class.[155]

People who called out to the Lord while being beaten by masters or overseers were beaten more severely; the lesson was that they were not "praying to the right man." As one slaveholder put it: "The Lord rule Heaven, but Jim Smith rule the earth."[156] Assumptions of slaves' inferiority were not, of course, all that influenced the design of their religious instruction. As Jim Smith and other slaveholders must have known, the slave who received the kind of instruction thought suitable for the slaveholding class or recognized a higher authority than the master was on the path of finding reason to rebel.

Despite being regarded as moral, intellectual, and political nonentities, enslaved people, understanding themselves to "have in Common with all other men a Natural and Unaliable Right to that freedom which the Grat Parent of the Unavers hath Bestowed equalley on all menkind,"[157] worked within and around the constraints of slavery to construct morally meaningful lives. The work of making moral meaning included coming to terms with the slaveholder's religion. Henry Bibb argued that white preachers taught "a pro-slavery doctrine. They say, 'Servants be obedient to your masters;—and he that knoweth his master's will and doeth it not, shall be beaten with many stripes;— means that God will send them to hell, if they disobey their masters." This kind of preaching, Bibb reported with obvious approval, "has driven thousands to infidelity. They view themselves as suffering unjustly under the lash, without friends, without protection of law or gospel, and the green eyed monster tyranny staring them in the face. They know that they are destined to die in that wretched condition, unless they are delivered by the arm of Omnipotence. And they cannot believe or trust in such a religion, as above named."[158] Lane recalled a "very kind hearted Episcopal minister" who was "very popular with the colored people. But after he had preached a sermon . . . in which he argued from the Bible that it was the will of heaven from all eternity we should be slaves, and our masters be our owners, most of us left him; for like some of the faint hearted disciples in early times we said,—'This is a hard saying, who can bear it?' "[159] Aptheker has concluded that many slaves regarded attention to this message as "merely another chore, another of the consequences of enslavement."[160] But, as he reports, some protested. As a Reverend Johnson was preaching the message of subservience to earthly masters, and slaves were sleeping and fanning themselves with oak branches,

> Uncle Silas got up in the front row of the slaves' pew and halted Reverend Johnson. "Is us slaves gonna be free in Heaven?" Uncle Silas asked. The preacher stopped and looked at Uncle Silas like he want to kill him 'cause no one ain't supposed to say nothing 'ceptin' "Amen" whilst he was preaching. Waited a minute he did, lookin' hard at Uncle Silas standing there but didn't give no answer.
>
> "Is God gonna free us slaves when we get to Heaven?" Uncle Silas yelled. Old white preacher pulled out his handkerchief and wiped the sweat from his face. "Jesus say come unto Me ye who are free from sin and I will give you salvation." "Gonna give us freedom along with salvation?" ask Uncle Silas. "The Lord gives and the Lord takes away, and he that is without sin is gonna have life everlasting," preached the preacher. Then he went ahead preaching, fast-like, without paying no attention to Uncle Silas.[161]

Uncle Silas stood throughout the service and never returned to church.

The unacceptability of the slaveholder's theology led slaves to study what they could read or hear of biblical texts, and to probe their minds, consciences, and homeland traditions in search of a theology of liberation and justice.[162] As Aptheker describes it, "slaves ... constructed a different religion. Their God had cursed man-stealers, had led slaves out of bondage, had promised the earth as an inheritance for the humble, had prophesied that the first would be last and the last would be first. Their God had created all men of one blood, and had manifested no preferences among those into whom He had breathed life."[163] This slave religion was developed and practiced in the family and in the secret networks of fictive kin and community where slaves found their moral and cultural voices: "My master used to ask us children, 'Do your folks pray at night?' We said 'No,' 'cause our folks had told us what to say. But the Lord have mercy, there was plenty of that going on. They'd pray, 'Lord, deliver us from under bondage.' "[164]

When the Reverend G. W. Offley wrote the story of his life, he described "[m]y mother's and father's theology, or the way we children were taught by our parents."[165] His description supports Gutman's view that slave children "were not socialized simply by an owner or an overseer; the choices they later made as adults were shaped by socializing experiences rooted within the developing slave community itself."[166] The Offley theology was a close step from the slaveholders', teaching that obedience to one's master was a key to salvation, but it also taught respect for family and for elders of all races. It taught that God "gave his son to die for all, bond or free, black or white, rich or poor." And, significantly for the process of making independent meaning in a context of enslavement, it taught that a person doing the will of God was beyond human control. Offley gives the example of Praying Jacob, a slave whose "rule was to pray three times a day, at just such an hour of the day; no matter what his work was or where he might be." When ordered with a gun at his head and to cease praying and return to work, Jacob "would finish his prayer and then tell his master to shoot in welcome." Praying Jacob was never shot, and he never abandoned his rule.

The moral lives of enslaved people were, of course, secular as well as spiritual. Just as spiritual meaning was created within real and fictive kinship groups, moral meaning developed in the working through of obligations to real and fictive kin. Within what critical race theory scholar Charles Lawrence calls home places, slaves forged opportunities for moral and intellectual self-definition. Parents and de facto spouses ran the risks of separation; closed their eyes to the obstacles slavery placed in the way of nurturing; bonded with their children, husbands, and wives; and created families unacknowledged and unprotected by law. Men like Westly Jackson, remembered in the words of his daughter, held "deep affection" for his kin, having "no other link to fasten him to the human family but his fervent love for those who were bound to him by love and sympathy." From the earliest days of slavery, adults forced to serve masters at the expense of their children did their best to extend their child-rearing capacities by developing "networks of mutual obligation." A child whose mother spent every daylight hour in the fields would be "minded" by an older woman who "looked after every blessed thing for us all day long and cooked for us right along with the minding." A teenager "sold from the Upper to the Lower South . . . [and] cut off from his or her immediate Upper South family" could expect nurturance from "many fictive aunts and uncles in the Lower South." An orphaned child was taken in by the mother's cabin mate or by some other member of the enslaved community. A 1661 petition by free blacks seeking to adopt a slave child reported that the couple had "reared child since mother died (4 weeks after baptism)," the wife having taken the child in "out of Christian affection" and "reared him as her own." Moral meaning assumed political and social scope as the slave network of mutual obligation developed into a net-work of African-American social responsibility. Free blacks in Phila-delphia reported in 1831 that they had formed more than forty-three mutual relief societies, dispensing nearly $6,000 in the preceding year. Free blacks in that same city (petitioning against a fugitive labor bill that would simplify the procedures by which "a man, a husband, a father, shall be torn from the bosom of his family and consigned to chains") reported in 1832 that they had "more than fifty beneficent societies . . . for mutual aid in time of sickness and distress." Moral meaning was made even in the working through of relationships with the slavemaster, as the slaves Betty and Jerry, husband and wife, ques-tioned whether it was right to take advantage of the indulgence of a last visit before Jerry's transfer to the hands of a slave trader and make their escape. Rose, assigned to Rufus for breeding, thought not only of the whippings she would endure if she refused, but also of an obligation she might owe to a "Master [who bought] me off the block and [saved] me from being separated from my folks." Slaves debated the morality of escaping without paying for themselves, some saying they would be willing to pay, others that they only owed themselves, still others that they were owed by their masters for uncompensated years of labor.[167] Similarly, some slaves thought it wrong to take food from their masters, while others thought it "not a violation of the commandment, 'Thou shalt not steal' but rather an exercise of the gospel, 'Where ye labor there shall ye reap.' "[168] Many would have agreed with Henry Turner, who grew up in the precarious condition of a free black in slaveholding Georgia, that it would be appropriate "to hurl thunderbolts at . . . men who would dare to cross the threshold of my manhood." Yet Josiah Henson abandoned an escape plan that required killing his master, deciding that "it was better to die a Christian death, and to have a quiet conscience, than to live with the incessant recollection of a crime that would destroy the value of life, and under the weight of a secret that would crush out the satisfaction that might be expected from freedom."[169]

The moral autonomy affirmed by being true to slave family values led to confrontations with the slaveholder's authority as often as it led to the kind of charity expressed by Henson. Studying the often rigid moral codes enforced by slave communities in general and slave mothers in particular, the historian Paula Giddings draws a connection between Linda Brent's refusal to accede to the demands of a master obsessed with winning her *voluntary* submission to his sexual advances and the values inculcated by her grandmother. Brent escaped to the North, where the master's pursuit continued. When a friend purchased her freedom and she felt safe against the master, Brent expressed an indignation made possible because she had been socialized not to slave authority but to moral responsibility: "The more my mind had become enlightened," she said, "the more difficult it was for me to consider myself an article of property."[170]

For many slaves and former slaves, acts of resistance grounded in autonomous thought were heroic. Samuel Ward wrote that when a slave determined to escape and conceived a plan to do so,

[h]e is more of a man for having conceived it. If it must be wrought out with his own unaided hands, it improves him to entertain the intention of doing it. If in the way of his resolution—and, still more, in the way of executing it—there stand many mighty obstacles of which he is well aware, but the extreme appals him not, he has in him all the elements of your moral or physical hero, or of both.

The "process of flight" was "improving," and it "fitted . . . [one] the more highly to appreciate, . . . more fully to enjoy, and . . . more wisely to use . . . liberty." Ward gave the example of Madison Washington, a slave in Virginia:

> He determined to be free. He fled to Canada and became free. There the noble fellow was dissatisfied—so dissatisfied, that he determined to leave free Canada, and return to Virginia: and wherefore? His wife was there, a *slave*. Freedom was too sweet to be enjoyed without her. That she was a slave marred his joys. She must share them, even at the risk of *his* losing them. So in 1841 he went back to Virginia, to the neighborhood in which his wife lived, lingered about in the woods, and sent word to her of his whereabouts; others were unfortunately informed as well, and he was captured, taken to Washington, and sold to a Negro-trader. One scarcely knows which most to admire—the heroism this man displayed in the freeing of himself, or the noble manliness that risked all for the freedom of his wife. One cannot help thinking that, as his captors led Madison Washington to the slave pen, they must have been smitten with the thought that they were handling a man far superior to themselves.[171]*

The moral necessity, and heroism, of constructing lives independent of the slaveholders' needs, dictates, and ideology fueled and explained the demand for emancipation. African-Americans denied the slaveholders' claim that "God [had] formed them to serve their fairer brethren [and] endowed them with faculties a little superior to the . . . orangutan."[172] Samuel Ward pointed out facetiously that "to say that the Negro is equal morally to the white man, is to say but very little," and thought that "call[ing] the names" of African-Americans like Henry Highland Garnett and Frederick Douglass was sufficient to meet the charge of intellectual inferiority.[173] African-Americans were peo-

---

*When the slave trader attempted to take Washington by schooner to New Orleans, Washington and two fellow captives staged a mutiny and commandeered the boat to the Bahamas, by which act they achieved freedom.

ple. In the jargon of the day, they were "men" and slavery was a "man-destroying system"—"a graveyard of the mind"[174]—man-destroying and mind-destroying because it frustrated the exercise of will and made human thought superfluous and moral choice impossible. As one contributor to the *Anglo-African Magazine* wrote: "the mind . . . is useless to the slave, or if of service to him, this thinking apparatus is not his own, it belongs to his owner. . . . Where liberty is, the head or mental part is presented to view. The slave—the chattel,—the thing is a *man.*"[175]

The slave, as a reasoning being, had a duty of moral responsibility that bondage rendered unfulfillable. A Presbyterian minister in Ohio argued this point to his slaveholding brother in Virginia, pointing out that moral obligation assumes liberty and that the denial of fundamental prerogatives, like the capacity to create and maintain families, was a denial of freedom of conscience.[176] As Massachusetts slaves had argued in 1774: "By our deplorable situation we are rendered incapable of shewing our obedience to Almighty God how can a slave perform the duties of a husband to a wife or parent to his child How can a husband leave master to work and cleave to his wife How can the wife submit themselves to there husbands in all things How can the child obey thear parents in all things."[177]

For the thinking, feeling, moral being, it was intolerable, as Lane put it, "[t]o know . . . that I was never to consult my own will, but was, while I lived, to be entirely under the control of another." When a fifty-year-old slave called Belinda petitioned the Massachusetts legislature for freedom, she said that "though she was a free moral agent, accountable for her own actions" she had not in fifty years of slavery "had . . . a moment at her own disposal." In the words of a declaration of the first National Negro Convention, the call for emancipation was fundamentally an insistence upon the right to "breathe the pure air of liberty . . . [to] *occupy that space, and enjoy those rights in the moral world, which God, in his wisdom has destined us to fill as rational beings.*" As Reverend Andrew Bryan wrote after he had purchased his freedom and that of his wife and children: "what . . . is so much . . . prized by myself [is that] we enjoy the rights of conscience to a valuable extent, worshiping in our families and preaching three times every Lord's day."[178]

''POOR JOSHUA!''

Doctrinal Stories of Public Duty to Children

"Poor Joshua!" is perhaps the most dramatic statement ever included in a Supreme Court opinion. It appears in the final passage of Justice Blackmun's dissent from the Court's decision that child welfare officials in Winnebago County, Wisconsin, were not liable for their apparently negligent failure to protect Joshua DeShaney during the first four years of his life from a father who repeatedly beat him, ultimately causing profound brain damage in addition to obvious but untold emotional trauma.[179] The Winnebago agencies had been aware of the father's violence, but failed time after time to intervene effectively. When, finally, Joshua was beaten so badly that his abuse was unquestionable, the father was convicted and Joshua was removed to an institution able to care for a child with the profound retardation that the beatings had caused. A civil suit was filed in behalf of Joshua and in behalf of his mother, seeking damages from officials. The question that reached the Supreme Court was not whether county officials, and the father, were liable under the tort principles which ordinarily govern cases of intentional or negligent infliction of harm. Those were matters to be determined under Wisconsin law and in the local courts of Wisconsin. The question was whether the government officials who had failed to protect Joshua were liable under *federal* law for having deprived him of civil rights guaranteed by the Constitution. The arguments on Joshua's side were difficult ones, for the Constitution's civil rights provisions have usually been interpreted as protecting against abusive or arbitrary government actions, rather than as establishing a right to government protection against abuses committed by private actors. A majority of the Court said as much, believing that, however tragic his situation, Joshua's *civil rights* had not been violated. They emphasized that although the Due Process Clause

> forbids the State itself to deprive individuals of life, liberty, or property without "due process of law," . . . its language cannot fairly be extended to impose an affirmative obligation on the State to ensure that those interests do not come to harm

through other means. . . . [The] purpose [of the Due Process Clause] was to protect the people from the State, not to ensure that the State protected them from each other.[180]

Three Justices dissented, taking the view that where government establishes systems and necessitates or encourages reliance upon those systems, it has a special duty of care. The government had set up a comprehensive system to protect against child abuse; it had encouraged, and in many circumstances required, that reports and concerns about child abuse be funneled through that system. Under those circumstances, it had a *constitutional* duty to protect children against reported perils. In addition to joining the dissent setting forth this theory of special constitutional duty, Justice Blackmun wrote a brief plea that the Justices understand "the broad and stirring Clauses of the Fourteenth Amendment" as a call to "moral ambition" in response to apparent injustice. It was in this context that he called for attention to the plight of "Poor Joshua."

DeShaney understandably divided the Justices. On the one hand, the idea that a national community must protect its children is deeply rooted in our common law traditions. A doctrine of *parens patriae* has served throughout the nation's history to establish government's right and duty to step in to protect the best interests of children, even against the wishes of their parents. On the other hand, as the Justices in the *DeShaney* majority pointed out (and as virtually every preceding page of this work has suggested), the very due process protections invoked in behalf of Joshua DeShaney are more commonly invoked to give families freedom to make their own choices and to function without state interference. The *DeShaney* majority did not believe that due process requirements should whipsaw state and local governments between the risks of liability for intruding too much in family affairs and liability for intruding too little.*

---

*In truth, no matter what interpretation the Due Process Clause is given, state and local officials are inevitably whipsawed in exactly the way the majority feared: they must constantly negotiate the narrow path between inordinate risks that children will be abused at the hands of their parents and inordinate risks that they will be subjected unnecessarily to the traumas of family separation and the inevitable deficiencies of public care.

That the government stood accused of a failure to intervene, rather than inappropriate intervention, makes *DeShaney* rare among federal cases involving parental rights. Notoriety periodically surrounds mistaken government failures to intervene, for failures to intervene are at times followed by conspicuous injury to children. But there are good reasons to believe that child welfare systems are at least as likely to intervene unnecessarily as to defer when action is required.[181] In the typical child welfare case before the Supreme Court, the state is accused of being too cavalier in deciding to intrude in pursuit of its idea of the children's best interests, not with being inordinately deferential to parental authority. *Stanley v. Illinois*[182] is a perfect example.

In 1972 Peter Stanley challenged what he regarded as a cavalier presumption of the state of Illinois that it was in the best interests of children left in the care of unmarried fathers for the state to assume their custody and make more suitable arrangements for their care. Peter and Joan Stanley, who were not legally married, lived together intermittently for eighteen years before Joan Stanley's death and had three children. When Joan Stanley died, the three children were taken from Peter Stanley under an Illinois law which said that children born out of wedlock became wards of the state upon the death of their mothers. He sought the children's return, presuming that he had a constitutional right to care for them unless he was found unfit to do so. As Justice Stewart has subsequently explained, the state is not justified in breaking up a biological family on no stronger basis than that it would be "in the child's best interests," the theory, borrowed from common law doctrine, being that government has no authority to break up families simply because of a judgment that the children would be better off in a different environment. Family disruption is permissible, the theory holds, only when parents prove themselves unfit by abandoning, abusing, or neglecting their children or are mentally incompetent to care for them. The statute that Illinois relied upon when it took the Stanley children seemed to skip the step of establishing unfitness or incapacity, simply presuming that an unwed father could not be a fit parent.

The case was closely decided. Some of the Justices thought the Illinois presumption entirely reasonable. They argued that the distinction between unmarried fathers and all other parents was consistent with the teaching of "[c]enturies of human experience" that "unwed fathers rarely burden either the mother or the child with their attentions or loyalties." But a bare majority disagreed and held that the Illinois statute violated due process requirements by summarily denying the parental rights of men in Stanley's situation. This was an essentially procedural critique of the statute, rather than a direct vindication of the substantive due process rights of family integrity and autonomy, but the constitutional status of the right to maintain custody of one's children was important to the judgment. As the Court has often held, the level of procedural protection required by the Due Process Clause varies with the seriousness of the stakes: in determining the sort of process due to Stanley's parental rights, Justice White, who wrote the Court's opinion, relied on the language and theory of *Meyer* and *Pierce* to characterize those rights as "essential," "basic," and "far more precious than property rights."[183]

In the real world, where parents have limited means and state officials have imperfect judgment, realization of these essential, basic, and precious rights is not automatic. Well-intentioned state officials are perceived as such by judges and other decision makers. They also have institutional experience and reasonable, although by no means luxurious, litigation resources. Without diligence, advocacy, and a thoughtfully structured procedural context, parents can easily be overwhelmed and rendered voiceless in proceedings in which such officials oppose them. Abby Gail Lassiter and John and Annie Santosky asked the Supreme Court to address this problem.

Lassiter's parental rights were terminated in a 1981 proceeding brought by the state of North Carolina on the claims that she was unfit to care for her children and it was in their interests to be freed for adoption. In *Lassiter v. Department of Social Services*,[184] she argued that parents facing termination of parental rights are constitutionally entitled to legal representation. The Court, which had earlier held forthrightly that people at risk of incarceration have a right to counsel, seemed unsure as it faced Lassiter's claim that the risk of losing one's children was comparably grave. As it weighed the justifications for appointment of counsel against the state's interests in proceeding without the expense and complexity of fully litigated proceedings, the Court seemed to teeter. It acknowledged the significance of parental

rights, weighing in the fact that prior decisions had "made plain beyond
the need for multiple citation that a parent's desire for the right to 'the
companionship, care, custody, and management of his or her children'
is an important interest that 'undeniably warrants deference and, absent a powerful countervailing interest, protection.' "[185] But in the end,
the Court punted, deciding that entitlement to counsel is necessary
only when the termination of parental rights litigation is complex, and
giving trial judges the authority to determine the matter case by case.
The Court seemed to forget that in an adversary system, complexity
in litigation is, more often than not, the product of the very thing its
decision precluded: the presence of trained and assertive advocates who
will investigate and articulate competing claims. Justice Blackmun,
writing in dissent for himself and Justices Brennan and Marshall, acknowledged the power of trained advocates in defining claims of right
and the constitutional importance of "family life as the focus for personal meaning and responsibility."[186] The dissent complained that the
Court's decision improperly left indigent parents at risk of losing forever, often as a result of "intimidation, inarticulateness or confusion,"
the fundamental right to contact and involvement with their offspring.[187] Justice Stevens, dissenting separately, distinguished himself
even more sharply from the majority, arguing that the parental right
is important enough to warrant the requirement of counsel in all termination cases regardless of the cost and inconvenience to the state.

   One year after *Lassiter*, Justice Blackmun wrote for a majority of
five (the *Lassiter* dissenters and Justice Powell) in a case establishing
the requirement that allegations by the state used to justify the
termination of parental rights be proved by clear and convincing evidence.[188] Once again, the Court unequivocally recognized the constitutional significance of the parental bond.[189] Observing that the
safeguard of a heightened burden of proof is in place when less significant interests are at stake, and knowing that this safeguard comes
without the expense associated with appointing counsel for the indigent, the justices easily concluded that parental rights could not be
terminated when parental failure had been demonstrated merely by a
fair preponderance of the evidence.*

---

*In the year between *Lassiter* and *Santosky*, Justice O'Connor had replaced Justice

The doctrinal significance of the Supreme Court's decisions in *Stanley, Lassiter,* and *Santosky* can be measured in the life story of Peter Stanley. After the Supreme Court held in Stanley's favor in 1972, the state did not return his children but began a neglect proceeding against him. He was apparently employed at that time and ineligible for the Legal Services representation that had served him in the initial litigation. Stanley lost the case, and the Legal Services office agreed to represent him on appeal. After the return of Stanley's counsel, the state dismissed the neglect charges and returned his children. The family had been separated for more than four years.[190]

"I'LL HAVE MY CHILD AGAIN!"

Motivating Stories of Parental Capacity

Walking the narrow path between reckless disregard of children's safety and reckless assumptions that state supervision and care are needed becomes more difficult the more diverse society is. Deciding what children need is not easy when subcultural differences, class differences, and diversities encouraged by freedom of thought and conscience yield a wide variety of approaches to life, learning, and child rearing. This difficulty—great enough in itself—is often compounded by prejudice. Justice Douglas warned in *Wisconsin v. Yoder* that liberty in constructing a life should not be compromised simply to discourage choices that disturb mainstream sensibilities. In many child welfare cases, a more insidious prejudice is at work—a prejudice expressed not in disapproval of life choices but in stereotypes of incompetence. The motivating

---

Stewart. In *Lassiter*, Justice Stewart's opinion so evenly balanced the arguments for and against the appointment of counsel in termination cases that it suggests a last-minute change of vote. In *Santosky*, Justice O'Connor gave no sign of being conflicted by the competing demands for state authority and private liberty, and she joined in a firm dissent written by Justice Rehnquist, which, although acknowledging the special constitutional status of parental rights, emphasized the importance of state autonomy in the governance of domestic affairs and argued that, as a whole, the statutes under which the Santowskys' parental rights were terminated were fundamentally fair. There remained, then, four members of the Court inclined to defer to state arguments that procedures protecting parents at risk of losing their children unduly complicated state efforts to secure the children's welfare.

stories that follow spotlight the perpetuation, after emancipation, of slavery's special myths of parental incompetence. They also establish that safeguarding family autonomy can help to cleanse slavery's residue of caste subordination.

In 1827, Sojourner Truth, the famous escaped slave and abolitionist activist, learned that her five-year-old son, Peter, had been sent by his owner from New York to Alabama. Truth protested against the loss of contact with her child; the likelihood that he would be put to unconscionably arduous service in the Deep South; and the risk that he would lose the opportunity, owed to him under New York law, of liberation at the age of twenty-one.[191] Initially, incredulous slaveholders dismissed Truth's insistent cry, "I'll have my child again!" As a slave, she had no enforceable claim of custody: if the sale of her son was otherwise legal, it did not become illegal because it deprived her of custody and Peter of his mother. But Truth's cry became a theme of struggle as she repeatedly walked miles on bare feet, resolutely demanding of lawyers, judges, and acquaintances with influence and goodwill that Peter be returned to New York.[192] And it became a cry of achievement when Truth finally recovered her child, seeming to vindicate the claim she had insistently pressed in unfamiliar, sometimes hostile forums.[193] Yet, even though Truth had become free by the time the matter was resolved in the courts, the decision to order the child returned to New York appears to have been grounded in New York's right to emancipate its slaves (and to hold them within her borders until the day designated for their liberation) rather than in a parental right of custody and guardianship.[194]

More than thirty years after Truth won freedom for her child, Union troops marched into the South, and hundreds of thousands of slaves deserted plantations and farms to join the war and seize their freedom.[195] As we have seen, this general strike by black workers, the contribution of their labor to the Union cause, and their belatedly accepted volunteer enlistment as soldiers were crucial to the Union effort. Black workers' withdrawal from the Southern slave system was also an assertion of civil status, and, as such, it centered on free exercise of family rights. From the first rumors of war, throughout the conflict, and well into the postwar years, Americans who had been slaves seized free citizenship by choosing how they would deploy their labor and demanding recognition of their bonds of blood and affection.[196] Workers and soldiers for the Union cause, emancipated first by self-help and later by law, grappled, as Sojourner Truth had, with unfamiliar and inhospitable systems in confrontations with the slaveholding class to win the custody and guardianship of their children. But, in a deeper sense than was possible for Truth, these parents acted as members of a civil society, claiming—and defining in the process—rights to form and maintain families and nurture and supervise their children.

The establishment of free families often began as Truth's saga had begun: with a cry of parental right. Deserting and emancipated slaves struggled to locate children held or traded by former masters, to negotiate or seize custody of the children, and to build self-directed lives for their reconstituted families.[197] Their stories, captured in some detail in army and Freedmen's Bureau records of the 1860s, give life to Truth's legacy and a more textured understanding of the Reconstruction Congress's concern that the former Confederacy would, if left to its own devices, establish de facto slavery by using the Black Codes to maintain control of children the former slave owners continued to believe they owned. Most important, the stories give deepened meaning to the constitutional concept of family autonomy.

At Camp Nelson, in the summer of 1864, "hardly a day passed without bringing . . . wives, children, and relatives [of black Union volunteers] into the camp, either on visits or in pursuit of new homes." Black soldiers regularly petitioned for legal rights of family. Those who had left wives and children in slavery returned to plantations to recover their kin, even though doing so entailed risks of violent retribution: one father returning for his family was described as having been "knocked down, whipped, and horribly bruised, and then threatened with shooting." It was in a spirit inspired by these actions that General John M. Palmer remarked to 20,000 black soldiers at an 1865 Independence Day gathering in Kentucky: "If any one has your children, go and get them. If they will not give them to you, steal them out at night. I do not think you will be committing any crime, nor do I believe the Almighty Ruler of the Universe will think you have committed any."[198] Striking slaves seemed to agree absolutely. In the face of substantial violence, emancipated Americans across the South who shared

John Palmer's sense of natural right replicated the "crime" of claiming one's children.

A Union officer described a soldier who "*demanded* his children at my hands." When the officer hesitated, the soldier said, "Lieut., I want to send them to school; my wife is not allowed to see them." The lieutenant protested that they had a good home with the former master, whereupon the soldier declared, "I am in your service; I wear military clothes; I have been in three battles; I was in the assault at Port Hudson; *I want those children*; they are my flesh and blood." The children were recovered.[199] A Missouri soldier wrote from an army hospital to his wife and her owner that if the wife were not permitted free choice as to whether or not to leave the owner and join the husband, the owner would be visited by ten or twenty soldiers. "You know," he wrote, "that a Soldiers wife is free read this letter to her and let her return her own answer I will find out whether this has been read to her in a full understanding with her or not, and if I should find out that she has never heard her deliverance I will undoubtedly punish you."[200]

Women seeking emancipation and control of their children in the years during and immediately after the war had less leverage, but their determination was equal. Writing two weeks after the Emancipation Proclamation of 1863, a Union captain reported to his command the case of a woman who had been "tied . . . to a tree her arms over her head & then whipped . . . severely." When he saw the woman, "the flesh on her arms where the ropes went was badly lacerated & her arms covered with blood," and all this for the "crime . . . that she demanded her daughter whom . . . [her assailant] retained in slavery."[201] In a letter petitioning for the freedom of a daughter indentured beyond emancipation, Lucy Lee wrote, "God help us, our condition is bettered but little; free ourselves, but deprived of our children, almost the only thing that would make us free and happy. It was on their account we desired to be free."[202] An Annapolis Union officer reported that every day he was "visited by some poor woman who has walked perhaps ten or twenty miles to . . . try to procure the release of her children taken forcibly away from her and held to all intents and purposes in slavery."[203] When Clarissa Burdett's husband enlisted in the Union Army, her owner "beat . . . [her] over the head with an axe handle"; when Burdett's niece fled to a Union camp and Burdett was unable to cause her to return, the owner "tied . . . [Burdett's] hands threw the rope over a joist stripped . . . [her] entirely naked and gave . . . [her] about three hundred lashes." Threatened with more abuse, Burdett fled, but she immediately took steps to rescue the children she had left behind. In an affidavit seeking the assistance of the Union Army, she said, "I have four children there at present and I want to get them but I cannot go there for them knowing that master who would whip me would not let any of my children go nor would he suffer me to get away."[204] Louisa Foster, wife of a Union Army soldier, traveled from Baltimore to Towsontown to recover her three children, whereupon their "owner" "threatened to chain . . . [her] down to the floor and whip . . . [her] if . . . [she] asked for her children any more." Some mothers were able, despite the risk of violence, to reclaim their children on their own. Jane Kemper reported, "[William Townsend] locked up my children so that I could not find them. I afterwards got my children by stealth and brought them to Baltimore. . . . My master pursued me to the Boat to get possession of my children but I hid them on the boat."[205] Amy Carrington, a Tennessee freedwoman who swore that she was "driven from home" by her "master" without provocation and without pay for work that she had done since emancipation, reported that her children were kept by the "master," who "hired them out, and . . . received compensation for their services." She described her ultimately successful efforts to recover the children:

> I had made several efforts since I was driven from home to get possession of my children but failed in every instance until the 23rd day of July 1865, when I succeeded in finding them and with the assistance of . . . [Union officers] brought them to Memphis. . . . My children were in a destitute condition with hardly any clothing on them and had been treated in a brutal manner.[206]

The violence and dissembling of those who would not willingly surrender control over the lives of black workers were supplemented by appeals to law. One of the primary purposes of the Black Codes of the former Confederate states was, as we have seen, to control the labor of newly freed slaves. Substituting state authority for that previously exercised by slavemasters, the Codes "defined [the former slave] as an agricultural laborer, barred or circumscribed any alternative occupations, and compelled . . . work."[207] As the Reconstruction Congress discovered, the Black Codes revived or enacted apprenticeship laws to hold young emancipated laborers against the protests of their families. Laws of this kind had in decades past served some slaveholders well, allowing them to get money for hiring out their slaves to craftspeople in need of capable hands.[208] "Some mechanics had been known to pay as much as six hundred dollars annually, in addition to providing food and clothing" for slaves hired out as apprentices. But black workers who were skilled as a result of apprentice service became irritants to their less skilled white overseers and a dangerous model, slaveholders feared, for slaves locked into a life of agricultural labor. As irritation and fear mounted, many states passed laws prohibiting masters from letting their slaves out.[209] Enthusiasm for apprenticeship schemes after emancipation therefore revived an institution that had been dying, at least as it pertained to African-American workers in the South.

But the institution was revived with a difference: black apprentices were not trainees in the trades, they were wards of individuals who became entitled to their menial service. Maryland laws, for example, gave local judges the power to place black children in the care and service of white people if placement was deemed "better for the habits and comfort of the child." Emancipation in Maryland freed approximately 90,000 slaves, 10,000 of whom, it has been estimated, were reenslaved under apprenticeship laws, as children were "carried . . . in ox carts, wagons, and carriages" to local courts to be bound, usually to former masters.[210] "[W]ithin a month of emancipation, . . . [Maryland] courts had apprenticed more than 2,500 black children and young adults, generally to their former owners." Parents and extended kin of these children responded as Sojourner Truth had responded to Peter's abduction. When the children of an ex-slave and former Union corporal named Berryman were bound to their former owner, Berryman simply "took the children." His wife expressed the family's feeling in the matter: "I told [the former owner] I did not want . . . [the children] bound out to any one as I was able to support them." Susan Thomas was able to take two grandchildren from a former owner, although they were later returned to his custody. Other Maryland parents turned to the courts, to state officials, and to federal agents. Leah Coston petitioned a local court to free her children from an unlawful apprenticeship; she prevailed, but only after a delay of fourteen months. Charles Henry Minoky brought a complaint to free his stepdaughter; it was denied (under the authority of *Dred Scott*) in an opinion subsequently reversed by a U.S. Supreme Court Justice sitting in circuit. "The complaints of black parents [about apprenticeship laws] filled . . . [a] record" submitted to the Maryland General Assembly. Three hundred parents petitioned President Johnson, complaining that "our homes are invaded and our little ones seized at the family fireside, and forcibly bound to masters who are by law expressly released from any obligation to educate them in secular or religious knowledge";[211] the remedy they sought was passage of the Civil Rights Act of 1866.

The views of African-American families with respect to Maryland's de facto reenslavement of their children were perhaps best expressed in the complaint from Charlotte Hall, wife of a Union soldier, to Freedmen's Bureau authorities: "I think it hard that my companion should be away from me in his country service and I am at the same time deprived of my only child, contrary to the free laws and institutions for which his father is fighting."[212] Her statement expresses an underlying ideology of freedom according to which adult citizens are presumptively able and legally entitled to take care of their children. Historian Rebecca Scott found evidence of the same ideology among North Carolina parents resisting indenture of their children. She reports that they "considered authority over their own children to be a part of their freedom."[213] As a North Carolina man petitioning for the release of his half brothers and sisters wrote: "Surely the law does not Call for Children to be bound out when their peopel is Abel to Keep them."[214] The planter class countered this ideology by revisiting the rationalizations by which it had justified slavery and retooling them to meet the circumstances of emancipation.

As is the case with most legal rules or arguments, the postemancipation apprenticeship system represented, and was defended in terms of, an ideology—in this case, the ideology of color-caste hierarchy.[215] This ideology undermined the liberating potential of apprenticeship training,[216] for it justified apprenticeship in terms of the slaves' categorical incompetence. It figured importantly in the story of Sojourner Truth's recovery of Peter. The most wrenching moment in the story occurred when Peter was brought to court and Truth appeared to identify and claim him. The child "cried aloud, and regarded her as some terrible being, who was about to take him away from a kind and loving friend. He knelt, even, and begged . . . with tears, not to take him away from his dear master, who had brought him from the dreadful South, and been so kind to him."[217] Seeing that the boy was badly scarred, the judge in Truth's case rejected this indirect assertion of her unfitness, declared Peter free as the result of his unlawful removal from New York, and awarded custody to Truth.[218] The judge must have sensed what Truth later confirmed: when she calmed Peter and was able to examine him, she "found, to her utter astonishment, that from the crown of his head to the sole of his foot, the callosities and indurations on his entire body were most frightful to behold," and the boy reported being "whipped, kicked, and beat."[219]* Truth won the battle to save her child, but she neither disproved nor silenced the general theme of African-American parental unfitness that Peter's cries had so poignantly sounded. After emancipation this theme was revived as part of the story of supremacy and paternalism that rationalized the apprenticeship system as it had rationalized slavery.

As we have seen, slavery in the United States—total subordination, without term and through the bloodline—had been justified, and

---

*Nell Irvin Painter suggests that Peter's fear of his mother may nonetheless have been genuine and a result of separation trauma he suffered in her absence. *Painter* at 34. This is plausible. Consider this recollection of former slave Sarah Debro:

One day my mammy come to the big house after me. I didn't want to go. I wanted to stay with Miss Polly. I begun to cry, and Mammy caught hold of me. I grabbed Miss Polly and held so tight that I tore her skirt binding loose, and her skirt fell down about her feets. "Let her stay with me," Miss Polly said to Mammy. But Mammy shook her head. "You took her away from me and didn't pay no mind to my crying, so now I's taking her back home. We's free now, Miss Polly. We ain't gonna be slaves no more to nobody." I can see how Miss Polly looked, now. She didn't say nothing, but she looked hard at Mammy, and her face was white.

Bullwhip Days at 532.

accepted, only on the assumption that the enslaved, a racially distinct caste, lacked the will or capacity for autonomous existence. The presumptions of intellectual and moral incapacity which I have described were but a piece of this ideology of racial hierarchy. By its terms, the African "race" was not only bestial and unintelligent, but also in need of the protection and supervision of the "white race." Slavery was a blessing and a system of support for beings incompetent to forge a decent existence for themselves. Jefferson Davis had argued that a Negro slave rebellion was possible only when "bad men [went] . . . among ignorant and credulous people." South Carolina legislators had reported in 1844 that with "[t]he animal predominating largely over the intellectual being, [the Negro] has no aspiration for liberty, and would never dream of revolt, or of elevating his social status, but for the machinations of those who, professing themselves his friends, are in fact his worst enemies."[220] This idea of beneficent subordination was deeply ingrained and easily revived.

Frederick Eustis, a Georgia plantation superintendent, testifying before the American Freedmen's Inquiry Commission in 1863, was asked whether "in making the transition from slavery to free labor" it would be "necessary for the government to establish some system of guardianship." He replied, "Yes, sir; that is my idea. I do not believe in absolute independence; the apprenticeship system is what is needed; they are not prepared for freedom yet." When asked whether it "[w]ould do at all to leave these people perfectly free to do as they liked in free competition with white men—taking white men as they are—without any guardianship adapted to their condition," he replied, "Not at all; white men of very low grade would outstrip them."[221]

The presumption that blacks were unfit for freedom and in need of supervision had as its corollary the presumption that they were incompetent to rear and socialize the children born to them. Edward Pierce, reporting on the War Department's administration of Port Royal, South Carolina, took a rather bright view of the intelligence of young slaves, but expressed concern about whether their parents could raise them properly. "While their quickness is apparent," he said of black schoolchildren, "one is struck with their want of discipline. The children have been regarded as belonging to the plantation rather than to a family, and the parents who in their condition can never have but a feeble hold on their offspring, have not been instructed to training their children into thoughtful and orderly habits."[222] This theory of black parental incompetence resonated with the arguments with which the South had dismissed protests that slavery destroyed family bonds, holding up the *slaveholding household* as "a paternalistic network of relationships which approximated a well-ordered [patriarchal] family," with a husband-father-owner at its head.[223]

The personal and social effects of the theories of black parental incompetence and paternalistic indenture are powerfully told in the story of three children who resided briefly in a Tennessee Union camp in 1864.[224] They were the children of a Union soldier, John Christian, and his wife, Pauline. A slaveholder by the name of Wheaton had owned the family and, with the assistance of sympathetic Union officers (who provided soldiers to guard his property and "keep his young slaves from running off"), retained custody of the children. One day, when the soldiers were absent from Wheaton's yard, Christian "took two black men with him, and watching their opportunity, they caught the children and ran off with them." Subsequently, the officer whose protection Wheaton enjoyed sent soldiers to the camp at which the Christian family had taken residence and forced the children's return. The scene was described by a witness in this way:

> What a fine subject for a painter was this! Dr. Wheaten [the name appears in this spelling as well in some documents], a slaveholder, and formerly, from the testimony of those who lived with him, a *traitor*, and Brig.-Gen. Buckland's aide-de-camp ride through our camp in a splendid carriage, and attended by three orderlies, in search of three children, aged respectively about ten, eight, and six years, who had been brought home to their father's house.
>
> ... [T]he aide-de-camp ... bore off the children from weeping and agonizing parents as triumphantly as was ever done in these States when the whole nation groaned and reeled under the rule of such men as this . . . slaveholder.

Officers at the camp apparently tried to protect the family, and an investigation ensued. The defense of Wheaton's protector was that he had acted in the best interests of the children:

> Those children were forcibly taken from the residence of Dr. Wheaton in his absence by armed soldiers and, *against the wishes of the children*, contrary to the written prohibition of Maj. Gen Hurlbut. I ordered them returned because they were forcibly taken away in violation of Military discipline and because I was well satisfied from my own knowledge and from information derived from others that *it would be for the good of the children.* They are well cared for and kindly treated in the family of Dr. Wheaton. They were not returned as slaves, nor do I believe they will ever be slaves. [Emphasis added.]

A subsequent report held open the claim that the children needed a "master's" protection. It said that Christian was on active duty, the mother was "on a plantation . . . working for wages having been sent there by order of [a Freedmen's Bureau officer]," and the children remained with Wheaton. It added that the mother had been "charged with abusing her children at times when with Dr. Wheaton but while in Camp she is said to have conducted herself with propriety."

Paternalistic sentiments about the children of former slaves, common at the time among American whites and used (however disingenuously) to justify seizures of this kind, were elaborated into a defense of former slaveholders' urgent efforts to have African-American children and young adults legally bound to their supervision and control. When questioned about the apprenticeship system, a planter testifying in Louisiana before a commission investigating the army-administered labor system in the lower Mississippi Valley complained that, as a result of emancipation, there was a difficulty:

> Here every man wishes to keep his negroes at home and then you incorporate on the same estate those in a quasi state of slavery—and you have their parents and the whole of the rest of the plantation to interfere with you [sic] exercise of authority over them. . . . If I went to correct these apprentices, under a

law, they say "I am not going to see my son or daughter punished and I will fight for it first," and nine out of ten are against
you, with a physical ability to resist you and they wont allow
you to punish them. If you threaten to send to the Provost
Marshal or to send them off the place,—or have reason to complain of one very decidedly, they are all against you at once.

He went on—ambiguously, but ominously: "if terms are made with the
people of the Southern states so that they can return under the Constitution to manage their affairs in their own way, subject only to the
Constitution of the United States, my impression is that the people
will return voluntarily to the Union."[225] The former slaveholders' idea
of managing affairs "in their own way" involved an elaborate rationalization for removing the impediment of parental interference with
their own supervision and control of young African-Americans.

Gutman reports that post-emancipation apprenticeship laws typically required a finding that the parent of the child was vagrant,
destitute, of poor character, or incompetent to instill habits of industry.
Although the rationale was belied by the fact that "younger children
. . . [were often] left to be maintained by the parents," children were
"taken from their parents under the pretence that . . . [the parents
were] incapable of supporting them." Claims of black parental incompetence were therefore featured—and the theory of black parental incompetence was reinforced—in legal actions to bind children to
former slaveholders or to secure their release. This pattern is apparent
from Rebecca Scott's analysis of post-emancipation apprenticeships in
North Carolina and from Gutman's similar analysis of Maryland.

Scott concludes that masters—who from the perspective of Bureau
agents had "the advantage of community standing, literacy, and a certain shared mode of argument"—were often able to undermine parental rights in the subjective and ad hoc process by which apprenticeships
were approved or reviewed. She reports that parents who as slaves had
not been able to marry lost children to indenture on the ground of
illegitimacy. Emancipated people able to earn only meager wages saw
their children indentured on the ground of parental poverty. When a
North Carolina freedwoman named Menice tried to reclaim her indentured child, she was rebuffed by a Freedman's Bureau agent who

counted against Menice that at the time of the indenture she was living with a man to whom she was not married, but did not count against the master a conviction for assaulting Menice while she was in his employ. Agents' sensitivity to the reputation and marital status of former slaves was exploited by masters who characterized parents appealing for return of their children as "worthless," "lazy," or less concerned than the master for the welfare of the child. When W. S. Swaringer was notified that his indenture of a freed child was being canceled, he complained bitterly that charges of his mistreatment of the child were false and that the parents were "not only liars but Rogues they hold connection with the devil dayly get their living by stealing."[226]

In Maryland, the pattern was the same. Benjamin Osborn held three black children against the claim of their grandmother, alleging that the grandmother was "incapable" of caring for them. A white woman held on to three children of a young freedwoman, alleging that the woman had married "a 'worthless' free black." Another Maryland man described his indenture of twelve black children as "an act of humanity," although he later admitted more selfish motives: "I am left with no body to black my boots or catch a horse. . . . I am now an old man, and in my younger days labored to raise these blacks."[227]

Gutman reports that some Maryland whites seeking to apprentice black children made the allegation of parental incompetence only implicitly, claiming that the children feared their parents, as Sojourner Truth's son had appeared to, and were eager to remain with their "masters." A Carroll County, Maryland, white man, for example, "claimed that a thirteen- or fourteen-year-old boy wanted to remain with him, but that the boy's parents opposed such an arrangement." When another planter said the same about the daughter of a Maryland freedman, the aggrieved father saw through the ruse:

This girl has been living with Wilson in her slave days, and they have got her so that she don't want to leave them, but I want to take her from them as they are not giving her any wages and holding her in slavery. I think I ought to take care of her as I am her father. I went to Mr. Wilson's for her and he drove me from his house, and said I should not have her without authority.

A mother spoke similarly:

> Mrs. Mills and her Son, holds my child in slavery. I went there
> and they ordered me out of the house to-day, and they locked
> the door and took the key out of the door, and they tell her
> not to live with me. I want her to come home and go to school.
> I feel myself perfectly able to support her.[228]

When the superintendent of Negro labor for the Mississippi Gulf area
tried to recover the children of one of his soldiers and was met with
arguments of black parental incompetence, he was blunter:

> I sent a soldier for the children, when the mistress refused to
> deliver them; she came with them to the office and acknowl-
> edged the facts; she affirmed her devotion to them, and denied
> that the mother cared for them; I told her even an alligatress
> would protect and nurse her young; she had bribed them to lie
> about their parents, but I delivered them up to the father.[229]

Representative Donnelly took the same stance speaking in 1866 on
the floor of Congress. He reviewed the Black Codes of South Carolina,
Mississippi, Alabama, Tennessee, and Virginia and concluded that the
children of emancipated people were being taken from them and "sold
into virtual slavery." "Having voted," he then said, "to give the negro
liberty, I shall vote to give him all things essential to liberty."[230]

THE DOCTRINAL STORY EVOLVES

In important respects, the Doctrinal Story about parental liberty and
autonomy has remained undeveloped since its beginnings in Meyer and
Pierce. Family courts across the nation struggle daily to reconcile the
values of autonomous family nurturance with public responsibility to
keep children safe. As we have seen, the Supreme Court has ruled,
albeit inconclusively, on the right of parents to have counsel when
they are faced with being separated from their children. It has also
ruled on the quantum of proof necessary to terminate a parent's legal

status. We know that when a state seeks to terminate a parent's rights and free his or her child for adoption, that parent is entitled to counsel if the issues are complex and entitled to have grounds for termination established by clear and convincing evidence. The Court has recently held that indigent parents must be provided means to appeal termination of their parental rights.[231] But the Court has not said how weighty the grounds for terminating or restricting parental rights must be. Is it enough to show, with clear and convincing evidence, that removal from the home would benefit the child? would be in the child's best interests? would protect the child from physical abuse? from corporal punishment? from psychological harm? from inadequate educational opportunities? What are the standards in neglect and abuse cases, in which the state wants to remove a child from the home but does not (or not yet) seek to terminate parental rights?

The Supreme Court has not directly confronted any of these questions about the scope of parental rights. It has, however, wrestled with the related and equally important matter of deciding which nuclear, extended, legal, common law, biological and affiliational family relationships are constitutionally protected. In the process of considering whether extended-family and psychological-family ties are entitled to the same constitutional protections afforded to biological-family ties, the Court has spoken indirectly about the scope of that protection. In the process of defining the constitutional status of unmarried fathers the Justices have done ideological battle, some arguing that states have a compelling interest in supporting "traditional" families and in placing children unambiguously under their protection, others arguing that parents who try to care for their biological children must be protected against displacement in the name of legitimacy or traditional form.

To round out the Doctrinal Story of parenting, we must trace the themes of family definition from psychological parenthood to unwed fatherhood, probing first for guidance concerning the limits of state authority over the family, and then for an understanding of the risks, merits, and complexities of making adherence to traditional family values a condition of constitutional protection.

The Court's most significant decisions about what family relationships are entitled to due process protection came in its 1976 term. *Moore v. City of East Cleveland*[232] raised the question whether extended-family members could be prohibited under local zoning laws from occupying the same household. This zoning case generated debate, and a measure of clarification, concerning the range of biological relationships encompassed by constitutional doctrines of family liberty. It was not the first time the Court had addressed the issue. *Prince v. Massachusetts*, the case holding that sales of *The Watchtower* could be proscribed by child labor laws, involved the rights of an aunt and guardian, not a biological parent and child. But the Court had not yet squarely addressed the possibility that family rights were inapplicable to extended-family relationships. Inez Moore was a grandmother residing with two grandsons who were not siblings. The zoning laws of East Cleveland excluded such a group from being considered "a family," entitled to reside in "single family" houses, and violation was a crime. Moore was convicted and sentenced to a jail term and a fine. Justices Powell, Brennan, Marshall, and Blackmun invalidated the ordinance, saying that it was unjustifiable because American traditions support due process protection for both nuclear and extended families.[233] Justice Brennan concurred specially to "underscore the cultural myopia of the arbitrary boundary drawn by the . . . ordinance."[234] The additional vote of Justice Stevens gave victory to Moore. Justice Stevens's opinion, a somewhat surprising reversion to the doctrine of fundamental *property* rights, seemed rather defiantly to evoke memories of the *Lochner* era. He reasoned that the ordinance bore no " 'substantial relation to the public health, safety, morals, or general welfare' " of East Cleveland residents, but "cut . . . deeply into a fundamental right normally associated with ownership of residential property—that of an owner to decide who may reside on his or her property."[235] Justices Stewart and Rehnquist dissented, arguing that "the interest . . . in permanently sharing a single kitchen and a suite of contiguous rooms with some . . . relatives" should not be equated with the constitutional right "to marry and to bear and raise children" and applying a rational-basis test to pronounce the ordinance a permissible exercise of state power.[236]

Justice White, who in the years before the Court's recognition of women's right to abortion choice in *Roe v. Wade* was a defender of constitutional rights of family liberty, wrote the first in a series of post-*Roe* dissents questioning, without flatly denying, the legitimacy of all family rights doctrine. Recalling the cautions voiced by Justices Holmes and Black with respect to substantive due process, he branded it as "nothing more than the accumulated product of judicial interpretation."[237] Granting that family rights are among the liberties with respect to which *procedural* due process protections are surely applicable, he urged that *substantive* due process protections be delineated with scrupulous restraint. Justice White acknowledged the appropriateness of exceedingly close judicial scrutiny of invasions of "freedoms of speech, press and religion, and the freedom from cruel and unusual punishments."[238] But he placed what he called privacy rights in a less favored category, alongside the rights to vote and to associate freely, as interests weighing "very heavily" against claims of state regulatory authority,[239] and he argued they should be narrowly defined to include only that measure of freedom "implicit in the concept of ordered liberty." White concluded that "the interest in residing with more than one set of grandchildren is [not] one that calls for any kind of heightened protection under the Due Process Clause."[240] Thus began an effort to find limits for a doctrine of substantive rights of family that had, in Justice White's view, produced alarming exercises of federal judicial power in the context of abortion cases.[241]

The issue of nonbiological family relationships was raised in *Smith v. O.F.F.E.R.*,[242] a 1976 case brought by New York foster parents to challenge the procedures by which children might be removed from their care. The foster parents cited the work of influential psychoanalysts and child welfare specialists who believe that children are irreparably harmed by separations from what are called "psychological parents," defined as persons who provide the children's day-to-day care and nurturing.[243] Arguing that strong psychological bonds between fostering adults and the children in their custody gave the foster family a social and psychological significance similar to that of traditional families, the foster parents claimed to be entitled to constitutional rights of family privacy and integrity.

Justice Brennan's opinion for the Court assumed, without deciding, that the foster parents were entitled to constitutional protections as scrupulous as those given to biological parents. Even so, the challenged procedures were found adequate. The foster parents lost in their effort to change New York's child placement procedures, but they won a concession from the majority that their claim of family status was plausible. Just as prisoners' marriages induced Justice O'Connor to probe deeply the meaning of legal protections of marriage, foster parenting caused Justice Brennan to probe deeply the meaning and purpose of legal protections of the parent-child relationship. What reasons beyond biology were there for safeguarding family autonomy? He found two: the importance to both children and adults of emotional attachments deriving from the intimacy of daily life and the unique role caregivers play in the socialization of children. As we shall see, Justice O'Connor and Justice Brennan found in their analyses of the special cases of inmate marriage and foster parenting an understanding of the meaning of family liberty that began to approach that of the antislavery activists who influenced the Reconstruction Congress. Justice Stewart, on the other hand, writing for himself, the Chief Justice, and Justice Rehnquist, argued that when a state threatened a fostering relationship, no due process liberty was at stake and no special scrutiny or protection was due.

Justice Stewart's opinion was doctrinally interesting for its brief but important discussion of the level of exigency necessary to justify disrupting the parent-child bond. With citation to *Meyer*, he opined that to break up a *biological* family on no greater showing than that it would be in the child's best interests, would "intrude impermissibly on 'the private realm of family life.' "[244] This statement was the first guidance that any member of the Supreme Court had offered to states attempting to develop child protection policies with appropriate respect for parental autonomy. Just as the Court's designation of marriage as a constitutional right resonated with common law pronouncements that marriage is a thing of common right, Justice Stewart's conclusion resonated with common law doctrine. The "best interests" standard, the most common measure for deciding child custody disputes, asks which among possible custodial arrangements will best foster the healthy physical, emotional, and social development of a child. Yet common law courts had long operated on the premise that a parent could not lose custody to a non-parent simply because the non-parent was thought able to provide a better environment. As the highest court of New York once put it: "In many cases the State may, and under some legal systems undoubtedly does, find 'better' parents for a child even though the natural parents may be willing and able to provide proper care. But it is fundamental to our legal and social system that it is in the best interest of a child to be raised by his parents unless the parents are unfit."[245] Justice Stewart spoke, then, with the support of common law tradition. But he spoke alone. The full Court has never addressed the question, and, as we shall see, it soon ruled, with Justice Stewart in agreement, that the "best interests" principle did not apply in the case of a noncustodial, unmarried father.

Peter Stanley, the common law father whose children were removed for no reason other than the death of their mother, preserved his parental status in 1972 when the Supreme Court accepted his constitutional claim, but he won his case with the votes of only five of the nine Justices. In 1977, a unanimous Court rejected the claim of Leon Webster Quilloin, another unwed father seeking the right to maintain responsibility for his offspring. Thus began a complicated and at times emotional effort to balance state interests in making appropriate custodial arrangements for what members of the Court still called "illegitimate" children against the desire of biological fathers to accept responsibility for and maintain a relationship with their offspring.

Peter Stanley, who had lived with his children intermittently, came to the attention of child welfare authorities only because of his partner's death. Leon Quilloin had not lived with his son but had supported him intermittently and maintained a visiting relationship with him. Then the mother consented to the son's adoption by a man whom she married some time after the child's birth. Both the child and the biological father expressed the wish to continue their relationship. Like Stanley, Quilloin faced termination of parental rights without any allegation of fault or wrongdoing—a fate against which mothers, but not fathers, were protected by state law. Although not required to do so, the trial judge gave Quilloin the hearing that Stanley had been denied. It did not find that Quilloin was unfit, but it did find that adoption was in the best interests of the child, and Quilloin's parental rights were extinguished. Stressing that the termination had protected the status and wishes of an intact family, the Supreme Court held that this state procedure did not violate due process. The Court explicitly adopted Justice Stewart's principle that the Due Process Clause would be violated were the state to force the breakup of a natural family "for the sole reason that to do so was thought to be in the children's best interests," but the relationship between Quilloin and his out-of-wedlock son was outside its conception of a "natural family."[246]

Two years later, in *Caban v. Mohammed*,[247] a bare majority of the Supreme Court vindicated the challenge of another unwed father. Like Leon Webster Quilloin, Abdiel Caban was a fit parent who sought to preserve his parental rights in the face of a stepparent's petition to adopt. His rights had been ordered terminated under a New York law that gave unwed fathers no genuine opportunity to contest, but gave unwed mothers and stepfathers a veto, when efforts were made to free their children for adoption. The Court applied "heightened scrutiny" because the statute used a gender-based classification and ruled that New York had violated Caban's right to equal protection of the law.[248] It made no mention of the possibility that rigorous scrutiny might be applied by virtue of the status of the parental right, and it "expressed no view" whether, in a case that did not involve gender discrimination, the state might order adoption over the objection of a fit parent.

Justice Stewart was among the dissenting Justices, and his opinion helps to reconcile the commitment he expressed in *O.F.F.E.R.* to protecting parents against unwarranted custodial interferences and his willingness, in *Quilloin* and in this case, to terminate the parental rights of a fit biological parent. He saw the issue as one of adoption policy, and took the view that adoption was clearly preferable to leaving a child in a nontraditional family constellation, arguing that the state's interest in addressing the "formidable handicaps" of illegitimacy is important and that the decision to permit adoption with the consent of one parent was easily justified. Parental rights for an unwed father, he thought, "do not spring full-blown from the biological connection" but must be earned, usually by marriage to the mother.[249]

Justice Stevens, joined by the Chief Justice and Justice Rehnquist, filed a more impassioned dissent, developing his argument, as Stewart had, from the perspective of child welfare officials, and vigorously defending the authority of states to terminate the rights of biological fathers in the process of settling their children in suitable homes. Stevens accepted fully the assumption that states are serving the interests of children when they extinguish ties with biological fathers in order to facilitate adoption. In his view, biological differences fully justify treating men and women differently with respect to parental rights outside of marriage, and requirements of paternal consent would merely disrupt the adoption process, with tragic consequences for children.

The dissenters in *Caban* have, it seems, been more influential than the majority, for each of the Court's subsequent opinions involving the parental rights of unwed fathers has rejected the father's claim.[250] In response to the *Caban* decision, the state of New York enacted a new statute, improving the chances for unwed fathers to contest proceedings to terminate their rights. In 1983, the Court heard the claim of an unwed father who had fallen between the cracks of this new system. Justice Stevens wrote for the majority, vindicating the claims he had pressed so vigorously in *Caban* and assuring that adoption procedures be no further complicated than *Caban* had strictly required. In fact, the opinion in this case, *Lehr v. Robertson*,[251] constricts the rights established in *Caban*. Abdiel Caban had received what Jonathan Lehr now claimed: the right simply to be heard concerning his child's best interests before adoption could be ordered. Lehr had filed a paternity proceeding, seeking orders of filiation, visitation, and support, but had not filed the bureaucratic paper needed to affect the adoption procedure—a notice of *intent to file a paternity proceeding*—and thus was not entitled to veto or to have notice of proceedings concerning the adoption of his child. Lehr alleged, but was never given the opportunity to prove, that he had lived with the mother for two years before the child's birth. The mother repeatedly acknowledged his paternity and told him she had reported it to the Department of Social Services. He visited the mother and child daily when they were hospitalized for the birth, but thereafter the mother hid her whereabouts and those of the child, and for a year Lehr was only occasionally able to find, and permitted to visit with, the child. Then the mother and child disappeared. When Lehr found them, with the help of a detective, the mother had married another man. She rejected his offers of financial assistance and threatened him with arrest if he tried to see the child. Having received notice from Lehr's attorney that legal action was contemplated, the mother and stepfather commenced adoption proceedings. The Supreme Court's majority failed to mention these allegations, but did mention with approval that state laws commonly prefer the "formal family." It then established for unwed fathers a sliding scale of constitutional protection:

> When an unwed father demonstrates a full commitment to the responsibilities of parenthood by "com[ing] forward to participate in the rearing of his child," his interest . . . acquires substantial protection under the Due Process Clause. At that point it may be said that he "act[s] as a father toward his children." But the mere existence of a biological link does not merit equivalent constitutional protection.[252]

Lehr's equal protection claim was dismissed for similar reasons: discrimination against those with no more than a biological link to a child was reasonable and lawful. Only three members of the Court—Justices White, Marshall, and Blackmun—thought Jonathan Lehr entitled even to be heard.

In 1989, the Supreme Court again addressed the parental rights of unwed fathers. The case, *Michael H. v. Gerald D.*, concerned Michael H.'s effort to maintain visitation rights with his daughter, Victoria D., and Victoria's efforts to preserve her relationship with him. Unlike Quilloin and Lehr, Michael H. had lived with his daughter for a time, but nonetheless, he was barred from establishing paternity or securing visitation rights. The impediment was a California law that had the effect of assigning those rights exclusively to the husband of the mother, even in the face of nearly conclusive evidence that Michael H. was the biological father.[253] Both biological father and daughter asked the Supreme Court to hold that they were constitutionally entitled to preserve their relationship. Justice Scalia announced the Court's judgment denying both claims.

The result was not surprising. The Supreme Court had already shown in *Quilloin* and in *Lehr* a disposition to let states restrict the rights of unwed fathers in order to facilitate settling children in traditional family units with traditional legal ties. The Justices had evidenced no appreciation of interests that children might have in maintaining ties to noncustodial biological parents. It would therefore have been unremarkable if they had found, rightly or wrongly, that

Michael H.'s and Victoria D.'s fundamental rights of family integrity were trumped by interests in protecting the bonds of the legally recognized family.[254]

But Justice Scalia's path to decision was different. It began with a worry that Justice White had repeatedly expressed in his post-*Roe* opinions questioning substantive due process family liberty: that the Court acts illegitimately when it protects rights not clearly specified in the text of the Constitution. It then argued that in order to be counted as a liberty interest under the Due Process Clause, an interest must be fundamental, and it must be "traditionally protected by our society." On the face of it, this truism places no significant obstacle in the path of most litigants seeking constitutional protection. The rights that Michael H. and Victoria D. claimed, for example—rights of family integrity and association—surely have found traditional recognition under the United States' laws. But Justice Scalia added a principle of maximum specificity: traditional protection had to be sought at "the most specific level at which a relevant tradition protecting, or denying protection to, the asserted right can be identified."[255] Traditions respecting general concepts like family liberty became irrelevant because, in Scalia's view, what mattered in connection with Michael H.'s claim was whether there was a tradition of allowing parental rights to a natural father *in his circumstances*.[256] And what mattered with respect to Victoria D.'s claim that she was entitled to maintain relationships with both her biological and her presumptive father was Scalia's belief that "[recognition of] multiple fatherhood has no support in the history or traditions of this country."[257]

Like the theory according to which state action is presumed constitutional if it was tolerated by the framers, this theory of due process adjudication draws the meaning of individual and family rights from majoritarian practice rather than from constitutional principle. The Court is not required to consider the relation between a constraint and our concepts of liberty, personhood, and governance as they have been understood over the nation's history. It is simply required to note whether the constraint has a precedent in our nation's laws.

All the Justices who joined Scalia's opinion in this case had been appointed or elevated by President Ronald Reagan in a process de-

signed explicitly to staff the Court with Justices who would overturn
the most controversial of all family rights decisions, *Roe v. Wade*, in
which it was affirmed that a woman has a constitutionally protected
right to decide whether to continue a pregnancy. Rehnquist, whom
Reagan had elevated to the position of Chief Justice in 1986, joined
without reservation; Justices O'Connor and Kennedy joined in most
of Justice Scalia's opinion but expressed clear reservations about a
footnote containing the most extreme version of the rule of specificity.
So two of the three Reagan appointees, it seems, were unwilling to
foreclose entirely on consideration of respect for general principles, like
family autonomy, in favor of an exclusive focus upon specific features
of the law, like presumptions of legitimacy—or prohibitions on miscegenation or abortion.[258] As we shall see, this difference signaled a
deeper difference concerning the Court's proper role in the protection
of individual and family liberty.

As one would expect, Justice Brennan, joined by Justices Marshall
and Blackmun, deplored the Court's departure from established due
process jurisprudence and its efforts to use closely specified tradition as
a complete measure of due process liberty. But even Justice White,
whose anxiety concerning the legitimacy of due process protection of
familial rights had served as Scalia's doctrinal starting point, sharply
disagreed with his conclusions. Although the autonomy claims of
women wishing to avoid motherhood had led him to question the
entire substantive due process rubric, the claims of men seeking to
embrace fatherhood inspired him to vigilance. In his separate dissent,
he cited the promise embedded in the wording (albeit betrayed by the
overall conclusion) of *Lehr*. The *Lehr* majority had seen constitutional
significance in the biological connection between unwed father and
child and conferred an opportunity to achieve legal recognition and
"the blessings of the parental relationship" in exchange for a demonstrated acceptance of parental responsibility.[259] In Justice White's
words:

It is as if this passage was addressed to Michael H. Yet the
plurality today recants. Michael H. eagerly grasped the opportunity to have a relationship with his daughter (he lived with

her; he declared her to be his child; he provided financial support for her) and still, with today's opinion, his opportunity has
vanished. He has been rendered a stranger to his child.
    . . . I respectfully dissent.[260]

As Justice White shows, the unwed father's right to earn a legally
secured relationship with his child has proved fragile indeed. It is capable of being extinguished, despite his best efforts, when a state
chooses to deny his legal existence in order to support nuclear families
that are legitimated—albeit through legal fictions—by marriage. It is
hard to review the unwed father cases without wondering how much
the Justices' willingness in those cases to compromise parental rights
has depended on the gender of the aggrieved parent. After all, it cannot
be irrelevant to the Court's reasoning that "fathering" is a term too
often limited in popular imagination to the procreative act, while
"mothering" is often (too often?) extended in our imaginations to create expectations of nurturing attention universalized beyond childhood
and beyond hearth and home. Light was shed on this question in 1996
as the Court decided, by a vote of 6 to 3, that when the fundamental
right to parent is extinguished, the state must provide an aggrieved but
impoverished litigant means to appeal. Like *Quilloin* and *Lehr*, the case
(M. L. B. v. S. L. J.) involved a termination to permit adoption by a
step-parent. But M. L. B. was a divorced mother rather than an out-
of-wedlock father, and her situation revived the Justices' perhaps lag-
ging sense of the enormity of a decision to extinguish a parental bond.
Justice Ginsburg, writing for the majority, approached the issues
"mindful of the gravity of the sanction imposed" on M. L. B. and prepared to shelter her rights of family "against the State's unwarranted
usurpation, disregard, or disrespect."[261] Perhaps traditional ways of
thinking about women have had as much to do with the Court's protection of family ties as commitment to the traditional nuclear family.

Troy 17th November 1807

I Hugh Teebles of Troy in the County of Rensselaer do Certify that I am Entitled to the service of a Negro Child a Male born of a slave since the Eight day of February one thousand Eight hundred & seven that the said Child is of the age of Nine Months & nine days & called by the Name of Peter. Witness my hand this day & date above written —

Hugh Teebles

Recorded 17th Novr. 1807
J. McCown Town Clk of Troy

4

"THEY HAVE NOT OWNED EVEN THEIR BODIES"

• ⬌ •

Stories about Procreation

We have seen that the Supreme Court's Doctrinal Stories of marriage and parenting did not develop in an entirely satisfactory manner. The first acknowledgment of a constitutional right to marry, in *Loving v. Virginia*, did not link the right to the text of the Constitution or to the United States' history or political traditions.

ABOVE: 1807 statement of ownership of a nine-month-old infant

168   "THEY HAVE NOT OWNED EVEN THEIR BODIES"

The first acknowledgment of a constitutional right of parental autonomy, in Meyer v. Nebraska and Pierce v. Society of Sisters, sketched the bare outline of a justifying theory with vague links to history and tradition, but it was a negative account, inspired by an uncritical fear of socialist measures, rather than a story of the value Americans have found in an ideal of family liberty. Subsequent cases acknowledging the rights of marriage and parental autonomy did little more than repeat the language of Loving, Meyer, and Pierce, and the Court has searched for opportunities to rest its decisions involving liberty in marriage and parenting on independent constitutional grounds, like freedom of religion or equal protection.

Nonetheless, until the 1970s, the Doctrinal Stories of marriage and parenting were relatively straightforward. Although the reasons for deferring to personal choice in choosing marriage partners and rearing children were not well articulated, deference was established: marriage was a thing of common right at common law and recognized under the Fourteenth Amendment "as one of the vital personal rights essential to the orderly pursuit of happiness by free men."[1] The Fourteenth Amendment was also held to encompass, as a "fundamental theory of liberty," the principle that "the child is not the mere creature of the State."[2]

Matters became significantly more complicated when the Supreme Court began to consider cases concerning procreation. The first consideration yielded, in the case of Buck v. Bell, one of the most notorious denials of individual liberty in American constitutional history. But the Court subsequently recognized the right of procreation in straightforward terms that echoed the formulations of Loving, Meyer, and Pierce. As the Court struggled with issues of contraception and abortion, however, it abandoned the straightforward approach of the early family rights cases in favor of a Doctrinal Story of privacy that depended, not on the fundamental importance of family as an aspect of human self-definition and moral choice, but on the right to be left alone and unobserved. Since then, the Court's family rights jurisprudence has wavered confusingly between Doctrinal Stories about privacy and those about family liberty and autonomy.

The Motivating Stories of slavery, antislavery, and Reconstruction speak less explicitly, but just as tellingly, to the meaning of the right to procreate as they did to the meanings of the rights to marry and to parent. Members of the Reconstruction Congress rose to advocate protection of the right to marry and the right to parent, but not to advocate protection of procreative liberty. Nonetheless, as the following Motivating Stories will reveal, the totalitarian control of slaveholders over their human property resulted in violations of procreative freedom that were as profound, and as inconsistent with the antislavery understanding of freedom, as were slavery's denials of marriage and parental autonomy.

"THERE ARE LIMITS"

Doctrinal Stories Concerning the Right to Continue One's Kind

In 1927, Justice Oliver Wendell Holmes wrote for a majority of eight in *Buck v. Bell* to affirm the authority of the state of Virginia to sterilize institutionalized people thought to be afflicted with hereditary forms of insanity or feeblemindedness. Under Virginia law, surgery to block the reproductive process could be authorized upon judicial findings that the subject was insane or feebleminded and that sterilization would serve his or her best interests or the interests of society. Carrie Buck was ordered sterilized on the grounds that she was herself feebleminded, was the child of a feebleminded woman, and was the mother of an illegitimate, feebleminded infant. She resisted the order on Fourteenth Amendment grounds, claiming that the Due Process Clause protected her right of bodily integrity and her "inherent right . . . to go through life without mutilation of organs of generation."[3] The Supreme Court rejected this claim summarily and without reference to the body of rights recognized only a few years before in *Meyer* and *Pierce*.

The language of the opinion shocks contemporary sensibilities, and only partly because we now know that the factual and scientific determinations upon which the state rested were false: as the Harvard scientist Stephen Jay Gould has been instrumental in establishing, there was in fact no feeblemindedness among the three generations of Bucks,[4] and most forms of feeblemindedness are not heritable.[5] We are also shocked by the disturbing casualness with which Holmes and his colleagues accepted the premises of a version of eugenics that became a "popular craze" of the 1920s, stimulated by the American Eugenics Society and encouraged by a surprising range of conservative and progressive thinkers.[6] The facts of *Buck v. Bell* seem in hindsight to prove the social biases implicit in their social Darwinist ideology:

> Carrie Buck was one of several illegitimate children borne by her mother, Emma. She grew up with foster parents . . . and continued to live with them, helping out with chores around the house. She was apparently raped by a relative of her foster parents, then blamed for her resultant pregnancy. Almost surely, she was (as they used to say) committed to hide her shame (and her rapist's identity), not because enlightened science had just discovered her true mental status. In short, she was sent away to have her baby. Her case never was about mental deficiency; it was always a matter of sexual morality and social deviance. The annals of her trial and hearing reek with the contempt of the well-off and well-bred for poor people of "loose morals." Who really cared whether [her daughter] . . . was a baby of normal intelligence; she was the illegitimate child of an illegitimate woman. Two generations of bastards are enough. [An expert witness for the state] . . . began his "family history" of the Bucks by writing: "These people belong to the shiftless, ignorant and worthless class of anti-social whites of the South."[7]

But our shock and disquiet are also attributable to the opinion's complete disregard of rights of personhood and family that we have come to take as granted. The decision reads:

> We have seen more than once that the public welfare may call upon the best citizens for their lives. It would be strange if it could not call upon those who already sap the strength of the State for these lesser sacrifices, often not felt to be such by those concerned, in order to prevent our being swamped with incompetence. It is better for all the world, if instead of waiting to execute degenerate offspring for crime, or to let them starve for

their imbecility, society can prevent those who are manifestly unfit from continuing their kind. The principle that sustains compulsory vaccination is broad enough to cover cutting the Fallopian tubes. Three generations of imbeciles are enough.[8]

The Court did not return to the subject of sterilization for fifteen years, but when it did, it spoke with new respect—both for the value of Holmes's notions of judicial restraint and for what Carrie Buck's counsel had referred to as "the inherent right of mankind to go through life without mutilation of organs of generation."[9]

Despite the casualness with which the eight-person majority approved the sterilization of Carrie Buck—and despite the chastening experience of the Court's Depression-era conversion from a policy of using the Fourteenth Amendment to protect property rights—the Justices were unanimous in 1942 in the view that a legislative judgment touching the right to procreate warranted "strict scrutiny" in the face of a Fourteenth Amendment challenge. Jack Skinner had been ordered sterilized upon the finding that he was a habitual criminal (having been convicted once of chicken stealing and twice of armed robbery) who could be rendered sterile without detriment to his general health. The Court concluded that the Oklahoma statute violated the Equal Protection Clause because it prescribed sterilization for an arbitrarily selected subcategory of habitual offenders, and, in language that carried a charge of class bias, asserted that "[s]terilization of those who have thrice committed grand larceny, with immunity for those who are embezzlers, is a clear, pointed, unmistakable discrimination."[10]

The majority opinion in Skinner is important, despite a number of doctrinal ambiguities. It was the first opinion to use the term "strict scrutiny"—a term that was used confusingly in Skinner, but later came to stand for the most searching review given by federal courts to the actions of legislative bodies. It is therefore important in the development of the post-laissez-faire-era notion that some laws deserve more critical judicial review than merely asking whether elected officials "could in reason have enacted [them]." Searching scrutiny of the Oklahoma sterilization law was justifiable under the terms of Footnote Four of the Carolene Products case. The Equal Protection Clause, upon which the majority relied, is an explicit provision of the Fourteenth

Amendment. Moreover, it can be argued that those who were vulnerable under the Oklahoma statute were less able to represent their views in the political process than those who were spared. Embezzlers may have more political clout than chicken stealers. But the words of the opinion suggest that the Court was prepared to give special scrutiny to the statute for reasons that went beyond the terms of Footnote Four. The statute was faulted not only because of the nature of the classification that separated those who were eligible for sterilization and those who were not, but also because of the importance of the right that was at stake. Although the Court made apparently respectful reference to Justice Holmes's earlier opinion in *Buck v. Bell,* it did not presume, as Holmes had, that a government that could demand combat service unto death could also demand sterilization, but, rather, that marriage and procreation are basic civil rights, "fundamental to the very existence and survival of the race," and that the power to sterilize is dangerous, both because of the finality of the procedure and because of the risk of policies that could "cause races or types . . . inimical to the dominant group to wither and disappear."[11]

Once again, Justice Stone, the author of Footnote Four and now Chief Justice, was specially vigilant in the protection of personal rights. In his separate opinion, he did not describe the case in equal protection terms at all but asserted a due process limitation upon the procedure by which a state might select candidates for sterilization: no person could be sterilized without the opportunity to challenge the claim that s/he was likely to transmit "socially injurious tendencies." The likelihood that an offender would transmit a socially injurious tendency did not figure in the Oklahoma statutory scheme. Chief Justice Stone's due process theory therefore implied a substantive as well as a procedural limitation upon state power: sterilization might be ordered only when it had been proved, in an adversarial context, that social harm was likely should the defendant reproduce. The requirement that the defendant be given an opportunity to be heard is clearly grounded in procedural aspects of the Due Process Clause. But the requirement that the parties address the heritability of the defendant's "condition" can only be grounded in substantive due process, for it enforces the substantive judgment that an unproved possibility of social harm is not reason enough for such an extreme interference with a defendant's life and liberty. Citing, and elaborating upon, his own language in the *Carolene Products* footnote, Chief Justice Stone reminded his colleagues, the bar, and the public, "There are limits to the extent to which the presumption of constitutionality can be pressed, especially where the liberty of the person is concerned."[12] Justice Jackson, who also concurred separately, echoed this in words and in spirit. "There are," he argued, "limits to the extent to which a legislatively represented majority may conduct biological experiments at the expense of the dignity and personality and natural powers of a minority—even those who have been guilty of what the majority define as crimes."[13]

Skinner did not invalidate sterilization laws per se, and the Supreme Court has never done so.[14] Nonetheless, *Skinner* marked a clear shift— from the nonchalant assumption that sterilization is a service owed those who "sap the strength of the State" to an announcement that one's reproductive liberties are basic, deserving of special constitutional protection. This shift was undoubtedly due, at least in part, to the Justices' exposure to European stories of eugenics movements turned deadly. The German Eugenic Sterilization Law of 1933, part of a program modeled upon the work of American advocates of genetic quality control,[15] required the sterilization of all "who suffered from allegedly hereditary disabilities, including feeblemindedness, schizophrenia, epilepsy, blindness, severe drug or alcohol addiction, and physical deformities that seriously interfered with locomotion or were grossly offensive."[16] By 1939, the German eugenics program encompassed euthanasia "upon certain classes of the mentally diseased or disabled in . . . asylums. Among the classes were all Jews, no matter what the state of their mental health." Seventy thousand patients were shot or gassed to death as "a river of blood . . . [ran] from the sterilization law of 1933 to Auschwitz and Buchenwald."[17] By the year of the *Skinner* decision, the horror of the German program was apparent, and religious and political opposition to the eugenics movement was mounting. The Court could not fail to see that the power to sterilize presented a grave risk to "races or types . . . inimical to the dominant group" or to bring caution and human sympathy to the consideration of claims of inappropriate usurpation of the power to control reproduction. But it remained blind to the relevance of older, domestic stories of comparable usurpations.

USED AS AVARICE OR LUST
MAY DICTATE

Motivating Stories of Reproductive Control

Slavery's intrusions upon reproductive liberty were more likely to involve coerced reproduction than denial of the freedom to procreate, which is in any case more a late-twentieth-century concept than a mid-nineteenth-century one. Enslaved people were considered, among other things, stock for breeding, and breeding was too often a requirement rather than a choice. What their condition illustrated was not the importance of the right to procreate but the importance of the overlapping but broader right of autonomy in decisions about having children.

The antislavery critique focused closely upon the "unnatural" and corrupting power that slaveholders held over the bodies and sexual lives of their human property. Antislavery advocates spoke of slavery as subjugation to a power so corrupt that it bred children, for passion or profit, outside the bonds of family, destroying natural (or, as some argued, divine) institutions as it disregarded them. We have seen the connection that these antislavery advocates drew between slavery and polygamy, conditions which their rhetoric described as "twin barbarisms," having in common an unnatural control by men over the lives of women. In the case of polygamy, control over the lives of a number of women was associated with lustful excess. The unnatural control of slavery reached further to include physical brutality, sexual exploitation extending to the breeding and marketing of one's own children, and a general debasement.

The extent of the physical abuse of slaves on American plantations is as much a matter of debate as the extent of their families' disruption. But it is clear that physical abuse occurred, and abolitionists saw this as a natural outcome of the unnatural physical dependency and legal and social subordination of enslaved people. They argued that what James Pennington called "the chattel principle"[18] led inevitably to brutality and depravity. Frederick Douglass demonstrated with examples from his experience as a slave the violence inflicted when masters and overseers worked to break a slave's will to resist or flee. Samuel Ward wrote that slaveholders "never, during life, lose the overbearing insolence, the reckless morals, the peculiarly inelegant manners, and the profligate habits" of their status.[19] A dissertation on the "political tendency" of slavery, published in *New York's Freedom Journal*, observed, "The man must be a prodigy who can retain his manners and morals undepraved by [the] . . . circumstances" of slavery and asked, "with what execration should the statesmen be loaded who, permitting one half of the citizens thus to trample on the rights of the other, transforms those into despots and these into enemies; destroys the morals of the one part, and the amor patriae of the other?"[20]

In 1856, when a South Carolina slaveholder, on the floor of the Senate, caned antislavery senator Charles Sumner until blood flowed, abolitionists thought the character of slaveholders had been amply demonstrated, if not proven. Ralph Waldo Emerson commented that this was the kind of behavior one expected from a slaveholder, who was both violent and slothful as a result of his immoral domination of other human creatures—"an animal, given to pleasure, frivolous, irritable, spending his days in hunting and practising with deadly weapons to defend himself against his slaves and against his companions brought up in the same idle and dangerous way." Sumner himself stated the case plainly four years after the attack (which had left him incapacitated for much of the intervening time): "Slavery must breed Barbarians," for it is "[b]arbarous in origin; barbarous in its law; barbarous in all its pretensions; barbarous in the instruments it employs; barbarous in consequences; barbarous in spirit; barbarous wherever it shows itself." Sumner saw moral, social, and cultural inferiority in the slaveholding states, and branded every slavemaster "a Bashaw, with all the prerogatives of a Turk," who kept "the bludgeon, the revolver, and the bowie-knife" as constant companions.[21]

Among the slaveholder's unnatural powers, power over the sexual functions of slaves ranked among the most dangerous and odious. In the words of Stephen S. Foster, the antislavery activist who married Abby Kelley, the slavemaster's "very position makes him the minister of unbridled lust," and leaves the slave woman vulnerable to being "used by her claimant as his avarice or lust may dictate."[22] Lust dictated rape of slave women; avarice, that laws granting ownership of children to the owners of their mothers would be used to their slave-breeding purpose.

Although sometimes overgeneralized and sometimes denied, it remains a fact that at times during the years when slavery was legal in the United States, "a laboring stock was deliberately bred for legal sale."[23] Frederick Douglass told of a slaveholder who was able to purchase only one slave, so he bought a woman as a breeder, hired a married man to impregnate her, and netted twins. Another former slave reported that sixty females were kept on the plantation where he lived solely for breeding with white men, producing twenty to twenty-five slaves a year to be sold as soon as they were ready for market.[24] In the last decade of slavery, as an intranational slave trade flourished, "fifty to eighty thousand slaves went from the Border States to the lower South." When Frederick Law Olmsted investigated Southern slavery, he received a report that said:

In the states of Maryland, Virginia, North Carolina, Kentucky, Tennessee and Missouri, as much attention is paid to the breeding and growth of Negroes as to that of horses and mules. Further south, we raise them both for use and for market. Planters command their girls and women (married or unmarried) to have children; and I have known a great many Negro girls to be sold off because they did not have children. A breeding woman is worth from one-sixth to one-fourth more than one that does not breed.

A planter "calculated that the moment a colored baby was born, it was worth to him $300."[25] The life consequences for slaves were harsh, especially for women who were forced by their masters into sexual relations with the slaveholders themselves or with other slaves the woman had not chosen:

After I been at he place 'bout a year, the master come to me and say, "You gwine live with Rufus in that cabin over yonder. Go fix it for living." I's 'bout sixteen year old and has no learning, and I's just ignomus child. I thought that him mean for me to tend the cabin for Rufus and some other niggers. Well, that am start the pestigation for me.

I took charge of the cabin after work am done and fixes supper. Now, I don't like that Rufus, 'cause he a bully. He am big and 'cause he so, he think everybody do what him say. We-uns has supper, then I goes here and there talking, till I's ready for sleep, and then I gets in the bunk. After I's in, that nigger come and crawl in the bunk with me 'fore I knows it. I says, "What you means, you fool nigger?" He say for me to hush the mouth. "This am my bunk, too," he say.

"You's teched in the head. Get out," I told him, and I puts the feet 'gainst him and give him a shove, and out he go on the floor 'fore he know what I's doing. That nigger jump up and he mad. He look like the wild bear. He starts for the bunk, and I jumps quick for the poker. It am 'bout three feet long, and when he comes at me I lets him have it over the head. Did that nigger stop in he tracks? I say he did. He looks at me steady for a minute, and you could tell he thinking hard. Then he go and set on the bench and say, "Just wait. You thinks it am smart, but you am foolish in the head. They's gwine learn you some-thing."

Rose, the woman who lived this story, held Rufus at bay on the second night. The next day, she learned the error of her ways:

The master call me and tell me, "Woman, I pay big money for you, and I's done that for the cause I wants you to raise me childrens. I's put you to live with Rufus for that purpose. Now, if you doesn't want whipping at the stake, you do what I wants."

I thinks 'bout Master buying me off the block and saving me from being separated from my folks and 'bout being whipped at the stake. There it am. What am I to do? So I decides to do as the master wish, and so I yields.[26]

When writers from the Federal Writers' Project interviewed the last survivors of United States slavery, they gathered similar stories. James Green explained the situation in which women like Rose found themselves:

More slaves was getting born than dies. Old Master would see to that, himself. He breeds the niggers as quick as he can—like cattle—cause that means money for him. He chooses the wife for every man on the place. No one had no say as to who he was going to get for a wife. All the wedding ceremony we had was with Master's finger pointing out who was whose wife. If a woman weren't a good breeder, she had to do work with the men. But Master tried to get rid of a woman who didn't have children. . . .

But the nigger husbands weren't the only ones that keeps up having children. The masters and the drivers takes all the nigger girls they want.

Hilliard Yellerday remembered: "A slave girl was expected to have children as soon as she became a woman. Some of them had children at the age of twelve and thirteen." John Smith attested to the success of the system:

My master owned three plantations and three hundred slaves. He started out with two woman slaves and raised three hundred slaves. One was called "Short Peggy," and the other was called "Long Peggy." Long Peggy had twenty-five children. Long Peggy, a black woman, was boss of the plantation. Master freed her after she had twenty-five children. Just think of that—raising three hundred slaves with two women. It sure is the truth, though.

Lewis Jones gave a more credible, but no less horrific account:

My mammy am owned by master Fred Tate and so am my pappy and all my brothers and sisters. How many brothers and sisters? Lord Almighty! I'll tell you, 'cause you asks, and this nigger gives the facts as it is. Let's see; I can't 'lect the number. My pappy have twelve children by my mammy and twelve by another nigger, named Mary. You keep the count. Then, there am Lisa. Him have ten by her. And there am Mandy. Him have eight by her. And there am Betty. Him have six by her. Now, let me 'lect some more. I can't bring the names to mind, but there am two or three others what have just one or two children by my pappy. That am right—close to fifty children, 'cause my mammy done told me. It's thisaway: my pappy am the breeding nigger.

Some were able to subvert the breeding system:

I is going to tell you how a nigger couple fools Master Buckham, once. 'Twas a colored gal—her name was Nancy—about seventeen years old, and her master told her to live with a certain nigger, named Tip. That gal, Nancy, detested that fellow, Tip. She won't allow him to come near her. Tip told his master about it, and the master gives the gal a whipping and told her that him owned her and that she must do as him wants. The colored fellow feels sorry about the gal getting the whipping, so Tip says to Nancy, "I don't want to see you whipped, so I sleep on the floor and you use the bunk. But you must promise never to tell the master." "I sure promise, hope to die," she says.

It was about three months after, the master see there am no children going to be born, so he takes her from that fellow and allows her to stay with the one she likes. That am about five years before Surrender, and every year there am a child born to Nancy while she am a slave. The master never did learn how come there weren't any children born with the first man.

Other enslaved women were brutalized by means that Rose and Nancy were perhaps spared; Mary Peters spoke of her conception:

My mother's mistress had three boys—one twenty-one, one nineteen, and one seventeen. One day, Old Mistress had gone away to spend the day. . . . While [my mother] was alone, the boys came in and threw her down on the floor and tied her down so she couldn't struggle, and one after the other used her as long as they wanted, for the whole afternoon. . . . and that's the way I came to be here.[27]

It was with an anger and contempt born of knowledge of these practices that antislavery people denounced the slaveholders for unseating the natural, familial order, for claiming or controlling sexual access to enslaved women, and for breeding human offspring for sale. This contempt is palpable in the words of a contributor to the *Anti-Slavery Record* of March 1836:

> Do the mothers of our land know that American slavery, both in theory and practice is nothing but a system of *tearing asunder the family ties?* Look at the map of the United States. Draw with your pen a line dividing between the fertile lowlands of the coast and the south, and the more sterile and mountainous uplands of the northern slave states. On one side of this line the principal business by which wealth is acquired is the *breeding of slaves,* to be driven over and worn out upon the cotton, rice and sugar plantations on the other side.[28]

As abolitionists saw the matter, exploitation of the labor, sexual and physical integrity, and reproductive autonomy of slaves violated the slave's "inalienable . . . right to his own body." It was "an audacious usurpation of the Divine prerogative, a daring infringement on the law of nature, a base overthrow of the very foundations of the social compact, a complete extinction of all the relations, endearments and obligations of mankind, and a presumptuous transgression of all the holy commandments."[29]

As Senator Trumbull said in his effort to describe the status that former slaves would share with other United States citizens in a reconstructed democracy true to the principles of the Declaration of Independence, "It is difficult to define accurately what slavery is and what liberty is."[30] If one follows the principle that freedom is slavery's opposite, one must conclude that the antislavery movement, and people like Trumbull, understood freedom to entail protection against totalitarian control over people's bodies and reproductive lives, and a social context within which family relations, endearments, and obligations could exist naturally and without coercion. For Rose Williams, who had been mated for breeding purposes with the enslaved man whom we know only as Rufus, liberty was the right of choice. After emancipation, she left Rufus, saying, "The Lord forgive this colored woman, but he have to 'scuse me and look for some others to 'plenish the earth."[31]

EMANATIONS AND PENUMBRAS

Doctrinal Stories of Procreational Privacy

In the 1870s, a Union Army veteran named Anthony Comstock spear-headed a campaign for sexual purity that inspired the enactment of state and federal laws prohibiting the sale, distribution, and discussion of contraceptive devices (and other materials deemed obscene by Com-stockian purists). The Comstockian movement has been described by the historian Ellen Chesler as a symptom of the social dislocation caused by a long and bloody civil war, and part of a campaign of or-thodoxy undertaken by "native white Americans concerned about the apparent threat to their hegemony from European immigrants and free blacks."[32] Anticontraceptive laws, enacted as a result of Comstock's vehement campaign and the cowardice of politicians who risked being branded as defenders of smut if they opposed it, challenged libertarian ideals of the First and Fourteenth amendments, but they survived years of infrequent enforcement before the Supreme Court addressed their constitutionality. Finally, in 1961, three married couples and a man who was physician to each of the women asked, in *Poe v. Ullman*,[33] that the Court pass constitutional judgment upon a Connecticut ver-sion of the Comstock prohibitions—a law forbidding the dissemination of birth control devices or information. Justice Felix Frankfurter, writ-ing for the majority and expressing his consistent resistance to sugges-tions that the Court invalidate legislative enactments, dismissed the case without discussing the merits, on the ground that threat of pros-ecution under the Connecticut law was so remote that the plaintiffs had no standing to challenge it. (Although the law had prevented the opening of family planning clinics, it had resulted in only one prose-cution since its enactment in 1879.) Four Justices dissented, believing the plaintiffs entitled to challenge the law, and two of the four—

Justices Harlan and Douglas—were prepared to say that the challenge should succeed. Their dissents articulated a basis for a right of procreative liberty.

Although *Poe v. Ullman* was decided more than twenty-five years after the demise of the *Lochner* era, many of the Justices who heard it remained under the influence of the questionable view that the Court in the 1930s had overreached because it failed to ground its opinions in the text of the Constitution. The Harlan and Douglas dissents wavered, as a result, between straightforward reliance upon a substantive due process right of family autonomy—a right subject to the criticism that it is not actually mentioned in the Constitution—and a more convoluted theory linked to the text of the Bill of Rights.

Both dissenting Justices created a text-based doctrinal story by drawing a concept of family privacy from explicit constitutional guarantees of security in one's person or home, describing that concept as a penumbra or shadow of the Bill of Rights.* Justice Douglas, for whom the now much derided penumbral privacy theory was primary, argued that the conception of liberty "gains content from the emanations of . . . specific guarantees [in the Bill of Rights]."[34] Raising the specter of bedroom searches, he declared the Connecticut statute inconsistent with a principle of privacy that radiates from the Fourth Amendment guarantee of security in "persons, houses, papers and effects" against unreasonable searches and seizures and the Third Amendment's restraint against the quartering of soldiers.[35]

Justice Harlan, who wrote a separate dissent, also made a cautious argument from the text and penumbras of the Bill of Rights, but that argument was embedded in—and secondary to—his principal thesis. Drawing upon the history and purposes out of which the Bill of Rights and the Fourteenth Amendment were formed, he articulated a carefully nuanced theory of substantive due process: the Constitution, "the only commission for . . . [the Court's] power" in a case such as *Poe*, was not like a tax code, to be read literally, but "the basic charter of our society, setting out in spare but meaningful terms the principles of

---

*Although Justice Douglas theorized that the entire Bill of Rights, consisting of the first ten amendments to the Constitution, cast a glow of liberty, he relied specifically on only two amendments.

government."[36] The Bill of Rights includes an instruction to the federal government against deprivations of life, liberty, or property without due process of law; the Fourteenth Amendment gives the same instruction to the states.[37] As the Supreme Court itself had done on prior occasions, Justice Harlan rejected the claim that the Due Process Clauses protect procedural rights only, and defined due process as a broader concept, protecting all rights fundamental to free government. Its meaning could not be reduced to formula. "The best that can be said is that through the course of this Court's decisions . . . [due process] has represented the balance which our Nation, built upon postulates of respect for the liberty of the individual, has struck between that liberty and the demands of organized society . . . having regard to what history teaches are the traditions from which it developed as well as the traditions from which it broke."[38] From this theoretical posture, Harlan reaffirmed the conclusions of *Meyer* and *Pierce* that state power to regulate the family is limited by due process restraints upon deprivation of family liberty. "I do not think it was wrong," he wrote, "to put those decisions on 'the right of an individual to . . . establish a home and bring up children,' or on the basis that [t]he fundamental theory of liberty upon which all governments in this Union repose excludes any general power of the State to standardize its children."[39] Applying the concept of "strict scrutiny" announced in *Skinner,* he had no difficulty in finding unconstitutional a law that sought directly to control conduct in the marital bedroom.

Although Justice Douglas did not articulate a theory of substantive due process, his opinion included—almost as an aside—a discussion of the nature of American democracy that forms an argument, independent of the text of the Bill of Rights but consonant with both the anti-Platonic language of *Pierce* and the traditions that inspired the Fourteenth Amendment, for protection of family liberty. Referring to "the totality of the constitutional scheme in which we live," he defined the American concept of liberty in contrast to the totalitarian idea. Quoting John Calhoun, he observed, "One of the earmarks of the totalitarian understanding of society is that it seeks to make all subcommunities . . . completely subject to control by the State," such that the families, the schools, the press, businesses, and religious communities all become organs of the government. Under the American theory of individual liberty, these "megatherian" (or statist) concepts of control are "rejected as out of accord with the democratic understanding of social good, and with the actual make-up of the human community."[40]

The Harlan and Douglas dissents offer, then, a two-layered challenge to state control of contraceptive choice. That challenge encompasses a story of privacy, legitimized by references in the Bill of Rights to the security of persons and homes against government intrusion, and a story of due process liberty and antitotalitarian democratic structure, legitimized by reference to national history and tradition.

Just three years after Justices Harlan and Douglas gave voice to these arguments for procreational choice, the Connecticut anticontraception statute was challenged in the context of an indisputably ripe controversy. *Griswold v. Connecticut*[41] was brought to the Court by two directors of Planned Parenthood who had been convicted and sentenced for giving a married couple contraceptive advice and material. Arguments seeded in the *Poe v. Ullman* dissents now took root, and the petitioners' claim was vindicated. Despite doctrinal differences, a majority of seven Justices voted to overturn the convictions and declare the prohibition unconstitutional insofar as it was applied to restricting contraceptive use by a married couple.

Justice Douglas, writing for the majority, elaborated his theme of emanations from the Bill of Rights, lengthening the catalogue of textual sources for a right of family privacy. As he had done in *Poe v. Ullman*, he relied on the Bill's prohibitions against unreasonable searches and seizures and unconsented quartering of soldiers. He also relied on the First Amendment right of assembly (which the Court had previously read to imply a right of association[42]) and on the Fifth Amendment right against self-incrimination. With these textual anchors, and a reference to the Ninth Amendment command that the enumeration of rights in the first eight amendments not be construed to deny the existence of other rights,[43] he concluded that the right of married couples to learn about and use contraception was "within the zone of privacy created by several fundamental constitutional guarantees."[44] Although the opinion contained a reaffirmation of *Meyer* and *Pierce*, it did not use the "antimegatherian" rhetoric from Douglas's dissent in *Ullman* or Harlan's reading of the independent meaning of

Fourteenth Amendment due process. It did not, in other words, assert that grounds for constitutional protection of family rights existed apart from the Bill of Rights and its "emanations."

Justice Harlan wrote separately to say that the Due Process Clause stands "on its own bottom" in its protection of family liberty, without regard to the language of the Bill of Rights.[45] Ironically, Justice White also wrote separately to reaffirm the teachings of *Meyer*, *Pierce*, and *Skinner* that the liberty protected by the Fourteenth Amendment includes a measure of autonomy in family life. The right "to be free of regulation of the intimacies of the marriage relationship" comes to the Court, White said, "with a momentum for respect lacking when appeal is made to liberties which derive merely from shifting economic arrangements."[46] He went beyond reaffirming the special constitutional status of family rights to argue that strict judicial scrutiny is required of laws that compromise family liberty: the state interest must be compelling, and the means chosen to further the state's interest may not be unnecessarily drastic.[47]

If we trace Justice White's subsequent positions with respect to family liberty, we learn a great deal about the effect that wrenching moral questions can have on how Doctrinal Stories develop. For he moved from being a strong and consistent supporter of the Doctrinal Story of a substantive due process right of family liberty to being one of its bitterest critics. And the issue that shook his commitment was abortion.

"A RIGHT BROAD ENOUGH TO ENCOMPASS A WOMAN'S DECISION"

A Doctrinal Story of Abortion Choice

In 1971, *United States v. Vuitch* came to the Supreme Court. It involved a doctor who practiced in the District of Columbia and who had been indicted under a law that prohibited abortions unless they were "necessary for the preservation of the mother's life or health."[48] The doctor claimed, and the lower court had held, that the law was unconstitutional in its vagueness, but a bare majority of the Supreme Court found it precise enough to be upheld. In a confusing tangle of dissenting and concurring opinions, only Justice Douglas mentioned, and no Justice squarely confronted, the implications of Griswold or the possibility that the law was unconstitutional not because it was imprecise but because it gave to agents of the state decision-making power that belongs, in a regime of ordered liberty, in private hands. Nonetheless, the case made the Justices imagine the effect of antiabortion laws upon the medical profession and upon pregnant women, and Justice Douglas noted that state involvement in the abortion decision might infringe the privacy rights that Griswold had delineated.

Two years later the Court confronted, in Roe v. Wade, the relationship between the power of states to proscribe abortion and Griswold's principle of family privacy. The Griswold principle was explicitly linked to an argument that there is a justifiable expectation of privacy in the marital home. As a result, the Justices might well have found it irrelevant to the abortion context: abortions do not, as a rule, occur in the home, and those who seek them are often unmarried. But in the two years between Vuitch and Roe, the Court had extended the Griswold principle beyond the marital domicile.

Eisenstadt v. Baird,[49] decided a year after Griswold, concerned the right of unmarried couples to use contraception. William Baird had given a lecture on contraception, at the conclusion of which he gave a woman a container of spermicidal foam. He was convicted for dispensation of the contraceptive device, that being a crime in Massachusetts unless one was a physician or pharmacist and the dispensee was married. The Supreme Court's somewhat perplexing opinion relies on Griswold, but seems studiously to ignore its limiting language. Giving Griswold an extremely generous interpretation, it assumes that married persons have a constitutional right of access to contraceptives and decides on equal protection grounds that the right must be available to the unmarried as well.*

---

*It is interesting to see how the argument—indeed the narrative of the Doctrinal Story—evolves. The Court assumed that the purpose of the challenged law was not to protect health, not to deter extramarital sex, but to prevent contraception per se. It thereby foreclosed a number of arguments that the state had special and legitimate interests in controlling extramarital sexuality. Then the Court set up two hypotheticals—either Griswold forbids the prohibition of contraception per se or it does not. Analyzing these possibilities on equal protection grounds—and studiously avoiding a

This tangle of argument is perplexing on the face of it, but comprehensible if one considers the composition and timing of the document. Justice Brennan, who wrote the opinion, was surely prepared to rest decision upon a due process right to privacy or autonomy in intimate affairs that was broader than any established in *Griswold*. But Supreme Court opinions are joint products, and the *Eisenstadt* opinion was crafted for endorsement by two Justices, Stewart and Blackmun, at least one of whom would have had difficulty with speaking in such broad, substantive due process terms. So Justice Brennan relied explicitly upon a theory of equal protection—the theory by which Justice Stewart had supported earlier decisions protecting family rights—but also included language suggesting that there were independent rights of privacy and autonomy. His opinion contains a statement that is a non sequitur in its equal protection context, but persuasively articulates a theory of constitutional liberty, placing decision making about contraception in private, rather than state hands: "If the right of privacy means anything, it is the right of the *individual*, married or single, to be free from unwarranted governmental intrusion into matters so fundamentally affecting a person as the decision whether to bear or beget a child."[50]

This amalgamation of due process and equal protection ideas may disturb one's sense of logic, but it is understandable and legitimate. Groundbreaking judicial opinions like *Griswold* often come to mean more than they have said, and as the meaning of a holding evolves over time, it is to be expected that different Justices will have in mind different doctrinal implications of it. *Brown v. Board of Education*, for example, was decided with an opinion that relied upon evidence that black children suffered psychological damage in segregated school en-

---

substantive due process analysis—it concluded that it doesn't matter whether or not the state may prohibit the distribution of contraceptives; the point is that if there is such a prohibition, it must apply equally to the married and to the unmarried.

None of this is self-evident. Nothing in *Griswold* says the state may not control unmarried, nonprocreative sex as a health risk. Moreover, every member of the *Griswold* Court speaking on the subject strongly suggested that the legislation of morality was permissible for its own sake, apparently leaving the door open for states to control unmarried sex as a vice. The only issue *Griswold* seems to insist on is that the state has no business intruding on the privacy of married life. It did not have anything to say about limitations on the distribution of contraceptive devices, even to the married.

vironments; the narrow holding was that separate schools are unequal as a result of psychological harm caused to the segregated child. But once the Court had repudiated the doctrine of "separate but equal" in the school context, equal protection discourse evolved, and the constitutional meaning of segregation was disentangled from the idea of subjective harm. It became clear that racial classifications that reinforce caste stratification and are based upon preference or custom (rather than upon some remedial or otherwise constructive function) are inherently stigmatizing and subordinating. The history of the Fourteenth Amendment supported the idea that caste subordination was among the evils the amendment was designed to address, and the Court was able to outlaw segregation in parks, trains, buses, and other public facilities by mere citation to *Brown*, in decisions that contained no findings of subjective harm but worked on the theory that *Brown* had come to represent: that racial segregation of public facilities perpetuated a system of caste subordination repudiated by the Fourteenth Amendment.

Just as *Brown* had, *Griswold* survived reflection and scrutiny, and it evolved. The idea of a constitutional right to be free of direct regulation of marital sex rang true to the American conception of individual liberty. In the minds of some Justices, the idea was more comprehensive, extending beyond the home and beyond marriage. And it affected the most pressing issue before the Court during the term in which *Eisenstadt* was decided: the constitutionality of abortion prohibitions. Thus, it is reported, Justice Brennan was willing to shape his opinion in *Eisenstadt* to win the broadest possible agreement with the proposition that the Constitution protects against government interference with "the decision whether to *bear or beget* a child."[51] The doctrinal bases for recognition of a woman's right to choose abortion had been established.[52]

When the Supreme Court affirmed, in *Roe v. Wade*, the right of abortion choice, it elaborated the special complications of this issue: the question whether the fetus has competing rights; the legitimacy of a state's interest in safeguarding the fetus; the pregnant woman's unique position of life-sustaining connectedness with the fetus; and the peculiar history of abortion regulation. But the Court's opinion is not elaborate in its description of the principles of liberty, privacy, and autonomy that underlie a woman's constitutional claim of a right to choose abortion. Echoing the language of *Eisenstadt* and drawing upon the penumbral privacy notions first accepted in *Griswold*, it characterizes family rights as aspects of the right of privacy, ranks them as "fundamental," and describes them as including the right to choose abortion. In the Court's language: "[A] right of personal privacy . . . does exist under the Constitution." It encompasses liberties that are "fundamental" or "implicit in the concept of ordered liberty," and it safeguards a measure of freedom with respect to "marriage, procreation, contraception, family relationships and child rearing and education." And it is "broad enough to encompass a woman's decision whether or not to terminate her pregnancy."[53]

Justice White, who had written so generously of rights of family liberty in *Griswold*, dissented bitterly in *Roe v. Wade*. For White, a pregnant woman claiming a right to choose abortion asserted "convenience, whim or caprice" as against a state effort "to protect human life."[54] In this "sensitive area"—as to which Justice White tellingly asserts that "reasonable *men* may easily and heatedly differ" (my emphasis)—he found "no constitutional warrant" for "valu[ing] the convenience of the pregnant mother more than the continued existence and development of the life or potential life that she carries." He did not mention the right of privacy or autonomy in matters of marriage and family life, and from the day of *Roe*'s decision, he did not support it without careful qualification.

As Justice White's reservations about the doctrine of family liberty and privacy swelled, those of Justice Stewart subsided. Justice Stewart agreed with the Court's conclusion in *Roe*, but he reached that conclusion by a very different route. For Stewart's brethren in the majority, *Roe* was a development in the evolving articulation of a doctrine of family privacy. For Stewart, it was a departure—a belated acceptance of *Griswold* and of the renaissance of substantive due process. Accepting due process family rights for the first time, Justice Stewart issued a concurring opinion that takes little for granted and therefore richly describes the doctrinal foundations of the right to choose. He may have been persuaded as he examined the issue over the years from the point of view of parents seeking autonomy, of interracial couples wanting freedom to marry, and of couples and individuals wanting protection of the right to reproductive choice. Perhaps his decision to join the majority in *Eisenstadt* was followed by an acceptance that the right asserted there entailed more than equal protection. Whatever the reason, Justice Stewart now asserted, "In a Constitution for a free people . . . the meaning of 'liberty' must be broad indeed." He embraced Harlan's view that due process liberty is not a summary of the terms of the Bill of Rights, but a guarantee against "all substantial arbitrary impositions and purposeless restraints," and a promise that purposes will be closely scrutinized when specially prized freedoms are at issue. Accepting the premise that had been avoided to win his support in *Eisenstadt*, he acknowledged that the Supreme Court has a special function to perform in protecting "freedom of choice in matters of marriage and family life."[55]

SLAVERY WILL NEVER OWN A CHILD OF MINE

Motivating Stories of Procreation and Freedom

The issue of procreative liberty had presented itself very differently a century and a half before when enslaved people struggled against the prospect of bearing and begetting children who would become a master's chattel. As free antislavery activists spoke out against this violation of a person's "inalienable right to his own body," enslaved people devised means of resisting claims made on their progeny. Means of resistance took sobering, sometimes chilling forms when slavery's domination extended beyond the body and mind to the bloodlines. J. W. Loguen did not marry because, as he put it in his autobiography, slavery must "never own a wife or child of mine."[56] Henry Bibb wrote that "if there was any one act of my life while a slave, that I have to lament over it is that of being a father and a husband of slaves," and vowed that the daughter whom he left in slavery was "the last slave that ever I will father, for chains and slavery on this earth."[57] Some slave women who shared this sentiment were abstinent or used a variety of substances and devices to prevent conception or to induce abortion;[58] emancipated slave Jane Blake commented that if "all bond women had been of the same mind, how soon the institution could have vanished from the earth."[59] Some women privately wished that their children would be stillborn; a few resorted to infanticide. The abolitionist Lydia Maria Child wrote of a mother facing the imminent sale of her children who "took an axe and chopped off their heads, and then ended her own life with the same instrument." Another woman in the same situation "threw her three infants into a well and then jumped in after them."[60] Margaret Garner, who tried to kill her four children to prevent their reenslavement and succeeded in killing one, was described by poet Frances Ellen Watkins Harper as "hew[ing] their path to freedom [t]hrough the portals of the tomb."[61] Harper marveled that Garner's act could fail to move her country to abolish slavery. (More than a century later, Toni Morrison immortalized Garner as the center of a novel, *Beloved*, that invites exploration of every implication of the child's killing and slavery's brutal arrogance.) A former slave told of a woman whose children were regularly sold at the age of one or two years: "When her fourth baby was born and was about two months old, she just studied all the time about how she would have to give it up, and one day she said, I just decided I'm not going to let Old Master sell this baby; he just ain't going to do it. She got up and give it something out of a bottle, and pretty soon it was dead."[62]

What can these century-old stories of celibacy, contraception, abortion, and infanticide tell us today about the right of procreative liberty or about family freedom? It is this: all of the participants— those who summon empathy and those who summon only horror— speak poignantly of the intertwining bonds of identification, affection, and responsibility that link us to our children. We love our children and take joy in their capacities to become independent beings. At the same time, we are responsible for their births. We are also responsible, in limited and ever-diminishing, but deeply felt ways, for the conditions under which they grow. To think through questions of procreative liberty completely, we must confront the truth that, for some, the deepest implication of responsibility is that there are conditions under which one cannot in conscience nurture young life.

THE DOCTRINAL STORY EVOLVES

Roe v. Wade is perhaps the most contested of all modern decisions of the United States Supreme Court. Justice White observed in 1976 that policing *Roe's* prohibition would be "a difficult and continuing venture in substantive due process."[63] He was right. Between 1973 and 1989, when the fundamental premises of *Roe v. Wade* survived their most recent assault, almost half the Court's cases (seventeen out of thirty-eight) touching on family rights were abortion cases, and they were often difficult and divisive. As Justice White's comment implicitly predicted, the evolving Doctrinal Story that began with *Roe v. Wade* defines, however confusingly, the Court's still unsettled understanding of substantive due process and of the family rights said to fall within its reach. It is a bitterly contested story of a search for coherence in the process of measuring personal and family liberties against important state interests, as a majority of the Court formulated a firm response to state and local governments bent on circumventing or overruling *Roe*, while a minority (growing as a result of appointments made by an anti-choice President) became insistent that *Roe* was illegitimate and should indeed be overruled. Ironically, the story may best be remembered for bringing an end to the Court's crisis of confidence over what is now agreed to have been judicial overreaching in the equally controversial *Lochner*-era cases.

In reviewing this Doctrinal Story, we must focus first upon the complicated and ambiguous standards that *Roe* set for judging invasions of procreational and sexual liberty. We will then turn to the majority's struggle to uphold *Roe* in the face of new antiabortion legislation from the states and persistent opposition from the Court's anti-*Roe* minority. In the end, we will see the Doctrinal Story of sexual and procreational choice retold in terms that reflect both the confident libertarianism of pre-*Lochner*-era due process jurisprudence and the respect the Great Depression brought for collectivist social welfare laws.

When *Roe v. Wade* reached the Supreme Court in 1973, there was precedent for recognizing that the Constitution protects freedom of reproductive choice, but there was no established standard by which claims to this freedom would be adjudicated. It seemed established by

Eisenstadt v. Baird that people in the United States are entitled to more in the way of procreational and sexual liberty than secrecy in the marital precincts, and that reproductive choice was among the rights to which the Justices were prepared to pay special deference. But recognition of a due process right was only the beginning of deciding an abortion case. The right of reproductive choice would have to be weighed against competing governmental interests. What were the governmental interests that might be served by prohibiting abortion? And how did they compare with a woman's right of choice? The outcome of *Roe* would turn as much on the standard by which those questions were answered as it did upon recognition of the existence of a due process right.

The *Lochner*-era family autonomy cases, like the subsequently discredited cases invalidating marketplace regulations, had been decided by a measure of "reasonableness"—a test moderate in language but searching in its application during the early twentieth century. Minimum wage laws, child labor laws, prohibitions of German-language instruction, and mandatory public schooling had all been condemned by the Court as arbitrary and unreasonable. With the 1930s repudiation of substantive due process, the Court virtually abandoned the more demanding requirement of reasonableness that had been applied to safeguard family rights in *Meyer* and *Pierce*. The sharply contrasting view that state laws touching on constitutionally protected liberties require only a "rational basis"—a standard most generous to government and most restrictive of civil rights—prevailed in the family rights context at least for the moment when compulsory sterilization laws were given such cursory scrutiny in *Buck v. Bell*. But most Supreme Court Justices in the post-*Lochner* era found that, as Chief Justice Stone predicted in his famous Footnote Four, the rational basis test was inadequate to judge reasoned government initiatives that infringe on fundamental rights of personhood and family. The search for alternatives was circuitous.

In the 1940s *Skinner v. Oklahoma* had introduced "strict scrutiny," the term by which the most rigorous of the Supreme Court's Fourteenth Amendment tests has been named. But the *Skinner* opinion's decisive language tracked the "rational basis" standard: the classification at issue was condemned as "artificial," "invidious," without "the slightest basis." Chief Justice Stone's and Justice Jackson's concurrences insisted that "[t]here are limits" to state actions impinging on liberties so personal and basic as the right to procreate. But none of the *Skinner* opinions made clear where the limits lay.

The meaning of the term "strict scrutiny" has grown beyond the implications it held in the *Skinner* case as it has been elaborated in opinions that are premised more purely on equal protection principles. Strict scrutiny is now most clearly associated with the kind of judicial analysis that is used in reviewing classifications based on race. Under a strict scrutiny analysis, classifications that are racial or otherwise "suspect" are considered unconstitutional unless they are necessary in the service of a compelling state interest. The test proceeds in two stages: the state is first required to show that its action serves a compelling purpose. If that is proven, the state must show the necessity of its action by establishing that there were no less drastic means available than its infringement of the complaining party's rights to advance the compelling interest. A Court decision that this two-stage strict scrutiny analysis must be applied is generally regarded as a decision to disapprove the government action at issue—the scrutiny has been jokingly referred to as strict in name but fatal in fact.[64]

Even though *Skinner* introduced the phrase "strict scrutiny," no Supreme Court family liberty case has been decided (and only one family liberty opinion has been reasoned) by a formula so rigid as the formula now associated with that phrase. Clear-cut application in family rights cases of what has come to be known as "strict scrutiny" would have clarified the limits of state power to compromise family liberty, but it would have imposed upon family rights cases a test far too rigid to meet the complexities of reconciling state and private interests in family governance. Moreover, as we have seen, *Skinner* was not a pure family rights case but one that depended on both family rights and equal protection principles: the Court's circuitous reasoning was that special scrutiny is due, *on equal protection grounds, to classifications resulting in* infringement of fundamental family rights. *Skinner* is not, of course, unique in its mixing of family rights and other, more developed, constitutional principles. Indeed, the Court's anxiety about the legitimacy of family rights jurisprudence has often left it straddling constitutional principles and borrowing rules of decision from cases involving the more established right.

When the school requirement to salute the flag was considered and upheld, for example, the Court approached the measure with "careful scrutiny," not in the name of family autonomy but because the requirement compromised the First Amendment freedom of religious choice. In doing an about-face on this question, the Court again announced the measure of freedom in First Amendment terms: state action infringing the right of free speech would be approved "only to prevent grave and immediate danger to interests which the state may lawfully protect."[65] In *Prince* just how far a state could go in infringing on the rights of children and parents to distribute religious literature was undefined, except for the Court's statement that because states have special obligations and authority with respect to children the appropriate measure was less stringent than the First Amendment's "clear and present danger test." The special complexities of approving an exercise of state authority in the presence and against the wishes of a fit parent were unexplored.[66]

The Court's invalidation of antimiscegenation laws was like its result in *Skinner*, a matter of both equal protection and due process. In its equal protection analysis, the *Loving* Court used the language of strict scrutiny,[67] but in its due process, family autonomy analysis it articulated no standard of review. The equal protection analysis of the plurality in *Eisenstadt* required, and failed to find, a "rational explanation" for discrimination between the married and unmarried in the prohibition of contraceptive sales.[68]

In family rights cases in which the Court did not rely upon standards appropriate to resolution of a parallel civil liberties or equal protection claim, it articulated an equally confusing variety of standards for judging the acceptability of state action. Justice Harlan's prophetic dissent in the first contraception case used the term "strict scrutiny," but defined that scrutiny as requiring a justification "stronger" than a rational basis for "intrusive" state measures affecting the fundamental right to privacy within the home.[69] When the full court confronted the contraception issue in *Griswold*, it produced a variety of tests. It presumed that the state's ends were acceptable (without articulating, let alone discussing them) and borrowed from a freedom of association case the rule that the state's means must not "sweep unnecessarily broadly and thereby invade the area of protected freedoms." Justice Goldberg, joined by Chief Justice Warren and Justice Brennan, filed a concurrence that stands as the only family autonomy opinion in which strict scrutiny analysis is fully applied. Justice White's analysis of the statute suggested that he found it irrational, but he wrote in language (including the term "strict scrutiny") that made clear his acceptance of a standard more rigorous than rational basis.[70]

The Court's procedural due process analysis in *Stanley* required, and did not find, a "powerful countervailing interest" to justify reliance upon a presumption of unfitness to deny the parental rights of an un-wed father.[71] When Amish parents challenged compulsory school attendance laws in *Yoder*, the invasion of free speech and family autonomy interests was measured in terms that had no clear lineage; the laws were deemed to require "searching examination" and a showing by the state of "more than a reasonable relation"—a "substantial threat to public safety, peace or order."[72]

So the Supreme Court faced the abortion controversy with a mix of borrowed and undeveloped measures of the legitimacy of state actions touching family rights. Looking to these, and to measures used in cases addressing the rights to travel, to vote, to speak, and to enjoy religious freedom, it emerged from the controversy with a test—more stringent than rational basis analysis and less stringent than strict scrutiny—that was applied for more than a decade within, but rarely outside, the abortion context.

The *Roe* Framework, as the Court's test has come to be called,* began with the assumption that states could restrict abortion choice in the name of a compelling purpose. The Court immediately designated the protection of pregnant women's health and the protection of unborn life as state purposes that become compelling at some point

---

*The term "*Roe* Framework" has often been used more narrowly to refer to *Roe*'s temporal criteria for determining when a state's interest in fetal life becomes compelling. I use the term in its broader sense, to encompass the whole of the *Roe* standard for assessing the legitimacy of infringements on the right of choice or on other personal and family rights.

STORIES ABOUT PROCREATION 197

during pregnancy.[73] Since the phrase "compelling state interest" was loaded with meanings associated with strict scrutiny analysis, the stature this designation conferred on the state's interests in pregnant women's health and unborn life was considerable. Since the Court's test contained no requirement of necessity or least drastic means in its second prong, the concession of a compelling state interest defanged the test as it was announced. In two swift strokes, the Court identified the right of abortion choice as being of such importance that states might not invade it except with the highest of justifications, and ranked unborn life and pregnant women's health among the highest of state interests—interests so worthy that they could justify the infringement of fundamental rights.

That protection of pregnant women's health is a compelling state interest in uncontroversial, although it raises specially knotty questions about autonomy. When is it right to curtail a person's liberty in order to protect her from herself? The harm principle, which is always a feature of discussions of autonomy and ordered liberty, plays out less simply when the only harms at issue are harms self-inflicted by an uncoerced actor.

That the state's interest in protecting unborn life is a compelling one is more complex, requiring a judgment about the state's relationship and responsibility to inchoate human life, and it is this aspect of the abortion issue that makes it morally wrenching and conceptually unique. Embedded in every legal issue concerning abortion is the question whether the fetus is to be counted as a member of the political community and entitled, on that ground, to have its life safeguarded by the state. Majoritarian conservatives, perceptively, see an analogy between *Dred Scott v. Sanford* and *Roe v. Wade*. Just as *Dred Scott's* result flowed from a decision that African-Americans were not members of the United States' political community and entitled to sue in federal courts, *Roe v. Wade's* result depended upon a determination that a fetus is not to be counted as a member of the political community entitled in its own right to life and liberty. It is this determination that we speak of when we ask in a legal context whether "life" begins at conception, viability, sentience, or birth. Were the fetus a political person, the state would be not only free but compelled to protect its life; because *Roe v. Wade* determined that it is not, abortion need not count as murder under our laws, and the state, as guardian of the life and liberty of its people, is not required to prevent it.

Despite its finding that the fetus is not a political person, the *Roe* Court compromised the pregnant woman's right to abort or continue her pregnancy, ruling that the state has *an interest in fetal life* and that *the interest is compelling.* This left the door open to an indeterminate but significant level of state regulation of abortion choice. But what was the nature of a state's interest in fetal life? The Court did not say. And why does it trump the pregnant woman's or the family's interest in reproductive autonomy? States have claimed that they have a responsibility both to each fetal being and to promoting a general respect for human life by disapproving contraception and abortion. But these claims are legitimate only if we answer in the state's favor the questions papered over by *Roe*: Where is the locus of procreational choice? Is the intimate, moral choice to continue or abort a pregnancy to be left entirely to pregnant women and their families, or is it to be left to, or somehow shared with, the state? Just as it had done in *Griswold* and in *Eisenstadt*, the Supreme Court in *Roe* ducked the fundamental question whether the United States Constitution requires us to conclude that procreational choice should be squarely within the family, rather than somehow shared between the family as rights seekers and the state as protector of human life.[74]

Having established, however conclusorily, that the state has a compelling interest in both pregnant women's health and fetal life, the Supreme Court offered three somewhat inconsistent statements of what it would substitute for the second leg of strict scrutiny analysis— what restraint a state would be required to show when it selected means to protect pregnant women's health and fetal life. In its general discussion, the Court said that the means had to be "narrowly drawn." In speculating explicitly about abortion control measures taken in the interest of pregnant women's health it described a more lenient standard, saying that they need only be "reasonably related" to that compelling purpose. It was more concrete, and arguably more lenient still, with respect to the means a state might adopt to further its compelling interest in unborn life, saying that legislatures "may go so far as to proscribe abortion . . . except when it is necessary to preserve the life or health of the mother."[75]

At this point, the Supreme Court's reasoning took an unusual turn: the compelling character of state interests in pregnant women's health and unborn life was given temporal limits. Because early abortions pose little risk to the pregnant woman, a state's interest in maternal health was deemed "compelling" only after the end of the first trimester of pregnancy. Government's interest in fetal life was said to become compelling at "viability"—the moment at which the fetus is capable of sustaining life outside the womb. This temporal aspect of the *Roe* Framework was ingenious, in that it provided the basis of a jurisprudence calibrated to account for the fact that abortion is increasingly problematic, in both moral and medical terms, as the pregnancy continues and fetal development advances. Still, *Roe*'s temporal criteria proved unsatisfactory when the Court wrestled in subsequent years to reconcile a compelling state interest in unborn life and a fundamental private interest in abortion choice.

To describe the doctrinal difficulties of *Roe* is not to condemn its architect or the majority for which he spoke. The ambiguity of the test established in *Roe* was unavoidable. In 1973, a majority of the Court was prepared to support an ambiguously limited individual right of abortion choice, and for that purpose the *Roe* Framework served as well as any clear alternative. The majority coalition was prepared to go no further. Doctrinal elegance would come, as it has come in most constitutional contexts, only with time and with reflection in the context of new controversies.

The Court's designation of pregnant women's health and of preservation of fetal life as "compelling interests" invited close state regulation of abortion seekers and abortion providers after the end of a pregnancy's first trimester. The invitation was accepted. States with strong antiabortion constituencies blanketed abortion seekers with regulations, and abortion rights advocates met each regulation with a legal challenge.

For ten years after *Roe*, the Court considered a series of complex state laws that expressed the determination of right-to-life constituencies to control abortion as much as possible given the *Roe* holding, or to invite its reconsideration. In what Justice White prophetically termed "a difficult exercise in substantive due process," these new abortion controls were set against the *Roe* Framework. States defending antiabortion laws drew upon *Roe*'s concession that the autonomy of pregnant women was incomplete and competing governmental interests were compelling. But the Supreme Court, perhaps seeing in abortion regulations shades of the reactions of Southern states to desegregation orders after *Brown v. Board of Education*, usually concluded that women's rights of abortion choice prevailed over the state interests in pregnant women's health and fetal life.

In the name of the "compelling" government interest in pregnant women's health, states enacted regulations prohibiting outpatient abortions or certain abortion techniques. A Court majority invalidated these regulations, saying that they impeded access to abortion services without furthering a reasonable concern for the health of the women undergoing abortion.[76] When states attempted to further their "compelling" interest in unborn life by imposing upon physicians performing both early- and late-term abortions a duty of care toward the fetus, the Court invalidated these requirements, saying that they were too broad and did not further in meaningful ways the life chances of the viable fetus.[77] *Roe* had characterized abortion choice as a medical decision to be left, in part, to the judgment of an attending physician. When states passed regulations that assigned the physician a prescribed counseling function with respect to the decision whether to abort, the Court invalidated them as interferences with pregnant patients' freedom of choice.[78] *Roe* acknowledged "the sensitive and emotional nature" of abortion decision making,[79] and its companion case acknowledged the relevance of "emotional, psychological [and] familial factors [as well as] the woman's age."[80] When states enacted regulations to inform and structure the pregnant woman's decision making, the Court approved a bare requirement that there be informed consent to the abortion procedure,[81] but invalidated statutes that went beyond this to require that abortions be postponed for twenty-four hours or that the woman be given information designed to deter her from choosing abortion.[82] When states made it a requirement that parents and spouses be involved in the abortion decision, the Court invalidated spousal consent regulations altogether and upheld provisions applicable to minors only insofar as they deferred to the wishes of "mature" minors and gave those who were unwilling to seek or unable to obtain parental consent the means to obtain judicial consent instead.[83] When states tried to extend the scope of their "compelling interest" in unborn life by structuring and influencing the determination of when a fetus was deemed viable to live on its own, the Court invalidated some but not all of the laws, finding that they were vague, or interfered inappropriately with medical judgment.[84]

The architecture and language of the Roe Framework complicated the efforts of Justices trying to protect the right of choice in the face of antiabortion laws. The reasoning of opinions striking down abortion regulations sometimes strained the apparent meaning of such concepts as "reasonable relationship" to pregnant women's health. If the state's interests in unborn life and women's health are legitimate and compelling, and abortion regulations that serve those interests need only a "reasonable relationship" to this purpose, it is not self-evident that second-trimester hospitalization, say, or viability determination procedures for late abortions are constitutionally proscribed. Yet, in opinions that were imprecise about the terms of the "special scrutiny" to be given to abortion restrictions, the majority struck down regulations of this kind on the authority of Roe.

There is, I think, a simple explanation for the Court's refusal to legitimate abortion control legislation that seemed to promote state interests which Roe had designated as "compelling." It was understood by the Justices in the Roe majority that these regulations not only burdened abortion choice but were intended to do so.* From their perspective, claims of a state's interest in maternal health and of a precise interest in the lives of viable fetuses masked a determination to deter abortion choice by simply making it as expensive and difficult as possible. Diplomacy counseled them against saying in the early cases that the laws at issue seemed insincere and designed more to inconvenience

---

*With the exception of Justice Burger, whose concurrence in Roe was based on an assumption that its holding was narrow, the Justices who voted in Roe to uphold the right to choose abortion voted consistently in the post-Roe decade to protect that right against erosion by abortion regulations.

and intimidate pregnant women than to protect fetal life, but the impression of insincerity undoubtedly affected the Justices' judgments as to these regulations' reasonableness.

From the perspective of states defending abortion regulations, it must have seemed that the Court was being insincere in its hypertechnical interpretation of the limits of government's interest in unborn life. The Court had, after all, designated that interest legitimate and, from the moment of viability, compelling. Why should a state legitimately interested in the life of a fetus be faulted for discouraging or impeding its abortion? Wasn't there a contradiction in the Roe Framework if it simultaneously endorsed and condemned efforts to protect a fetus against women contemplating abortion? These questions generated frustration and anger in the early post-Roe years; in subsequent years, they caused dismantling of the Roe Framework.

For a brief moment in the late 1970s, it appeared that Roe might provide a measure against which a broad range of personal and family rights claims could be evaluated. Justice Brennan clarified and broadened its Framework in an opinion concerning restrictions on contraception sales in New York.* Speaking in 1977 for five members of the Court in Carey v. Population Services International, he reaffirmed, "The decision whether or not to beget or bear a child is at the very heart of . . . [a] cluster of constitutionally protected choices," and described the measure of protection in terms that strengthened the language of Roe: " 'Compelling' is . . . the key word; where a decision as fundamental as that whether to bear or beget a child is involved, regulations imposing a burden on it may be justified only by compelling state interests, and must be narrowly drawn to express only those interests."

In Brennan's reading, the Roe Framework required compelling justification and narrowly drawn measures whenever government action touched on intimate, constitutionally protected choices. But this straightforward measure of the realm of family liberty was not broadly endorsed. Four Justices were unwilling to apply it even in Carey: Justices Burger and Rehnquist dissented; Justice Powell found the com-

---

*The provisions that were invalidated, on the ground that they violated a right of autonomy, had prohibited sale of contraceptives to minors and required that they be sold by licensed pharmacists. The opinion also invalidated, on First Amendment grounds, a law prohibiting advertisements for contraceptives.

pelling interest test too restrictive when put to measures less inhibiting of contraceptive use than direct prohibition; and Justice White saw "no need . . . to agree or disagree with the Court's summary of the law."[85]

In any case, just as the *Carey* majority was endorsing and clarifying the special scrutiny standards of the *Roe* Framework, its temporal aspects were beginning to break down. In 1977, the year of the *Carey* decision, a Court majority, consisting of the *Roe* dissenters and Justices Powell, Burger, Stewart, and Stevens, gave to states the freedom to further their "compelling interest" in unborn life through legislation that affected a pregnancy long before the fetus was viable, and had no purpose but the coercion of procreational choice. The case was *Maher v. Roe*.[86] The *Maher* Court approved a state decision to give financial assistance for costs associated with childbirth but withhold it, except in cases of medical necessity to preserve the life of the mother, for costs associated with abortion, an exemption that applied to *all* abortions, regardless of the stage of fetal development. The opinion was written by Justice Powell, a member of the *Roe* majority who had begun to express reservations.[87] The laws at issue might have been upheld, without challenge to the *Roe* Framework, on the argument that the right of procreational choice does not imply a right to financial support for implementing a particular choice. But the Justices in the majority approached the matter differently: they did not argue that government has no duty to fund abortion; they argued that it has a clear right to *discourage* abortion. Expanding upon *Roe*'s admission that the state has a compelling if ill-defined interest in fetal life, the *Maher* majority found it "abundantly clear that a state is not required to show a compelling interest for its policy choice to favor normal childbirth over [abortion]."[88] The reasoning was that *Roe* implied "no limitation on the authority of a state to make a value judgment favoring childbirth . . . and to implement that judgment by the allocation of public funds."[89] The *Roe* majority had held that the right of privacy was broad enough to encompass the decision whether to bear a child; the *Maher* majority held that the sovereign's interest in unborn life was broad enough to legitimate the use of state power to encourage childbirth over even early-term abortion and to do so on exclusively moral grounds.[90]

The change that *Maher* wrought in the Doctrinal Story about procreational choice has been largely overlooked. *Maher* was severely—and properly—criticized for effectively excluding poor women from *Roe*'s constitutional protection. But it was equally important as the occasion of a crucial shift in abortion discourse. *Roe* had spoken of nontherapeutic abortion as a difficult choice as to which reasonable people might differ, at least up to the time of viability. It had not explicitly acknowledged a role for the state in protecting the nonviable fetus. *Maher* directly conceded the state's power to brand all abortion as an evil to be officially discouraged. This shift was most apparent when the *Maher* majority approved an incidental requirement, without analogue outside the abortion context, that medical necessity be specially demonstrated if a woman sought to take advantage of the law's exception for cases in which abortion was needed to preserve the woman's life. In justification, the Court said, "The simple answer to the argument that similar requirements are not imposed for other medical procedures is that such procedures do not involve the termination of a potential human life."[91]

Despite *Maher*'s disregard of the temporal aspects of the *Roe* Framework and its validation of the state's role as an advocate for fecundity, the Supreme Court continued to review direct regulations of abortion according to the Framework and continued to invalidate regulations that directly constrained abortion choice. Yet it was a small step from the majority's stance in *Maher* to Justice White's subsequent statement that *Roe* was premised on the notion that "the evil of abortion does not justify the evil of forbidding it."[92] This characterization of abortion as an evil, rather than as a difficult moral choice, was a prelude to retrenchment from *Roe*. In the years after *Maher*, cases in which the Court invalidated what the majority Justices surely thought were anti-abortion laws became the occasions for increasingly bitter struggles over the legitimacy of *Roe*'s decision to protect abortion choice and the workability of its Framework.

This increasing bitterness developed in a political context that must be considered if we are to understand fully subsequent choices the Justices made. Political opposition to *Roe v. Wade* was, of course, a motivation for the legislatures that enacted abortion control laws. But it also affected the very composition of the Court, as Justices retired and a President outspokenly opposed to *Roe* tried to create an anti-*Roe* majority. The first of President Reagan's three appointees, Justice O'Connor, brought the special credibility of a woman's voice to the abortion debate, and early in her tenure she began to criticize the *Roe* Framework. The President's second nominee, Robert Bork, was a well-known critic of the entire line of family privacy and autonomy decisions, who regularly decried the Court's interferences with legislative will in the 1930s and equated them with its later invalidations, in cases like *Roe*, of laws thought to inhibit individual or family liberty. For Bork, you will recall, it was improper to distinguish constitutional adjudication laws that interfered with a corporation's right to pollute the air from laws that interfered with a married couple's right to use birth control. Under the Constitution, states were equally free to regulate marital sex and the toxic emissions of a chemical plant.[93] When the Senate declined to confirm Bork's nomination, it was thought that political forces had ratified the rights of privacy and personhood he found illegitimate. For the millions of people in the United States who regarded contraception and early abortion as appropriate aspects of family planning, and for millions more who opposed one or both of those measures but agreed with the Court that they were matters for individual conscience rather than state control, retrenchment from *Griswold* or *Roe*—not to speak of Court decisions about marriage and parenting—was unthinkable. Also, people were deeply troubled by the President's thinly veiled efforts to use his powers of judicial appointment to ensure that *Roe v. Wade* would be overturned. True, people appointed to the Supreme Court have views, histories, and political and social values, and Presidents are likely to choose Justices whose views, histories, and values they find appealing. Nonetheless, efforts to pack a Court in order to achieve a specific judicial outcome conflicted with ideals of open-minded and impartial adjudication that live, however incongruously, with our realism about judicial predilections. It was against this background of controversy that Justices Scalia and Kennedy joined Justice O'Connor, in 1986 and 1988, as President Reagan's second and third appointments to the Supreme Court bench.

As anti-*Roe* Justices grew in number and vehemence, the theme of evasion and defense of abortion choice became explicit. Justice Blackmun, the author of the majority opinion in *Roe*, said in 1986, speaking for a majority then reduced to five: "In the years since this Court's decision in *Roe*, States and municipalities have adopted a number of measures seemingly designed to prevent a woman . . . from exercising her freedom of choice."[94] Justice White defended the states. Finding their efforts to legislate access to abortion wrongfully condemned as "some sinister conspiracy," he argued that efforts "to pursue permissible policies through means that go to the limits allowed by existing precedent is no sign of *mens rea*" or evil intent. Justice Blackmun's direct criticism of the motives of state legislatures was matched by Justice White's questioning of the motives of the Court's majority. White charged that the majority was insecure about *Roe*, aware that it had "created something out of nothing" and produced an unpopular and "illegitimate" ruling, and was now reaching, defensively and indiscriminately, to invalidate abortion control measures that were offensive only from its "warped point of view."[95]

Beneath this bitter quarrel lay fundamental doctrinal differences. The debate had never died over *Roe*'s underlying premise that rights of family privacy and autonomy encompass a woman's right to choose abortion. *Roe*'s ambiguity and compromises seemed not to mitigate doctrinal differences but to deepen them. A framework that pitted a *compelling* interest in unborn life or pregnant women's health against a *fundamental* right of procreational choice encouraged absolutist rhetoric on both sides and left no common ground between them. And *Roe*'s temporal distinctions seemed arbitrary to those who viewed a mother's health and a fetus's life as worthy of protection throughout pregnancy.

When Justice O'Connor replaced Justice Stewart in 1981, she had quickly announced that she believed the temporal aspects of the *Roe* Framework unworkable and analytically flawed. The verdict of unworkability rested on a belief that measures of constitutionality should not be keyed to concepts, like the moment of fetal viability or the safety of later-term abortion procedures, in constant flux as medical knowledge advances. This was rather unpersuasive as an attack upon the *Roe* Framework, for it exaggerated both the difficulty of assessing the reasonableness of abortion requirements related to pregnant women's health and the likelihood of imminent medical advances that would significantly change the point at which a fetus could have a viable independent life. But in any case the unworkability argument was secondary to Justice O'Connor's more fundamental claim that the Framework was analytically flawed. Dissenting from the Court's invalidation of a set of abortion restrictions enacted by the Akron, Ohio, City Council, O'Connor argued that Roe's temporal framework was not only unworkable but inappropriate, for, in her view, the state's interests in unborn life and maternal health were "compelling throughout pregnancy." Relying heavily on Justice Powell's opinion in *Maher*, and disregarding or rejecting Roe's formula for "heightened scrutiny" of all abortion restrictions, she argued that in light of the states' continuous and compelling interests in fetal life and their compelling interests in women's health, "heightened scrutiny" was appropriate only with respect to state actions that constituted an "unduly burdensome interference with . . . freedom to decide whether to terminate . . . pregnancy."[96] In her view, none of the Akron regulations was unduly burdensome.* Justices White and Rehnquist joined her opinion, and, for the first time, there was a clear alternative to the *Roe* Framework.

In 1986, the majority again ruled against a state that was seeking to justify a complex mix of abortion regulations, deliberately obstructive of abortion choice or reasonably related to maternal health and the protection of viable fetal life, depending on one's point of view. On this occasion, Chief Justice Burger joined Justices White, Rehnquist, and O'Connor in dissent, arguing that the state acted under the reasonable assumption "that [the] Court meant what it said in *Roe* concerning the 'compelling interest' of the states in potential life after viability," and announcing the belief that *Roe* should be reexamined.[97]

By 1989, Justices Kennedy and Scalia had replaced Justices Burger and Powell, and Justice Rehnquist was Chief. By the end of the term, the *Roe* Framework was hanging by the thread of Justice O'Connor's reluctance to join a new majority that was even more tolerant than

---

*The Akron law required hospitalization for second-trimester abortion; parental or judicial consent for all patients under fifteen; a prescribed counseling procedure; consent informed in a closely prescribed way; a twenty-four-hour waiting period; and "humane" disposal of fetal remains.

she of abortion control. The unraveling occurred in *Webster v. Reproductive Health Services*,[98] a case concerning the constitutionality of a Missouri law that announced in its preamble the "findings" that human life begins at conception and the unborn have "protectable interests in life, health and well-being." The Court had to determine the constitutionality of this preamble, as well as of requirements concerning the determination of viability and a proscription against the use of public facilities for abortions (except those necessary to save the life of the mother). Each provision was approved, but the anti-*Roe* Justices were unable to gather a majority, either to overrule *Roe*'s basic premise or to announce a new framework. Justices Rehnquist, White, and Kennedy formed the plurality. They found it unnecessary to reconsider the *holding* of *Roe*, but directly rejected its temporal framework, taking the view that the state's interest in potential life existed without regard to a fetus's viability.[99] Justice Scalia wrote a concurrence that took the others to task for tinkering with the *Roe* Framework rather than taking the opportunity to reconsider its basic premise. Justice O'Connor took an independent path, finding the Missouri law constitutional even under the standards established by *Roe* and its progeny.

In the 1989 term, the Court approved parental notification provisions of the abortion laws of two states, but still it failed to pronounce definitely on *Roe*'s premise or its framework. To the relief of pro-choice constituencies and to the consternation of right-to-life constituencies, the precision with which Justice O'Connor examined the notification statutes suggested that she was unwilling to provide the fifth vote necessary to remove entirely constitutional restrictions upon state interference with the right of choice. The thread held.

Finally, in 1992, Justice Scalia's insistent demand that the Supreme Court reconsider *Roe*'s fundamental premises was met—at least in part. The Court did reconsider *Roe*'s conclusion that women have a constitutional right of abortion choice, but it rejected Scalia's argument that *Roe* was the product of the Court's "self-awarded sovereignty over a field where it has little proper business"[100] and should be overruled. Upon sober reflection nineteen years after the fact, in one of the most significant constitutional cases of the twentieth century, the Justices affirmed *Roe*'s central holding by a majority that included both

Justice O'Connor and Justice Kennedy. And it struggled once again with the task of settling upon a workable framework.

The case that occasioned reconsideration of *Roe* was *Planned Parenthood v. Casey.*[101] The various issues in *Casey* were decided by close margins, and the case produced three opinions, one of them a caustic dissent written by Chief Justice Rehnquist and joined by Justices White, Scalia, and Thomas. But the three centrist Justices— O'Connor, Kennedy, and Souter (appointed by President Bush in 1990)—spoke in a single voice* to accomplish two somewhat incongruously related objectives: (1) to reduce the level of constitutional protection for pregnant women seeking autonomy in the management of their pregnancies and (2) to end the Court's post-*Lochner* crisis of confidence by explicitly restoring substantive due process to mainstream constitutional jurisprudence.

In the world of abortion rights jurisprudence, the O'Connor-Kennedy-Souter opinion in *Casey* is significant because it greatly expands the *Roe* compromise. It designates states' interest in fetal life as compelling *from the moment of conception*; it abandons the *Roe* Framework in favor of a version of the "undue burden" test developed in earlier opinions by Justices Powell and O'Connor;[102] and it gives unqualified approval to state measures designed to influence a pregnant woman's choice by making known an official "preference for childbirth over abortion." The centrist Justices drew a conceptual line between manifestations of state disapproval and constitutionally "undue" burdens on abortion choice.[103] A burden on abortion choice was defined as constitutionally "undue" only if it had "the purpose or effect of placing a substantial obstacle in the path of a woman seeking an abortion of a nonviable fetus." States were free, then, to condemn abortions, to regulate them closely, but not to place "a substantial obstacle" in the way of women who wanted them. This new framework was applied in the case at hand to uphold an informed consent provision that had been designed to discourage abortion, a twenty-four-hour

---

*As the full Court had done to show its solidarity in *Brown v. Board of Education*, these Justices deviated from the tradition of individual authorship to produce a jointly authored opinion.

waiting period (both similar to measures invalidated under the *Roe*
Framework in prior cases), and a variety of reporting and record-
keeping requirements, but invalidate a requirement of spousal notification.[104]

Yet, despite these clear retreats from the *Roe* Framework and
from the first post-*Roe* decade of abortion jurisprudence, the Supreme
Court's new abortion rights majority took pains to reaffirm *Roe*'s central
holding. In portions that were joined by Justices Blackmun and Stevens
and therefore expressed a majority view, the *Casey* opinion decisively
reaffirmed *Roe*'s conclusion that rights of personal and family liberty
encompass the right to choose abortion. These sections of the opinion
are thoughtful, thorough, and broad, reaffirming not only *Roe*'s central
holding but all of the due process, personal and family rights jurisprudence from which it drew. As Justice Stevens had done in *Roe*, this
new majority avoided the circumlocutions of the penumbral privacy
rationale and rested its holding directly upon the understanding that
democratic liberty, as defined by the United States Constitution and
traditions, guarantees independence and choice in shaping personal
and family life. Going back to Justice Harlan's time-honored reasoning
in *Poe v. Ullman,* the Court agreed that despite the breadth and ambiguity of its terms, the Due Process Clause rests on its own bottom to
guarantee personal and family rights that are not specified in the Constitution.

The five Justices joining this opinion pronounced themselves fully
prepared to take on the process of reasoned judgment, guided by history, tradition, and precedent, necessary to discern the contours of
ordered liberty. They definitively rejected Justice Scalia's argument
that constitutional liberties are restricted by principles of initial toleration or maximum specificity. And, most significantly for the Court's
sense of mission and character in the years to come, the majority cast
aside the doubt that had clouded constitutional jurisprudence since
the *Lochner* era with respect to the legitimacy of affording substantive
due process protection to personal and family rights. These Justices
understood that the *Lochner* Error was far narrower than had been
feared: the early-twentieth-century Justices who overruled marketplace
regulations in defense of freedom of property and contract were right

to acknowledge substantive liberty interests, though wrong in the balance they struck between those liberties and governmental interests. The *Lochner*-era Court had made what the *Casey* centrists called "fundamentally false factual assumptions about the capacity of a relatively unregulated market to satisfy minimal levels of human welfare"; although marketplace regulations may impinge on constitutionally protected liberties, they are often justified by the need to protect the polity's general welfare.[105]

As Charles Black's test of laughability might have shown long ago, in a humane and civilized nation constitutional protection of liberty of contract does not imply that employers and workers must be "free" to agree upon eighty-hour workweeks and unhealthy working conditions.* To state the case in the context of family rights, in a humane and civilized nation the right to marry does not imply that spouses must be "free" to remain in a battering relationship. Having recognized this, the Court's new majority could, without fear that it would force them to stymie good government, embrace a substantive concept of Fourteenth Amendment liberty. It said:

> Our law affords constitutional protection to personal decisions relating to marriage, procreation, contraception, family relationships, child rearing, and education. Our cases recognize "the right of the individual, married or single, to be free from unwarranted governmental intrusion into matters so fundamentally affecting a person as the decision whether to bear or beget

---

*This view is consonant with antislavery understandings of liberty. Freedom, as slavery's opposite, did not preclude collectivist social welfare measures. To take the case of labor reforms, many antislavery advocates thought it possible to liberate slave labor without leaving former slaves and other workers vulnerable to exploitation in an unregulated marketplace. One Union general wrote to Gerrit Smith: "There must be no rule contracting the labor of the negro for one year or one month, it is strength contracting with weakness and results in oppression." Letter from Brigadier General John P. Hawkins to Hon. Gerrit Smith, October 21, 1863, in *Berlin II* at 745. Another proclaimed: "It is the conviction of my command . . . that labor—manual labor—is inherently noble; that it cannot be systematically degraded. . . . Our motto and our standard shall be . . . FREE LABOR AND WORKING-MEN'S RIGHTS." Proclamation of Brigadier General J. W. Phelps to the Loyal Citizens of the South-West, December 4, 1861, *id.* at 201.

a child." Our precedents have respected the private realm of family life which the state cannot enter. These matters, involving the most intimate and personal choices a person may make in a lifetime, choices central to personal dignity and autonomy, are central to the liberty protected by the Fourteenth Amendment.[106]

5

A NEW APPRECIATION OF
FAMILY RIGHTS

• ⟺ •

I have gathered together these Motivating Stories of slavery and antislavery in the belief that they enrich public discourse, the arguments of lawyers, and the decisions of judges about families, family values, and personal freedom. It remains to confront and neutralize forces that have suppressed these neglected stories and then suggest

ABOVE: Extract and drawings from Louisiana's Reconstruction constitution

more precisely how our thinking can be nourished as we return them to public consciousness. My discussion is structured around Fourteenth Amendment jurisprudence, but, as is so often the case, the jurisprudential questions have parallels in public discourse and in political debate.

What are the reasons for neglect of antislavery history and tradition in Fourteenth Amendment jurisprudence? I offer two: First, the Court has been influenced, albeit only to a limited extent, by a flawed judicial philosophy that emphasizes legislative practice over democratic principle. In addition, the Court has been unwittingly susceptible to outdated and unworthy cultural influences that mute the historical significance of antislavery and Reconstruction.

How, then, is our thinking affected if we clear these impediments and analyze important questions of due process jurisprudence in light of Reconstruction and antislavery history? Two demonstrations will serve as partial answers in what must be an ongoing inquiry. The first concerns the legitimacy of what I call moral legislation. Using as a case example the Court's increasingly infamous decision in *Bowers v. Hardwick*, we shall consider whether an antislavery understanding of moral autonomy calls into question the Court's deference to state efforts to control matters of conscience. The second concerns the difficult problem of properly allocating, as between parents and the state, responsibility for the care and socialization of children. Using as case examples the Court's treatment of abortion regulations that require parental consent when the pregnant patient is a minor, and its failure to address standards for state intervention in cases of neglect and abuse, we shall consider whether our new, antislavery understanding of due process liberty supports or challenges the choices the Court has made.

RECAPTURING ANTISLAVERY HISTORY
AND TRADITION

What is the object of writing the history of Reconstruction? . . . [I]t is simply to establish . . . Truth . . . on which Right in the future may be built.[1]

In the search to understand what the Constitution promises with respect to family liberty, Justices of the Supreme Court have consistently
gravitated to Justice Harlan's dissent in *Poe v. Ullman*, in which he
wrote that due process liberty represents "the balance which our Nation, built upon postulates of respect for the liberty of the individual,
has struck between that liberty and the demands of organized society."
There is a broad consensus that this balance is to be understood in
terms of "what history teaches are the traditions from which [the Na-
tion] developed as well as the traditions from which it broke."[2]

To be sure, Justices disagree as to how history and tradition are to
be read. As we have seen, Justice Scalia, in *Michael H.*, applied a rule
of specificity that set the meaning of due process liberty by reference
to a tradition of narrowly defined *practices* rather than to a national
tradition of commitment to broader *principles*. This vision of the uses
of tradition in due process adjudication is disturbingly limited. By Justice Scalia's measure, *Brown v. Board of Education*'s challenge of official
segregation would have failed in the face of a history and tradition of
separatist legislation; *Loving v. Virginia*'s challenge of antimiscegenation laws would have failed in the face of a history and tradition of
laws designed to protect the purity of the white race; and we would be
forced to agree that Myra Bradwell's challenge of laws barring her from
law practice should have failed in the face of a history and tradition
of laws restricting women to the domestic sphere.

The question of tradition must not be whether *the state action* was
traditional or traditionally tolerated, but whether toleration of it is
consistent *with the history that produced, and the traditions that support,
the relevant constitutional provisions.*[3] Laws and practices consistent with
a challenged state action may shed light on the relevant history and
traditions, but they do not constitute them. In themselves, they are
like medieval annals: they are lists of data with no narrative structure,
no "notion of a social center by which . . . to charge them with ethical
or moral significance."[4] When we try to place them in a story about
the Fourteenth Amendment, we can imagine them carrying a variety
of meanings—they might be manifestations of a constitutional ideal,
but they might also be manifestations of the mischief against which
the Constitution protects us.

In *Michael H.*, Justice Scalia seemed to imagine laws enforcing a presumption of legitimacy as a self-justifying tradition. He wrote as though there were no Constitution and traditional practice carried the force of inviolable law. But this is surely a mistake. The United States is not a constitutionless nation. It is a nation with a rich *constitutional* tradition that should, at times, preempt legislative traditions. The analysis of history and tradition in due process adjudication should highlight the traditions that animate the principles expressed in the constitutional text. Historical facts illuminate constitutional meaning only when they are understood as part of a story, or history, of why and how the Constitution came to say what it says.

The history and traditions most pertinent to interpreting Fourteenth Amendment liberty comprise a story of why and how the amendment came to be—a story of conflict, war, and reconstruction. Although the causes of conflict and war were multiple,[5] the words of support for the Reconstruction Amendments make clear that they were inspired by the rejection and repudiation of slavery, in turn the product of a successful political movement led by slaves, former slaves, and other antislavery advocates. The movement was grounded in human rights traditions that had been enshrined in the nation's founding documents and stood throughout the slaveholding years in increasingly explicit challenge to the commodification of human beings. The Fourteenth Amendment is, then, illuminated by the history of slavery, antislavery, war, and Reconstruction—by repudiation of the traditions of slavery, and by the human rights traditions that drove antislavery and Reconstruction.

To say that the amendment is illuminated by history and tradition is not to say that the latter shed light on the intent of any historical actor to legitimate or repudiate particular kinds of state action. Intent so defined is unknowable in most cases. Intent also varies among actors; members of Congress, state legislators, and voters participating directly or indirectly in the constitution-making process will not have had uniform or equally developed understandings in these matters. But even if intent with respect to the *particular effects* of a constitutional provision were knowable and monolithic, it should not freeze constitutional interpretation. For, as the Court's jurisprudence teaches with respect to official segregation, miscegenation, and gender discrimination, constitutional principles may be broader and nobler than long-tolerated official practices can measure. Most members of the Supreme Court have understood this and have taken a broader view of history and tradition than Justice Scalia's rule of specificity would require. In most cases raising questions of due process liberty, the Justices have gone beyond asking whether a challenged deprivation of liberty had a historical precedent and asked whether it was consistent with an understanding of liberty that made sense in light of the United States' broader traditions. Yet the story of the nation's wrenching struggle to reconcile its tradition of commitment to human freedom with its practice of chattel slavery has been virtually ignored in that process.

At the end of the last century, there was a glimmer of recognition of the importance of antislavery history to Fourteenth Amendment interpretation. Justices who lived during and immediately after Reconstruction wrote of the Fourteenth Amendment as a repudiation of slavery and a triumph of antislavery. The dissenting Justices in *Slaughter-House* placed it squarely in the history of slavery, antislavery, war, and Reconstruction.[6] In 1895, the first Justice Harlan, dissenting in *Plessy v. Ferguson*, described the Thirteenth Amendment as having decreed "universal civil freedom" as it "struck down the institution of slavery." The Fourteenth Amendment was added, he continued, to complete the work of safeguarding "all the civil rights that pertain to citizenship."[7] The *Slaughter-House* and *Plessy* dissents described the Fourteenth Amendment as a guarantor of rights essential to freedom, and placed it in the context of rejecting and repudiating slavery. But these were, after all, dissents, and one need not look beyond the majority opinions in *Slaughter-House* to see the beginning of the process of muting their stories. The *Slaughter-House* majority did not, of course, deny that the Reconstruction Amendments were responsive to slavery and abolition. Its opinion is elaborate in its explanation that the amendments were the product of, and must be understood in terms of, a rebellion that had slavery as its "overshadowing and efficient cause." It acknowledges that they were written to ensure that emancipation was undergirded by constitutional decree, observing that former slaveholding states had passed "laws which imposed upon the colored race onerous disabilities and burdens, and curtailed their rights in the pursuit of life, liberty and property, to such an extent that their freedom was of little value."[8]

But the *Slaughter-House* opinion focused upon the history of slavery and antislavery not to illuminate a code of freedom, but to justify a narrow reading of the Fourteenth Amendment by highlighting the fact that the *Slaughter-House* plaintiffs were not former slaves, not African-Americans, and therefore not readily imagined as beneficiaries of Fourteenth Amendment protections. Although the majority Justices rejected the idea that "no one else but the negro can share in . . . [the] protection of the Fourteenth Amendment," they shuddered at the thought of placing state governments under close constitutional control. They therefore found the right to work that the plaintiffs claimed—and all rights not pertaining to *federal* citizenship—to be outside the scope of federal power.[9] This conclusion was unreasonable, but it is not incomprehensible.

The majority's denial of what Justice Swayne remembered in dissent as "deliberately adopted"[10] measures to place basic civil rights under federal protection is consonant with the misgivings that arose in the postwar years concerning the wisdom of congressional Reconstruction. Indeed, the majority's opinion contains evidence of these misgivings. As the Court described the reports of Southern practices that led Congress to conclude that "something more [than the Thirteenth Amendment] was necessary"[11] to emancipation, it allowed for speculation that "falsehoods or misconception may have been mingled with their presentation."[12] The Court further undermined congressional credibility by characterizing Congress as acting, when it considered the Fourteenth Amendment, "[u]nder the pressure of all the excited feeling growing out of the war."[13] The tone of the opinion then assumed an edge as the Court insisted that "whatever fluctuations may be seen in the history of public opinion on this subject . . . this court . . . has always held, with a steady and an even hand, the balance between state and federal power, and we trust that such may continue to be the history of its relation to that subject."[14] It would not be a mistake to take these words to indicate that the majority thought congressional Reconstruction so misguided that it could be repudiated by judicial fiat. True to its commitment to protecting state power against federal will, the Court reduced the history of the Fourteenth Amendment from a story in which civil freedom was understood through the experience of slavery and guaranteed as an aspect of national citizenship to a story of the end of a specific, peculiar institution.

The decision to restrict the reach of the Fourteenth Amendment in this, the first case in which its meaning was tested by the Court, may not have been entirely determined by, but is surely consistent with, the disenchantment with Reconstruction that surfaced and spread as the United States adjusted to reunion. Imagine the context. The antislavery banner carried by the Reconstruction Congress was held ambivalently, both by members of Congress and by most of the people of the reunited states. To be sure, antislavery sentiment abounded in the United States: long and bloody battle had required the development of a "moral justification . . . able and worthy to sustain the will and morale of the North through a punishingly long and bloody war."[15] Antislavery was the obvious candidate. Antislavery commitment had spread during the war as a result of the massive slave resistance that undermined the stability of the Confederacy[16] and the eagerness and crucial effectiveness with which African-American troops fought on the Union side.[17] But many considered the war in its opening years, and President Lincoln had baptized it,[18] to be a war to save the Union, not a war to free the slaves,[19] and in the years after the war, caste prejudice and feelings of unity and empathy among whites threatened the nation's moral commitment to freedom.

Most United States citizens who were not African-American were apprehensive about at least some aspects of emancipation. Among Union supporters, there were many who had fought to eliminate the competition of free African labor rather than to include slaves in the United States' economic and political systems.* Even the most ardent

---

*A Civil War song expresses this sentiment well:

Oh! give the slaves their freedom,
You surely do not need them
And no longer clothe and feed them,
In these United States.

Then the slave no longer belabor
But act the part of neighbor
And hire white men to labor
In these United States.

white antislavery advocates were often uncomfortable in the embrace of a new, multiracial polity.[20] And in the South, people felt deeply wronged by this most brutal of American wars. Southern whites of means continued to regard African-Americans as property and were prepared to adopt any method short of resumption of war with the North to preserve their hegemony.[21] Southern white workers fell into a competitiveness with black workers that led them to eschew efforts to advance the status of all working people and, instead, support the color-caste system and the "subordination of colored labor."[22]

The Fourteenth and Fifteenth amendments—and the civil rights laws that they were designed to constitutionalize—had drawn the implications of freedom. While the Thirteenth Amendment simply ended slavery, the Fourteenth and Fifteenth explicitly made Africans who had so recently been slaves voting African-American citizens. For racialist white citizens, the ideal of universal—now more fully comprehended as multiracial—civil freedom paled, and sentiment for compromise with the former rebels deepened. Ratification of the Fourteenth Amendment became more difficult because of "racial attitudes" and states' rights traditions.[23] The Democratic Party consistently and vocally resisted Reconstruction, counseling "magnanimity and generosity to a fallen foe."[24] In 1872, the year of the Slaughter-House decision, white Republicans in substantial numbers joined Democrats in support of Horace Greeley's campaign for "reconciliation and purification," the latter meaning restoration to (white) Southerners of all the rights of citizenship.[25] For the next four years, Greeley, a Radical Republican turned Democrat and editor of the New York Sun, made "No Negro domination!" a constant cry of the paper.

The charge of "Negro domination" had substance that was pertinent to evolving sentiment concerning Reconstruction and the Fourteenth Amendment. In 1867, every Southern state but Tennessee had refused to ratify the Fourteenth Amendment, and Reconstruction was faltering.[26] Charles Sumner then won congressional approval of a provision imposing a "requirement of suffrage irrespective of race or color

Mrs. Parkhurst, "The New Emancipation Song," in The Civil War Songbook 138 (Richard Crawford, ed., 1977).

in the election of delegates to the Reconstruction conventions, and as the basis of suffrage for the constitutions of the rebel states."[27] When the provision was agreed upon in committee, Senator Wilson of Massachusetts remarked, "Then and there in that small room, in that caucus, was decided the greatest pending question of the North American continent."[28] This bitterly resisted provision survived presidential veto and became law in the last days of the congressional session. As a result, American-born people of African descent constituted 25 percent of those electing delegates to the constitutional conventions by which states of the former Confederacy were reconstituted;[29] electoral majorities in the Alabama, Florida, South Carolina, Mississippi, and Louisiana delegate elections;[30] delegate majorities in South Carolina and Louisiana; and 290 of the Southern convention delegates who ratified the Fourteenth Amendment.[31] Black voter turnout in the late 1860s was overwhelming, approaching 90 percent in many elections.[32] In coalition with white Republicans, black people, many of whom were former slaves or children of slaves, were responsible for ratification of the amendments that constitutionalized national citizenship and specified its attributes.

This assertion of African-American political status and power unsettled many white Americans. There were repeated expressions of contempt for the multiracial constitutional conventions and legislative bodies that reconstituted Southern state governments and ratified the Reconstruction Amendments. Disgruntled racialists contemptuously referred to "black and tan conventions"; they described the delegates as "baboons, monkeys, mules," or "ragamuffins and jailbirds." The South Carolina convention, according to a local newspaper, was "the 'maddest, most infamous revolution in history.' "[33] A Northern journalist described the South Carolina legislature as a "mass" permeated with unimaginable "ignorance and vice." Immediately after Reconstruction, African-American legislators were omitted from the Georgia legislative manual on the ground that "[i]t would be absurd . . . to record 'the lives of men who were but yesterday our slaves, and whose past careers, probably, embraced such menial occupations as bootblacking, shaving, table-waiting, and the like."[34]

There is now a consensus among historians that interpretations of the work and thought of Reconstruction's political figures were tainted for several decades by culturally embedded versions of the sense of Reconstruction's illegitimacy that produced these invectives.[35] As Du Bois argued in 1935[36] and Foner reaffirmed in 1988, United States historians first told the story of Reconstruction with "prevailing disdain," grounded in a judgment that Radical Reconstruction was a product of Republican opportunism and vindictiveness and that its implementation of multiracial democracy was folly in the face of "negro incapacity."[37] As Du Bois established in detail, generations of students and scholars were taught to view Reconstruction as a frenzy of misrule and corruption. A history text used in the 1930s reported, "In the exhausted [Southern] states already amply 'punished' by the desolation of war, the rule of the Negro and his unscrupulous carpetbagger and scalawag patrons, was an orgy of extravagance, fraud and disgusting incompetency."[38] Reviewing the legacy of the historians James Ford Rhodes, John W. Burgess, William A. Dunning, and their students, Du Bois confirmed the conclusion of Will Herberg, a young labor leader in the 1920s and 1930s:

> The great traditions of . . . Reconstruction are shamelessly repudiated by the official heirs of Stevens and Sumner. . . . [H]ardly a single book has appeared consistently championing or sympathetically interpreting the great ideals of the crusade against slavery, whereas scores and hundreds have dropped from the presses in . . . measureless abuse of the Radical figures of Reconstruction. The Reconstruction period as the culmination of decades of previous development, has borne the brunt of the reaction.[39]

Negative interpretations of Reconstruction had, as Foner puts it, "remarkable longevity and [a] powerful hold on the popular imagination."[40] A well-received book of the late 1950s reinforced the understanding of Reconstruction as a process by which narrow political motivation led the Republican Party, acting with "hatred of the white South," to give "the Negro more rights than he possibly could exercise with profit to his advancement," and establish "carpetbag governments based upon Negro suffrage." This influential work concludes that abandonment of the tenets of Radical Reconstruction facilitated a healing process that was necessary and noble, albeit grounded in acceptance of a "credo" of white superiority which the author justified, saying, in the final paragraph of a chapter titled "The Negro Problem Always Ye Have with You," "Once a people admits . . . that a major problem is basically insoluble they have taken the first step in learning how to live with it."

Despite the deep appeal of the interpretative work begun by Rhodes, Burgess, and Dunning, in the years following publication of *Black Reconstruction* historians began a process of research and rethinking by which the derisive view of Reconstruction was "completely overturned."[41] As Foner reports: "Today, not only has the history of the era been completely rewritten, but most scholars view Reconstruction as a laudable, though flawed, effort to create a functioning interracial democracy for the first time in American history, and view Reconstruction's overthrow as a tragedy that powerfully affected the subsequent course of American development."[42] This revival of the ideals of antislavery and Reconstruction in historical literature has facilitated a revival of the ideals of antislavery and Reconstruction in legal thought. Jacobus tenBroek began in the 1950s to argue that constitutional liberty should be understood in terms of antislavery ideology.[43] My own work linking abolition and individual and family autonomy was first published in 1988.[44] More recently, David Richards has argued that "the moral, political, and constitutional arguments forged by the abolitionists in the antebellum period [are] crucial hermeneutic background for the proper interpretation of the Reconstruction Amendments,"[45] and Christopher Eisgruber has complained that "constitutional jurisprudence [wrongfully] slights the Civil War and Reconstruction."[46]

The Supreme Court, on the other hand, has not returned to the traditions of antislavery and Reconstruction as sources of the meaning of civil freedom. The *Slaughter-House* Court's evisceration of the Fourteenth Amendment was remedied; the spirit of civil freedom was breathed back into the amendment and given life as substantive due process.[47] But when controversy concerning the New Deal's constitutional legitimacy made the Court apprehensive about recognizing substantive due process rights, the idea of civil freedom was preserved in the concept of penumbral privacy, which, as we have seen, allowed the Court to claim support in the Constitution for its reading of due process liberty by incorporating ideas suggested by the Bill of Rights, the Founders' charter of civil freedom vis-à-vis the federal government, into the Fourteenth Amendment. More recently, the Court has returned to the rhetoric of substantive due process, yet in *none* of the cases recognizing civil freedoms guaranteed by Reconstruction's Fourteenth Amendment, either as matters of substantive due process or as matters of "penumbral privacy," has the Court found guidance in the history of slavery, antislavery, or Reconstruction.

The nation that adopted the Reconstruction Amendments was deeply influenced by the ideals of the nation's founders. Indeed, a long trail of evidence suggests that the antislavery movement was nearly obsessed with the contradictions it saw between the ideals of the Declaration of Independence and the practices of slavery. Virtually every abolitionist relied explicitly and repeatedly on the Declaration as authority for the slave's entitlement to life, liberty, the pursuit of happiness, and a government dependent upon the consent of the governed. Du Bois concluded in his study of Reconstruction: "The colored people had read the Declaration until it had become part of their natures."[48] In a petition presented to the New Hampshire legislature in 1779, nineteen slaves urged abolition, arguing that the "God of Nature gave them life and freedom, that freedom is an inherent right of the human species, not to be surrendered, but by consent, for the sake of social life."[49] When Anthony Burns had difficulty deciding whether it was morally right to abscond from his master, he turned not only to the Bible but also the Declaration. Assured that the Bible justified no claim of property in human beings, he "applied himself to the recovery of his inalienable right to liberty and the pursuit of happiness."[50] Frederick Douglass reported that he had "frequently seen in . . . [abolitionists'] houses, and sometimes occupying the most conspicuous places in their parlors, the American Declaration of Independence."[51] The narrative of a slave named Zamba accused white citizens of "bursting asunder with the one hand the chains and fetters of King George the Third—which weighed so heavily upon their own limbs—whilst with the other hand they were firmly and cruelly riveting chains and fetters, ten times more weighty and galling, around the limbs of their coloured fellow-men." An article written in 1789 by "A Free Negro" argued that while white revolutionists were hailed as heroes and martyrs, African-Americans who likewise attempted to obtain their freedom were met with derision and treated like depraved criminals."[52] A slave executed for planning rebellion said at his trial, "I have nothing more to offer than what General Washington would have had to offer, had he been taken by the British and put to trial by them. I have adventured my life in endeavouring to obtain the liberty of my countrymen."[53] William Grimes began his autobiography with the words "I was born in the year 1784 . . . in a land boasting its freedom, and under a government whose motto is Liberty and Equality. I was yet born a slave."[54] William Lloyd Garrison used these words in christening the *Liberator*: "Assenting to the 'self-evident truth' maintained in the American Declaration of Independence 'that all men are created equal, and endowed by their Creator with certain inalienable rights—among which are life, liberty, and the pursuit of happiness,' I shall strenuously contend for the immediate enfranchisement of our slave population."[55] Samuel Ward joined fellow abolitionists in demanding "the simple application of the principles of the Declaration of Independence to the black as well as the white."[56] Elizur Wright wrote that "[t]he American Revolution was incomplete" so long as slavery continued.[57] At least some officers on the Union side in the Civil War were of the same mind. General Phelps noted: "It is nearly a hundred years since our people first declared to the nations of the world that all men are born free; and still we have not made our declaration good,"[58] and Colonel Utley refused to return a young slave to his Confederate "owner," saying, "The same God made him that made you, and endowed him with the same natural rights to life, liberty and the pursuit of happiness that you possess."[59]

The Reconstruction Congress was similarly influenced, and similarly determined. Thaddeus Stevens vowed that there would be no representation for the Southern states "before Congress has done the great work of regenerating the Constitution and laws of this country according to the principles of the Declaration of Independence."[60] Charles Sumner told a packed Senate chamber, "Our fathers solemnly announced the Equal Rights of all men, and that Government had no just foundation except in the consent of the governed; and to the support of the Declaration, heralding these self-evident truths, they pledged their lives, their fortunes, and their sacred honor. . . . And now the moment has come when these vows must be fulfilled to the letter."[61]

The antislavery movement's reliance on the nation's founding ideology must not, however, reduce our appreciation of how much our understanding of the meaning of freedom was enriched and deepened by the nation's experiences in slavery and antislavery struggle. The inspiration for Reconstruction's charter of freedom was not the Bill of Rights, which the Supreme Court has so dutifully "incorporated" into the meaning of the Due Process Clause, but an ideal of civil freedom that might be best defined as an interpretation of the Declaration's promise of equality, life, liberty, and the pursuit of happiness by a people who had known civil death.

It is understandable that the Supreme Court did not take the lead in challenging the derisive view of Reconstruction history. That work was properly done by historians and other students of the United States' culture. But more than sixty years of scholarly work stand to give the Court confidence in returning to the traditions that reconstructed our nation and its constitutional premises. The burden of the next two sections is to demonstrate ways in which reference to the antislavery ideal of civil freedom might affect our understanding of the meaning of due process liberty.

DEFINING THE SELF AND DEFINING THE COMMUNITY

Antislavery and the Value of Moral Autonomy

Frederick Douglass said in 1861 that antislavery meetings had been the very best schools in the nation—schools in which the nation had learned, as it had learned nowhere else, about law and morality.[62] The schools that antislavery meetings had become taught most vividly that something about the unique consciousness of humankind causes us to seek meaning in life through the exercise of moral choice. At the heart of the antislavery idea was a protest against regimes that so overbear the will of human beings that moral choice is precluded. To be deprived of moral autonomy is, according to the antislavery critique, to be treated not as a human being but as a beast. This comparison between humans and beasts was ubiquitous in antislavery rhetoric. Slaves petitioning in 1773 for freedom complained that they were unable to enjoy life but forced to live "in a manner as the Beasts that perish."[63] Samuel Ward said, more than eighty years later, that in slavery he was "like a wild beast, chained and caged."[64] Linda Brent described slaves as "God-breathing machines" who were, in the sight of their masters, "no more . . . than . . . the horses they tend."[65] To be free was to have the autonomy that is the natural right of humankind. It was, as the first National Negro Convention proclaimed, "to occupy that space, and enjoy those rights in the moral world, which God in his wisdom has destined us to fill as rational beings."[66]

Freedom, understood in this way, is equally compromised whether moral choice is preempted by a slavemaster or by a state. State coercion of moral choice may nevertheless be entirely appropriate. To take an easy case, the state may surely constrain its citizens from visiting physical harm on one another. In prohibiting murder and assault, the state constrains moral choices, but it does so in the course of serving a protective function that we readily concede it should have. Similarly, mandatory public education, prohibitions against violence, *parens patriae* protection of children in medical crisis, and family support requirements are all justifiable in service of the state's authority to protect its citizens from harm, exploitation, or extreme deprivation. Rights of family autonomy do not exist to shield perpetrators of family violence, to prevent the requirement that children have a basic education or lifesaving medical treatment, even if their parents do not wish it for them, or to preclude requirements of alimony or child support.

But there are times when the state tries to constrain moral choice without advancing a secular or public welfare rationale. There are times, that is, when it tries to impose that we have come to call family values on the ground that they are values to which the people collectively subscribe—values in terms of which the political community wishes to define itself. It is this category of moral legislation that antislavery traditions challenge.

In striking the balance between order and liberty, one of the greatest difficulties is to assess a state's claim to a right of collective moral self-definition. This difficulty is apparent, for example, in the case of proscriptions of certain forms of marriage. The prohibition of marriages between family members has been defended on public health grounds as a protection against birth defects and on child welfare grounds as a measure to assure that children develop in environments in which they are safe from sexual attention. But medical science has taught us that the genetic risks of incest are less than had been thought, and medical science has found ways to protect us against the risks that do attend procreation by partners who have a close blood relationship. Moreover, many people who marry do not wish to have children. The risk that the child-rearing environment might be sexualized may be great with respect to parent-child or sibling relationships, but remote or nonexistent with respect to more distant relations. Nonetheless, some people count marriages between first or second cousins as incest and forbid it on grounds of moral approbation or religious proscription. As we have seen, the requirement that marriages be monogamous has been defended as a measure protective of women's social status and autonomy, but also on the ground that polygyny is morally odious or contrary to divine law.

The legitimacy of legislating morality has been long debated as a matter of democratic theory, of course. Competing arguments were thoughtfully and prominently presented as the English debated the issues of sexual conduct and new reproductive technologies, official regulation of each being the subject of a Royal Committee of Inquiry. In 1963, the Wolfenden Committee, asked to consider the appropriateness of prohibitions upon homosexuality and prostitution, took a position akin to that of John Stuart Mill:

> [The law's] function, as we see it, is to preserve public order and decency, to protect the citizen from what is offensive or injurious, and to provide sufficient safeguards against exploitation and corruption. . . . It is not, in our view, the function of the law to intervene in the private lives of citizens, or to seek to enforce any particular pattern of behavior, further than is necessary to carry out the purposes which we have outlined. . . . There must remain a realm of private morality and immorality which is, in brief and crude terms, not the law's business.[67]

In the debates that followed the Wolfenden Committee's Report, the jurisprudence scholars H. L. A. Hart and Patrick Devlin had a famous exchange about the appropriateness of legislating public morality. Lord Devlin claimed a basis for state legislation that went beyond protecting against harm or providing for the public welfare—a basis that he thought sufficient to justify the legislation of morality. That basis was, in essence, community self-definition. A sense of community requires, according to his argument, a set of shared values, and an ability to protect against the changes in the community's character that would result if those values were challenged. This requirement of shared and stable values is legitimately met, he said, by insisting that people follow certain basic moral precepts. Hart, on the other hand, challenged the notion that moral differences are socially intolerable and argued that individuals cannot legitimately be bound by majoritarian moral claims that are unsupported by arguments of harm to others.

The Warnock Committee, sitting twenty years after the Wolfenden Committee to consider the appropriateness of regulating new reproductive technologies and fetal research, placed itself on Lord Devlin's side of the Hart-Devlin debate, for it acknowledged no restraint on the authority of government to legislate morality. Although many of its recommendations were made on public welfare grounds, the Warnock Committee recommended that the government prohibit a variety of practices squarely on the ground of the community's moral opposition. With liberty to recommend state action on an exclusively moral basis, the Committee decided, for example, that reproductive technologies should be made available only to heterosexual couples, since it believed that "many" people thought that "the deliberate creation of a child for a woman who is not a partner in [a loving, stable, heterosexual relationship] is morally wrong." Finding surrogacy "totally ethically unacceptable" in some circumstances and "liable to moral objection" in others, it recommended that surrogacy agreements be unlawful and void, and that participating in arrangements for surrogate births be criminalized. It is arguable that the Warnock Committee could have found public welfare justifications for all the prohibitions it recommended, but the Committee saw no need to justify its recommendations in those terms or, to the extent that it relied upon public welfare rationales, to disentangle its moral and public welfare judgments. The Committee proceeded according to a process that it referred to as "moral reasoning," by which it sought "to discover the public good, in the widest sense."[68]

On the few occasions when the United States Supreme Court has addressed the question of official morality, it has seemed to take the Warnock-Devlin rather than the Wolfenden-Hart view. In the contraception cases, the dissenting Justices in *Poe v. Ullman* and the majority Justices in *Griswold* all conceded the authority of the state to prohibit contraception on moral grounds. Justice Harlan observed in his *Poe* dissent that traditional laws proscribing sex outside lawful marriage touch family life but are "so deeply pressed into the substance of our social life" as to be presumptively constitutional. He observed, without apparent disapproval, that state laws contain "many proscriptions of consensual [sexual] behavior having little or no direct impact on others," and express controversial moral judgments concerning marriage, divorce, abortion, homosexuality, sterilization, euthanasia, and suicide. Justice Douglas took a similar stance, conceding (with a bow to the Court's post-1930s position of deference with respect to economic regulation) that prohibition, on moral grounds, of the manufacturing of contraceptives would be an appropriate regulation of commerce.[69] The majority opinion in *Griswold* overturned Connecticut's prohibition of the *use* of contraceptives, but said that prohibition of manufacture or sale might be justifiable on moral grounds.*[70] Although it acknowledged in the 1990 case of *Cruzan v. Director of the Missouri Department of Health*[71] that patients have a fundamental liberty interest in controlling the extent to which their lives are extended by life support systems, the Court also acknowledged that the state has a legitimate *moral* interest in preserving human life. Finally, in the abortion cases the Court has repeatedly supported what it referred to as states' compelling interest in inchoate human life, an interest that

---

*When the Court subsequently struck down statutes governing contraceptive sales, it rather blatantly ignored the distinction between use and sale. Indeed, as we have seen, it fudged all questions of state justification by relying upon a rather incoherent equal protection rationale. It is possible that this incoherence is a symptom of unresolved ambivalence concerning the constitutional legitimacy of moral legislation.

many hold to be exclusively moral. Only Justice Stevens has taken a view of these matters that is consistent with the Hart-Wolfenden position. Stevens has argued in dissents from the Court's decisions in *Cruzan* and *Webster v. Reproductive Health Services* that infringements of individual and family liberty must be justified by a *secular*—by which he seems to mean a nonmoral or public welfare—purpose.[72]

Cases concerning contraception, abortion, and the right to die are special in that they all involve a state interest in preserving actual or inchoate human life, and the temptation to blur secular and moral concerns, as the Warnock Committee did, is especially great. The protection of human life is so basic to appropriate government functioning that the distinctions between secular and moral justifications can seem beside the point. Moreover, one can argue that any act that seems to treat human life as if it were cheap causes a brutalization that places all members of the community at risk. On this view, promoting a "moral" respect for human life by defining the political community as pro-life is inherently instrumental to protecting the state's subjects from physical harm. We might say, then, that the Supreme Court's recognition of the state's legitimate and compelling interest in human life should not be read as a general endorsement of moral legislation. But we would still have to explain the deeply troubling case of *Bowers v. Hardwick*, where the Supreme Court upheld state authority to define the political community in terms of a moral commitment to heterosexuality and to outlaw homosexual expression.

In 1982, Michael Hardwick was apprehended in his bedroom and charged under Georgia laws that criminalized private, consensual sodomy and made it punishable by imprisonment for up to twenty years. He challenged these laws in a case that reached the Supreme Court in 1985. Although the charges had been dropped, Hardwick sought a declaratory judgment so that he could be secure against arrest and prosecution in the future. Justice White spoke for a majority deciding by only one vote to uphold the Georgia law, in an opinion (which one now retired member of the Court has said that he no longer supports[73]) that hinged on saying that Hardwick could claim no specially protected or fundamental liberty interest. Hardwick argued, of course, that he had rights of privacy and personal autonomy, and that these had been violated by the police officers' invasion of his bedroom and the criminal law's regulation of his sexual practices. The majority responded as Justice Scalia later responded to the family rights claims of Michael H. and Victoria D.—by applying a principle of specificity. Justice White's opinion concerned not a right of autonomy but a right to homosexual sodomy. Although the sodomy prohibition was applicable without regard to gender, Justice White relied upon Hardwick's sexual preference to narrow the question before the Court to "whether the Federal Constitution confers a fundamental right upon homosexuals to engage in sodomy."* Since recognition of fundamental rights must be grounded in constitutional text, in history, or in national traditions, and this right was not in the text of the Constitution, White turned to history and tradition for the answer to his narrow question. What he found was a history of prejudice and a tradition of aversion.

Justice White's recitation, without qualification or disapproval, of the history of aversion and condemnation with respect to homosexual conduct is biting—particularly so when the imagined reader is homosexual. Nonetheless, Chief Justice Burger filed a concurrence that embellished White's description of the disrespect of and aversion to homosexual expression. As the Court had earlier called upon Western tradition to justify prohibitions of polygamy, he searched the history of Western civilization to find characterizations such as "crime against nature" and " 'deeper malignity' than rape."[74] In the majority's view,

---

*This formulation is as problematic as Justice Scalia's formulation in Michael H. The Court has settled upon two tests of the fundamental character of unenumerated rights: whether they are "implicit in the concept of ordered liberty" and whether they are "deeply rooted in this Nation's history and tradition." There is no national tradition of respect for the right of homosexual expression. There is, as Justice White had earlier pointed out, no national tradition of respect for the right of a grandmother and two nonsibling grandchildren to share a dwelling. Justice Rehnquist reminded us in Carey, the post-Roe contraception case, that there is no national tradition of respect for "the right of commercial vendors of contraceptives to peddle them to unmarried minors through such means as window displays and vending machines located in the men's room of truck stops." There is but a short national tradition of respect for the marital bonds of interracial couples or for the contraceptive choices of the unmarried. Ordered liberty is imaginable without recognition of any of these narrowly defined rights. If rights of privacy and autonomy are to be taken seriously, these matters must be considered in terms of a national tradition of autonomy rather than being evaluated only in their most particularized terms.

this tradition of intolerance established that homosexual sodomy could not command special constitutional protection.

From the majority's holding that the Georgia statute infringed no specially protected right, it followed that the statute required no special scrutiny; the law was satisfactorily justified if it was enacted with a rational basis. Hardwick's lawyer argued that even on a rational basis analysis, the Georgia statute was unconstitutional, for the proscription of consensual sodomy has no purpose other than the illegitimate one of regulating morality. Possibly misunderstanding this argument, the majority rejected it in the following terms: "The law . . . is constantly based on notions of morality, and if all laws representing essentially moral choices are to be invalidated under the Due Process Clause, the courts will be very busy indeed."[75]

The majority was correct, of course, in saying that the law is constantly based on notions of morality, but this misses the point that Hardwick and his lawyers were surely making. None of us would argue that the law must be *without moral basis*, but one *can* argue that although a law may be moral in impetus and effect, it must have what Justice Stevens called a secular purpose—a purpose *beyond* controlling the moral choices of the citizenry. Since the majority did not acknowledge a distinction between legislation that is moral and the legislation *of morality*, it easily found that Georgia had a legitimate moral interest in prohibiting homosexual sodomy.

What light might Motivating Stories of slavery, antislavery, and Reconstruction shed upon such questions of due process liberty as are raised by the legislation of morality in general and the prohibition of same-sex intimacy in particular?

The Motivating Stories we have considered speak most obviously to the legitimacy of Fourteenth Amendment protection of rights to marry, to parent, and to procreate. The link between the Fourteenth Amendment's antislavery history and the right to marry is evident: we have heard the voices of spouses who saw their partners sold and shackled into slave coffles, and the voices of congressmen who decried slavery's abrogation of the marriage bond and vowed that it would not be repeated. This history—unmentioned in *Loving*, or *Zablocki*, or *Safley*—confirms the conclusion of those cases that the right to marry is a fundamental aspect of the liberty conferred by the Fourteenth Amendment. The link between the Fourteenth Amendment's antislavery history and the right to parent is evident in the protest poetry of Frances Ellen Watkins Harper, the complaint of an emancipated father outraged that a stranger's authority had been imposed upon his child, and the declaration of Senator Wilson that in the reconstructed Union "the sharp cry of the agonizing hearts of severed families would cease" and "the hallowed family relations of husband and wife, parent and child [would] be protected by the guardian spirit of the law." This history—unmentioned in *Meyer*, or *Pierce*, or *Prince*, or *Stanley*, or *Lassiter*, or *Santosky*—confirms the judgment of those cases that the right to parent has fundamental constitutional status. And the link between the Fourteenth Amendment's antislavery history and the rights of procreative choice is apparent in the declarations of a woman named Rose, who was mated in slavery for breeding purposes, that in freedom she would *choose* not to procreate, of J. W. Loguen and Henry Bibb, that they would not be responsible for bringing into the world children who would be enslaved, and of the abolitionists who insisted that every person has an inalienable right to control his or her own body. These voices—unmentioned in *Skinner*, or *Griswold*, or *Roe*, or *Casey*—support the judgment of those cases that the right to control one's sexual and procreative choices is fundamental to the liberty protected by the Fourteenth Amendment.

But the Motivating Stories go beyond this. They also tell us how rights of family autonomy function within a dialectic of constraint and choice, to produce a society that balances the need for stability against the need for openness to individual choice and social change. Let me explain first the dialectic and then the relationship between the dialectic and the lessons of antislavery.

We humans are social beings. This rather simple fact has far-reaching implications. The psychologist Jerome Bruner has a transactional model of the mind that reflects a consciousness as old as human discourse but felt with special keenness in the wake of what Bruner calls the cognitive revolution: human meaning is actualized when it becomes "public and communal rather than private and autistic."[76] The self is thus defined in its relationships to others.

There is a dialectic between the individual self and the community.

On the one hand, individual development is constrained by the community's shared cultural forms; we are all very much products of our cultures and inclined to share culturally determined predispositions. But on the other hand, cultural forms are the sum of, and are incrementally altered by, individual acts of meaning; each of us is a unique manifestation of slightly different cultural influences and capable of effecting some degree of change in cultural norms.

Most of what a culture does to structure or constrain individual choice is informal, subliminal, and outside the reach of constitutional protection. It is manifested by the very nature of the culture's markets, customs, scripts, words, and stories. Still, explicit and official constraints upon individual choice are significant. The state controls private behavior with blunt effectiveness. Moreover, intrusiveness or restraint in the official control of private behavior is an important marker of a society's character. As the dialectic between individual choice and cultural form plays out in a culture, official restraints on private choice make the social environment more stable, predictable, and controlled. Protection of civil liberty, on the other hand, makes the social environment more open, responsive, and dynamic. Extremes in either direction are problematic. Without social controls, government cannot protect its citizens against internal or external harms or mobilize resources for the common good. Moreover, a measure of stability and predictability may be necessary as a nucleus for the sense of oneness that makes the social contract viable. But excessive social controls inevitably become intolerable, for they leave government unresponsive to the needs and values of its differing citizens, and they unduly inhibit citizens' efforts to make meaning. Moreover, rights of moral autonomy and self-definition seem necessary to the realization of human potential. Rational, morally conscious beings seem to require a place in the social dialectic and a balance between its competing forces, such that community and cultural constraints do not freeze individual acts of meaning or foreclose incremental social change.

The Doctrinal Stories of personal and family liberty address this dialectic between personal choice and social constraint. On the one hand, they help to define the space that the United States' polity allows for individuals to express their own values and to reshape cultural forms that have hardened into legal rules. On the other hand, they delineate the community's authority to impose direct constraints on individual choice.

Motivating Stories of slavery and antislavery enliven the justifications for structuring the social dialectic so that official constraints do not overwhelm opportunities for personal choice. Subjects in a rigidly totalitarian state are frozen in the social dialectic that I have described—unable to effect change or express individuality. The image of the totalitarian subject gives life to arguments for individual autonomy and choice by forcing us to contemplate their lack. The experience of slavery has had the same effect. The sociologist Orlando Patterson argues that people in Western societies "came to value freedom [and] to construct it as a powerful shared vision of life, as a result of their experience of, and response to, slavery." As Toni Morrison has observed: "What was distinctive in the New [World] was, first of all, its claim to freedom and, second, the presence of the unfree within the heart of the democratic experiment—the critical absence of democracy, its echo, shadow, and silent force in the political and intellectual activity of some not-Americans."[77] The presence of the unfree was a profound argument for recognition of human autonomy.

Enslaved people were positioned *outside* the dialectic of cultural constraint and change. They were constrained, of course, but as cultural outsiders. They were expected to observe not the cultural forms of the dominant culture but the cultural forms imposed upon their caste and the private "law" of their masters. And, perhaps most importantly, in the slaveholder's legal and cultural scheme there was no room for the individual agency of enslaved people to reshape either the dominant culture or the public and private codes governing the slave caste. This was the nature of what Patterson calls social death.

The Motivating Stories of marriage, parenting, and procreation are stories about the starkness of social death and about constitutional measures that confer social agency. They are, then, about political as well as personal issues. On a personal level, enslaved people were haunted by the knowledge that they might, on any day, look up to see a partner or parent or child being shackled and taken away for service to a distant master. Children lacked the comfort of adequate parental attention and the security of knowing that their parents spoke and acted from a position of social authority. Adults endured the indignity of sexual exploitation. Parents endured the frustration of being unable to nurture, protect, or direct their children.

But quite apart from the personal costs of enslavement, enslaved people were denied legal and social recognition as individual members of civil society, as partners, or as families. They could not combine property as partners in life or bequeath it in death. If, as partners, they made commitments of monogamy, the law and the larger culture gave those commitments no formalized (and little de facto) reinforcement. If they made commitments of mutual support, the law and the larger culture could choose to ignore them. They could not provide a home for children that the law and the larger culture would regard as "legitimate" and acknowledge as the appropriate primary site for the children's socialization.

At the same time, enslaved people had only a very limited ability to affect the character of the larger culture. The quality and character of their lives had little effect upon institutional definitions of the family. The law's understandings of obligations of support, loyalty, common enterprise, and monogamy within marriage and of the privileges and responsibilities of parenting were developed and interpreted in response to the experiences and situations of free people. Enslaved people were precluded not only from claiming the protections of laws governing marriage and parenting, but also from arguing the applicability or inapplicability of the law to their situations, and from challenging the law's terms, as Henry Blackwell and Lucy Stone were able to do, in formal exercises of civil freedom.

Enslaved people and antislavery advocates responded to the civil death that slavery inflicted with demands for universal civil freedom that encompassed the right to form a legitimate and socially recognized family. The right of family formation was necessary for the fulfillment of moral and religious obligations and necessary for self-realization through lasting affiliations. When, in the midst of the Civil War, enslaved people began to claim the right to have their marriages recognized, they claimed it as a component of the broader right to unseat the color-caste system and be established as a people. A soldier equated recognition of his family and acknowledgment of his humanity. Another said that legalized marriage was at the foundation of all rights. Another demanded that the children who were his flesh and blood be surrendered by a former master so that they could be educated and socialized to the values of their birth parents. Marriage was seen as a step in the direction of responsibility and honorable citizenship. The stability of family life was a badge of freedom.

The Reconstruction Amendments were a culmination of struggle, not only to assure that no person's labor was owned, but also to assure that each person was autonomous and self-defining—free to act within and to act upon the culture. Slaves demanded freedom to make meaning by taking chosen, rather than dictated paths. Antislavery ideology demanded universal freedom such that every citizen would have a role in the collective that could be chosen, rather than prescribed. Democracy seen through the experiences of slavery and antislavery contemplates what Du Bois called "domination of political life by the intelligent decision of free and self-sustaining [people]."[78]

These Motivating Stories identify the right to form a family as an aspect of a more general right of autonomy and self-definition. They give us an impetus to leave the convoluted reasoning of "penumbral privacy" behind and continue the work of understanding the implications of the autonomy principle that is at the heart of the antislavery critique and the Fourteenth Amendment's promise.

There are seeds of an autonomy principle in the Supreme Court's family rights cases. Meyer alluded to principles touching the relation between individual and state that caused the United States to reject the Platonic idea of creating ideal citizens through official control of marriage and parenting. Pierce identified a fundamental theory of liberty according to which the child must not be the creature of the state or subject to standardizing practices. Harlan's Poe dissent also made a cautionary reference to such practices, but argued that the Due Process Clause requires a balance between order and liberty that is appropriate to a nation "built upon postulates of respect for the liberty of the individual."[79] Justice Douglas, also writing in Poe v. Ullman, echoed Pierce's caution against state standardization and pointed out that the United States' constitutional scheme is antitotalitarian. The Casey centrists came closest to offering a satisfactory rationalizing principle for close protection of individual autonomy when they added to these concerns an articulation of the effect that totalitarian control has on individual human lives: "At the heart of liberty is the right to define one's own concept of existence, of meaning, of the universe, and of the mystery of human life. Beliefs about these matters could not define the attributes of personhood were they formed under compulsion of the State."⁸⁰ In these words, the Court's centrists echo the meaning of the antislavery claim that it is the right of all people "to organize their lives in accordance with their own sense of propriety [and] establish their families as independent units." Enforcement of this vision of due process liberty would assure that individual self-definition is not unduly sacrificed to collective self-definition. It would safeguard what anti-slavery activists called "rights of conscience," vouchsafed to all who "occupy space . . . in the moral world . . . as rational beings."

Lord Devlin was right to assume that a society would change in unpredictable ways if its laws went from legal prohibition to tolerance of homosexual intimacy. Social norms would cease to be officially frozen with respect to the gender of sexual intimates or life partners, and they might, and might not, change with respect to a host of related matters, such as the perceived link between procreation and life satisfaction or the proper allocation of roles and responsibilities within a household. The society might or might not continue to be predominantly heterosexual. The definition of the community would be more open to influence by homosexual people, who, in a climate of prohibition, are subjected to civil disabilities akin to the civil death of the enslaved. The ramifications of those civil disabilities are both personal and political—personal because homosexual couples are haunted by the knowledge that their bedrooms can be raided and they can be arrested, prosecuted, and punished; political because whether or not homosexual couples are prosecuted, they are denied legal and social recognition as partners or as families. They can, with some difficulty, combine property in life and bequeath it in death, but if they make monogamous commitments, the law and the larger culture give those commitments no formalized (and little de facto) reinforcement. If they make commitments of mutual support, the law and the larger culture can choose to ignore them. Homosexual couples cannot make a home for children that the law and the larger culture will predictably regard as "legitimate" and acknowledge as the appropriate primary site for the children's socialization.

In 1996, the Supreme Court had to decide whether the state of

Colorado violated the Fourteenth Amendment when it amended its constitution to forbid the passing or enforcement of laws protecting homosexual people against discrimination. The Court ruled that Colorado could not impose this sweeping civil disability upon a group of its citizens, and it noted that the measure was so crudely matched to legitimate state purposes that it seemed born of animus. Justice Scalia, joined in dissent by Justices Rehnquist and Thomas, said, "This Court has no business . . . pronouncing that 'animosity' toward homosexuality . . . is evil." For him, the case was about "a rather modest attempt by seemingly tolerant Coloradans to preserve traditional sexual mores against the efforts of a politically powerful minority." He said that homosexual people, whom he described (without offering evidence and against available evidence) as disproportionately wealthy and concentrated in cities, are engaged in a campaign for first tolerance, then affirmation of their lifestyle. He thought it appropriate for the majority to use its electoral strength against that effort. He quoted an 1885 polygamy case in which the Court, relying on *Reynolds*, approved a state's decision to deny polygamists the right to vote:

> Certainly no legislation can be supposed more wholesome and necessary in the founding of a free, self-governing commonwealth, fit to take rank as one of the co-ordinate States of the Union, than that which seeks to establish it on the basis of the idea of the family, as consisting in and springing from the union for life of one man and one woman in the holy estate of matrimony, the sure foundation of all that is stable and noble in our civilization, the best guaranty of that reverent morality which is the source of all beneficent progress in social and political improvement.[81]

And he wondered that Justices in the majority might think the perceived social harm of polygamy, but not that of homosexuality, a "legitimate concern of government." The majority conceded that this 1885 polygamy case warranted rethinking, but it did not say what the result of that rethinking would be, nor did it respond to Justice Scalia's entirely apt complaint that invalidation of the Colorado initiative challenged the reasoning and result of *Bowers v. Hardwick*.[82]

When the Supreme Court revisits these questions of civil freedom, as surely it must, what guidance might the history and traditions of antislavery provide? They would, I think, counsel that official sanctions against homosexual or polygamous conduct compromise the autonomy, choice, and civil agency that the Fourteenth Amendment was designed to guarantee. We would therefore be compelled to demand that the state provide worthy justification. And we would have to count it against the state if the proffered justification were nothing more than a political majority's wish to define and freeze the moral character of the polity. I have said that protection of the welfare and autonomy of women may provide justification beyond moral approbation for restrictions against polygamy. But the case is not self-evident, and we must be wary of the cultural myopia that informed the Justices' thinking in *Reynolds.** In the case of homosexuality, social welfare justifications are far harder to imagine.

THE CHILD-CARE FUNCTIONS OF
PARENT AND STATE

Antislavery and the Value of Family Socialization

Stories about autonomous authority in child rearing are poignant and complex. Jacob Stroyer's disillusionment when his father could not protect him from being whipped by the man who was master to both father and son; the humiliation of a slave whipped on bare buttocks in front of his wife and children for the offense of visiting them beyond his leave; the rupture caused in the Pennington family when the father was publicly whipped—all these make vivid the feeling of an absence of parental authority. The Bradford cook's assertion of responsibility to choose whether to take her child to a meeting about emancipation; the rage of James Jeter when, after emancipation, an employer and former master whipped his son; the insistence of a newly freed North Carolinian that his child not be ordered about by white strangers; and

---

*Nelson Mandela, surely one of the greatest moral leaders of our age, grew to maturity in an apparently healthy family that included a husband, four wives, and nine children. The justifiability of antipolygamy laws seems reduced if we imagine prosecution of a Mandela family emigrated to the United States.

the struggles of newly freed people to recover their children from apprenticeship systems that were de facto reenslavements—all these attest to the connection between civil freedom and parental autonomy. Moreover, they show how parental autonomy provides a context within which children learn to function as free and self-defining democratic citizens.

Yet, despite the commitment to parental autonomy that stories like these engendered, antislavery advocates shared with their compatriots a sense of communal responsibility for children. The extended care networks of enslaved and emancipated African-Americans have a common root with state public-welfare systems in the recognition that it often takes both a family and a supporting community to raise a child. The possibility of disagreement between family and community over how child rearing should go raises profound social and constitutional questions, to which we now turn.

At times, concern for children's basic care and nurturance inspires community action. Child welfare systems in every state of our Union authorize official action to remove children from their homes or supervise their care when it has been established that the family is not safeguarding its children's basic well-being. When this happens, the children's and the parents' Fourteenth Amendment rights of family autonomy should assure that the official actions are justifiable and measured.

But justifiability and restraint are difficult to assess. As the Supreme Court once observed, a child welfare system that some observers see as "a class-based intrusion into the family life of the poor" strikes other observers as making sound and necessary interventions that are rendered less effective by deference to ill-conceived ideas about parental rights.[83] Moreover, apart from the dictum that a state should not disrupt a traditional family unit just because intervention seems to be in a child's best interest, the Court has given states no guidance in deciding what kind of circumstances warrant official intervention to supplant or supervise a family's child rearing.

The Court's failure to speak to these questions cannot be entirely explained away by want of opportunity. Federal courts have deliberately adopted a policy of deference to state judgments in family matters, so questions of federal jurisdiction are narrowly construed. This position of deference to state authority in child welfare and other matters of family law is grounded in a claim that states are the appropriate arbiters of family issues and federal protection of family rights inappropriately fetters states' rights to control the exercise of local police power. Ironically, this very claim was made in Congress by members who spoke in *opposition* to Reconstruction's constitutional amendments and civil rights acts; in their insistence that states' rights was too important a principle to be sacrificed for federal guarantees of individual liberty, they, too, argued that state and local governments were specially competent in the domestic sphere. The claim is not typically offered with empirical support, and one suspects that it is supported less by reason than by an unfortunate tendency among lawyers to trivialize family law questions and, literally, avoid making "federal cases" of them.

A 1982 case illustrates how a special deference to states' rights continues to thwart the definition and enforcement of family liberty. Marjorie Lehman's parental rights were terminated by order of the courts of Pennsylvania, and her children were placed for adoption. Her case was decided under the "best interests" standard that some Justices had said was inadequate to justify family disruption. The Supreme Court nonetheless declined to review Lehman's case, whereupon she sought to demonstrate in federal habeas corpus litigation that her constitutional right of family autonomy had been violated. When this second challenge reached the Supreme Court, a majority of six ruled that the prospect of federal habeas corpus proceedings in this context would inappropriately inhibit state power over domestic affairs and undermine state family-planning processes by throwing a cloud of uncertainty over adoption results.[84] We cannot know whether the termination of Lehman's parental rights violated due process standards for family disruption, for deference to the state twice precluded review of her claim, and no similar claim has ever been deliberated by the Court.

Because the Court has failed to review child welfare cases and set standards for judging when it is appropriate to supplant parental authority or separate children from their families, the Fourteenth Amendment gives little tangible protection in this domain against government overreaching. The all too frequent consequence of such overreaching is that children are removed from their homes and placed in the care of the state or of substitute families chosen by the state. When this happens, children suffer the trauma of losing their first home, parents suffer the loss of their children, and—more subtly, but just as importantly—a family's freedom to develop and foster its own character and values is compromised. Still, when child welfare interventions, based as they are on concern for a child's health and safety, undermine a family, they do not challenge directly the family's civil and moral autonomy; their effect on the family as a unit of democracy is incidental to their goal of safeguarding the family's children. It sometimes happens, however, that a state's intervention seems motivated by concern as much for the child's life-defining moral or value choices as for the child's physical or emotional well-being. To be sure, these issues are difficult to disentangle. It is hard to say, for example, whether Wisconsin was concerned, in Yoder, about the physical well-being and developmental progress of Amish children or about their religious and lifestyle choices when it sought to assure that they had schooling beyond the eighth grade. Equally, it is hard to say when a state wants to terminate the parental rights of a mildly retarded parent whether it is protecting the child against gross neglect or changing the child's vision of life's chances.

There is, however, one area of the Supreme Court's personal and family rights jurisprudence in which it is clear that states have been permitted—indeed, encouraged—to appropriate directly the family's role in guiding children's moral development and life-defining choices, and to do so in the absence of any showing that the children's families had failed to provide for their well-being. This has happened in cases concerning abortion and parental consent. That it was allowed to happen is evidence of the shallowness of our thinking about family freedom.

The pregnant child seeking an abortion without parental consultation or consent and, to a lesser extent, the pregnant wife seeking abortion without consultation or spousal consent raise profoundly difficult questions of family liberty. One of Justice Harlan's enduring rules for establishing the fundamental character of asserted rights is, you will recall, that a right is fundamental if it is "implicit in the concept of ordered liberty." It is fair to say, as most members of the Supreme Court from the time of *Roe* have said, that in a world where personal and life-defining choices such as whether to have an abortion are removed from private hands, there is order without genuine liberty. But in a world of ordered liberty, who is entitled to validate or reject a *child's* decision to have an abortion? To give power to the parent is to permit a significant qualification of the right of individual choice. To give power to the state is to undermine the premise that abortion choice should be a private, not a state affair. To give power to the immature minor is irresponsible.

When the Supreme Court first dealt with the issue of parental and spousal consent requirements, it relied on *Eisenstadt v. Baird* for the idea that procreational choice is an individual, not a family right, and held that since the state could not directly control the abortion decision, it could not delegate control to the parent of a mature minor or to a spouse. This "delegation" theory failed to account for the great difference between family and government influence over abortion choice. As three members of the Court pointed out, the family member appropriating or sharing in a decision about abortion is not vindicating a state interest but exercising an independent and private interest.[85] Thinking all the way through this question, one must acknowledge the difference between state action to reconcile or protect competing interests within the family and state action to impose an official judgment. The Court overlooked this difference in *Belotti v. Baird* when, taking the view that parental consent requirements for abortion may not be absolute, it ruled that states enacting such requirements must offer an alternative in the form of a "judicial bypass"—a procedure by which a pregnant child can, without notice to her parents, take the matter to a judge. The doctrinal difficulty arises in the details of this judicial bypass procedure. The Court has held, quite reasonably, that judges in bypass procedures should be authorized to waive parental consent if they think the pregnant minor is mature enough to make an independent decision. But the Court has made the more questionable judgment that in cases where the pregnant minor is *not* mature enough, the judge should be authorized to give or withhold the required consent, deciding the matter in terms of the child's best interests.[86]

With this approval of judicial consent provisions in cases involving pregnant minors, the Supreme Court accepted a subtle but important compromise of *Roe*'s underlying principles. Whereas the *Roe* decision was initially intended to protect against state interference with private moral choice in family matters, it became, ironically, a justification for state action that could *undermine* the family's private moral values. The state, which the Court originally cast as a threat to individual privacy and autonomy, was now a protector of the minor's privacy and autonomy and, in that role, was given power to decide the abortion question for her, without reference to her wishes and values or the wishes and values of her parents. This result caused alarm across the Court's ideological spectrum. Justice Stevens, who had consistently voted to protect the right of abortion choice, found the requirement of what he termed "consent of the sovereign" more pernicious than the requirement of consent of a family member.[87] Justice White, who had consistently opposed *Roe*, took no pains to conceal his outrage: "Until now, I would have thought inconceivable a holding that the United States Constitution forbids even notice to parents when their minor child who seeks surgery objects to such notice and is able to convince a judge that the parents should be denied participation in the decision."[88]

The majority required bypass provisions because, in the aftermath of *Roe*, it feared that parental consent requirements were parts of schemes to put obstacles in the path of pregnant women who wanted abortion. This fear was reasonable.[89] Antiabortion constituencies urging parental consent requirements may well have been motivated by a desire to deter minors from obtaining abortions rather than by a desire to encourage family involvement in the abortion decision. But consent of the sovereign provisions were a shortsighted means of addressing that possibility. Before *Casey*, the new provisions left judges in bypass proceedings with little but their own value judgments to rely upon. As it happened, they tended rather routinely to approve the minor's choice to undergo abortion, but that result bears no apparent relationship to the design of the bypass scheme.

Under the modified framework for evaluating abortion regulations that was announced by the centrist Justices in *Casey*, consent of the sovereign becomes a more threatening idea. *Casey*'s modified framework rests, you will recall, on a judgment that the state's interest in protecting unborn life is compelling from the moment of conception. It is consistent with the Devlin-Warnock view that the state may act to advance a moral judgment—in this case, a judgment that fetal life is sacred and abortion morally wrong. On this view, one might argue that a state may authorize judges hearing bypass petitions to follow a state-mandated presumption in favor of childbirth over abortion in cases in which an immature girl is unwilling or unable to obtain consent from her parents. Or, conversely, a state might be permitted to decide—based on the value judgment, endorsed by the Warnock Committee, that it is wrong to rear a child outside of traditional wedlock—to enforce a presumption in *favor of abortion* in cases involving immature, unemancipated (and therefore, by definition, unmarried) minors.

Antislavery history and traditions are particularly instructive with respect to the constitutional legitimacy of state actions that compromise, in direct or indirect ways, the family's ability to serve as the locus for value choices about issues like abortion. As we have seen, the antislavery movement dismantled a system within which human beings were denied the self-defining exercise of independent will and subjected to the authority of a master. They dismantled this system because they thought it unconscionable to subject rational, self-reflective human beings to totalitarian control. Working from an understanding of human rights as they related to human capacities, the people of the United States adopted a reconstructed Constitution that balanced order and liberty. It is no accident that the establishment of families was seized upon by emancipated people as a badge of civil freedom. Slavery had elevated the master vis-à-vis the enslaved so that he assumed both the role of the state and the role of the family. Civil death was a consequence both of isolation from the privileges and protections of citizenship and of the abrogation of natal ties. Freedom meant the right to form a legally recognized family within which one might develop a "family theology," as the Offley family did; worship freely, as Praying Jacob insisted upon doing, or not at all; consult one's own will, as Lunsford Lane longed in slavery to do; supervise the socialization, learning, and value formation of one's children; and enjoy, as the emancipated Bryan family did, rights of conscience.

To think of family liberty as a guarantee offered in response to slavery's denials of natal connection is to understand it, not only as an end in itself, but as a mechanism of democracy. In the antislavery vision, people are not meant to be socialized to uniform, externally imposed values. People form families and other intimate communities within which children might be differently socialized and from which adults will bring different values to the democratic process. These ideas give coherence and legitimacy to the themes of autonomy and family function sounded in *Meyer, Pierce, Skinner, Barnette,* and *Prince.* The antislavery ideal of family autonomy is a necessary component in any design to permit individuals to affect their culture and to embrace, advocate, and act upon freely chosen values, because it is in families that people are socialized to varied values, rather than uniform ones. And it is in families that the socialization process can be flexible and individualized enough to nurture autonomous thought and permit intrafamilial, as well as interfamilial differences. As Philip Heymann and Douglas Barzelay explain in a brilliant essay on the doctrinal legitimacy of *Roe v. Wade,* free and self-sustaining people *require a certain context.* They require "private realms," not so that they may be secluded, but so that they can develop along chosen paths.[90] They require an opportunity to grow to maturity under the influence of intimate caretakers rather than under the tutelage of the state. As Heymann and Barzelay have said, if government controlled one's family life and the development and inculcation of values within one's home, "the substance of our system would be radically altered, for the government would . . . be vested with the capacity to influence powerfully, through socialization, the future outcomes of democratic political processes."[91]

If we were to reconsider, in light of these principles, the federal courts' policy of deference to states in their regulation of family life, we would, I think, weigh more heavily the need to enforce the Fourteenth Amendment's guarantee of autonomy, for we would understand that protections of the integrity and independence of families are central not only to the preservation of cherished relationships but also to the health of our democracy. If we were to reconsider, in light of antislavery principles, the strategy of leaving a pregnant minor's right of abortion choice to the discretion of a judge, we would surely be concerned that by imposing a sovereign's choice, government had appropriated and standardized the moral searching that free and rational people are entitled to do in the intimate and various places they call home.

AFTERWORD

• ⟵⟶ •

I have focused on neglected stories of slavery and the capacity they have to enrich our interpretations, in constitutional theory and in public debate, of the value and place of family. If you have been persuaded that these neglected stories give richness and depth to our constitutional and public discourse, then I ask that you count that enrichment as evidence in support of a principle that transcends controversies about the constitution, political debate, and family values: the principle that cultures become richer and evolve in directions of social equity and human freedom when they attend to their neglected stories—to those people, ideas, and events that its members were once somehow predisposed to neglect.

Ralph Ellison spoke of an underground logic of the democratic process, in which "that which is ignored defies our inattention by continuing to grow and to have consequences."[1] This is a lesson worth remembering in all aspects of our lives in this many-layered and (to borrow a silver-dollar word from Jerome Bruner) schismogenic culture.

Just as stories of slavery inform a balanced sense of family, they inform a balanced sense of work, of community, of due process, and of equality. The meanings of war and commerce will not be told in stories cast only with men. The reach of our obligations cannot be measured unless we tell stories of children and of other easily neglected members of our polity.

The final word, then, is a plea for what my colleague Sarah Burns calls a willing suspension of belief—for the courage to rethink doctrine and other canonical stories in light of the stories we have been apt to forget.

NOTES

• ⟺ •

Introduction: A Path to Appreciation of Family Rights

1. The shining exception to the pattern of early neglect is, of course, W. E. B. Du Bois, whose *Reconstruction* remains a model for contemporary work.
2. *Pace v. Alabama*, 106 U.S. 583 (1883); *McLaughlin v. Florida*, 379 U.S. 184 (1964); *Loving v. Virginia*, 388 U.S. 1 (1967).
3. *Skinner v. Oklahoma*, 316 U.S. 535 (1942). See also *Stump v. Sparkman*, 435 U.S. 349 (1978).
4. *Meyer v. Nebraska*, 262 U.S. 390 (1923); *Pierce v. Society of Sisters*, 268 U.S. 510 (1925).
5. *Stanley v. Illinois*, 405 U.S. 645 (1972).
6. *Poe v. Ullman*, 367 U.S. 497 (1961); *Griswold v. Connecticut*, 381 U.S. 479 (1965); *Roe v. Wade*, 410 U.S. 113 (1973).
7. The notion that the Fourteenth Amendment requires a judicious mediation between order and liberty is especially well stated in Charles Black's "The Unfinished Business of the Warren Court," 46 *Washington Law Review* 3, 32 (1970).
8. As Pierre Bourdieu argues: "Legal discourse . . . creates what it states . . . by producing the collectively recognized, and thus realized, representation of existence." *Language and Symbolic Power* 42 (1991 ed.).
9. The necessary incompleteness of historical accounts is beautifully examined by Louis Mink:

   [T]he particular *history* of [anything] escapes theoretical understanding simply because to envision that history requires the attribution of indefinitely many descriptions of it as they are successively relevant or irrelevant to the sequences that intersect its career. . . . On the one hand, there are all the occurrences of the world . . . in their concrete particularity. On the other is an ideally theoretical understanding of those occurrences that would treat each as nothing other than a replicable instance of a systematically interconnected set of generalizations. But between these extremes, narrative is

the form in which we make comprehensible the many successive interrelationships comprised by a career.
Louis O. Mink, "Narrative Form as a Cognitive Instrument," in *The Writing of History: Literary Form and Historical Understanding* 129 (Robert H. Canary & Henry Kozicki, eds., 1978).

10. *Roe* at 113, 169 (Stewart, J., concurring).

11. Felix R. Frankfurter, "Can the Supreme Court Guarantee Toleration?" in *Law and Politics, Occasional Papers of Felix Frankfurter 1913–1938* 195 (A. MacLeish & E. F. Prichard, Jr., eds., 1939).

12. *West Virginia v. Barnette*, 319 U.S. 647, 648 (1943).

13. *Griswold* at 479, 516 (Black, J., dissenting).

14. Robert H. Bork, "Neutral Principles," 47 *Indiana Law Journal* 1, 9–10 (1971).

15. The important insight that constitutional doctrine undergoes a process of political ratification is the central contribution of Bruce Ackerman's work. See *We the People* (1991).

16. 505 U.S. 833, 851 (1992).

17. Michael Sandel, *Democracy's Discontent* 91–103 (1996).

18. Sylvia A. Law, "Rethinking Sex and the Constitution," 132 *University of Pennsylvania Law Review* 955 (1984); Ruth Bader Ginsburg, "Some Thoughts on Autonomy and Equality in Relation to *Roe v. Wade*," 63 *North Carolina Law Review* 375 (1984–85). See also Kenneth L. Karst, "The Supreme Court, 1976 Term—Foreword: Equal Citizenship Under the Fourteenth Amendment," 91 *Harvard Law Review* 1, 53–59 (1977).

19. For discussions of the feminist critique of rights-based liberal constitutional theory, see Robin West, "Supreme Court Foreword: Taking Freedom Seriously," 104 *Harvard Law Review* 43 (1990) (*West*); J. M. Balkin, "Nested Oppositions," 99 *Yale Law Journal* 1669 (1990) (*Balkin*); Catharine A. MacKinnon, "Feminism, Marxism, Method, and the State: Towards Feminist Jurisprudence," 8 *Signs: Journal of Women in Culture and Society* 635 (1983).

20. See Balkin at 1687; West at 45–46.

21. Justice Brandeis coined this now famous phrase in *Olmstead v. U.S.*, 277 U.S. 438, 478 (1928), *overruled*, *Katz v. U.S.*, 389 U.S. 347 (1967), as he dissented from an interpretation of the Fourth Amendment that left government wiretaps beyond constitutional control. His words convey an important but undeveloped sense of the meaning of autonomy rights:

> The makers of our Constitution undertook to secure conditions favorable to the pursuit of happiness. They recognized the significance of man's spiritual nature, of his feelings and of his intellect. They knew that only a part of the pain, pleasure and satisfactions of life are to be found in material things. They sought to protect Americans in their beliefs, their thoughts, their emotions and their sensations. They conferred, as against the Government, the right to be let alone—the most comprehensive of rights and the rights most valued by civilized men.

22. John Hart Ely, "The Wages of Crying Wolf: A Comment on *Roe v. Wade*," 82 *Yale Law Journal* 920, 935–36 (1973).

23. People of color in the academy have long argued—often to uncomprehending audiences—that the ideals of United States constitutional democracy were born and nurtured in struggle, first against slavery and then against caste oppression. For a review of the arguments, see Derrick Bell, Address at the Schomburg Center for Research in Black Culture, December 7, 1991 (on file at the Schomburg Center). For a recent, and well-received, version of the arguments, see Orlando Patterson, *Freedom in the Making of Western Culture* (1991).

24. Akhil Reed Amar, "The Bill of Rights and the Fourteenth Amendment," 101 *Yale Law Journal* 1193, 1275 (1992) (*Amar*).

25. Henry Bibb, *Narrative of the Life and Adventures of Henry Bibb, an American Slave, Written by Himself* 192 (1850) (*Bibb*).

1. "A Wide Field for Ambition": Stories about Work

1. *Bradwell v. Illinois*, 83 U.S. 130, 137 (1872).

2. *The Slaughter-House Cases*, 83 U.S. 36 (1872).

3. *Bullwhip Days: The Slaves Remember: An Oral History* 349–50 (James Mellon, ed., 1988).

4. From a lecture on slavery by Frederick Douglass, in Philip S. Foner, *The Life and Writings of Frederick Douglass* vol. II, 135. (1950).

5. William Hamilton, "An Address to the New-York African Society, for Mutual Relief," delivered in the Universalist Church, January 2, 1809, in *A Documentary History of the Negro People in the United States* vol. I, 52–53 (Herbert Aptheker, ed., 1951).

6. Constitution of the American Society of Free Persons of Colour, for improving their condition in the United States; for purchasing lands; and for the establishment of a settlement in Upper Canada, also the Proceedings of the Convention, with their Address to the Free Persons of Colour in the United States (Philadelphia, 1831), in Aptheker, *Documentary History*, at 106–7.

7. Address from the Convention of North Carolina Negroes, 1865, in Aptheker, *Documentary History*, vol. II at 546.

8. 39th Cong., 1st Sess. 111 (December 21, 1865) (Senator Stewart).

9. *Slaughter-House* at 128–29.

10. *Id.* at 83–130.

11. *Bradwell* at 130, 141. For an account of Bradwell's life after the Supreme Court decision, see Jane M. Friedman, *America's First Woman Lawyer: The Biography of Myra Bradwell* (1993).

12. Dorothy Sterling, *Ahead of Her Time: Abby Kelley and the Politics of Antislavery* 108 (1991) (*Sterling*).

13. Paula Giddings, *When and Where I Enter: The Impact of Black Women on Race and Sex in America* 60–61 (1984) (*Giddings*).

14. *Sterling* at 104.
15. *Id.* at 275.
16. *Id.* at 268.
17. *Id.*
18. *Loving Warriors: Selected Letters of Lucy Stone and Henry B. Blackwell, 1853–1893* 45 (Leslie Wheeler, ed., 1981).
19. *Id.* at 27.
20. *Id.* at 46.
21. *Black Women in White America: A Documentary History* 15 (Gerda Lerner, ed., 1972) (*Lerner*), quoting Abbie Lindsay, an ex-slave from Louisiana.
22. *Black Women in Nineteenth-Century American Life* 235 (Bert James Loewenberg & Ruth Bogin, eds., 1976).
23. *Id.* at 239, quoting an 1867 speech for the American Equal Rights Association.

   Although black women abolitionists were strongly feminist, and some, like Truth, insisted upon linking women's rights and the rights of blacks (arguing, for example, that the Fifteenth Amendment should be expanded to enfranchise women or be defeated), others ranked black liberation as a concern that took precedence over women's liberation. See *Giddings* at 65–68.
24. *Sterling* at 265.
25. See *Giddings* at 55; Ellen Carol Du Bois, *Feminism and Suffrage: The Emergence of an Independent Women's Movement in America, 1848–1869* 32 (1978).
26. *Slaughter-House* was not overruled, but evaded by a shift in focus from the Privileges and Immunities Clause that was the most natural vehicle for enforcement of civil rights, to the Due Process and Equal Protection Clauses. This unfortunate perversion of the constitutional text is well described in Laurence Tribe, *American Constitutional Law* 548–59 (2d ed., 1988) (*Tribe*).

2. "A Thing of Common Right": Stories about Marriage

1. *Meister v. Moore*, 96 U.S. 76 (1877).
2. *Id.* at 78.
3. *Id.* at 81.

   In taking this course, the Court relied upon the principle, regularly applied in constitutional decision making, that a legislature will not be understood to have intended a compromise of a constitutional right—or, in some cases, of a natural right—unless that intention has been clearly stated. See Amar, "The Bill of Rights and the Fourteenth Amendment," 101 *Yale Law Journal* 1193 (1992) (*Amar*) (discussing the "clear statement rule" as it was applied in the nineteenth century to protect rights declared in the Bill of Rights against state infringement).
4. Moses I. Finley, *Ancient Slavery and Modern Ideology* 75 (1980) (emphasis added) (*Finley*).

5. Thomas R. R. Cobb, *An Inquiry into the Law of Negro Slavery in the United States of America* x (1858).
6. *Id.* at 242–43.
7. *Id.* at 245–46 (citations omitted).
8. William Goodell, *The American Slave Code in Theory and Practice* 91 (1853) (*Goodell*).
9. B. A. Botkin, *Lay My Burden Down: A Folk History of Slavery* 86 (1989) (*Botkin*).
   For a description of slave marriage rituals and suggestions concerning their origins, see Herbert Gutman, *The Black Family in Slavery and Freedom, 1750–1925* 273–81 (1976) (*Gutman*).
10. *Bibb* at 192.
11. *Gutman* at 318.
12. Deborah G. White, *Ar'n't I a Woman?* 147 (1985), (*White*), quoting J. W. Loguen, *The Reverend J. W. Loguen as a Slave and as a Freeman* 223 (1859).
13. Frederick Douglass, *The Life and Times of Frederick Douglass* 95–96 (Collier, 1962) (1881).
14. *Lerner* at 8.
15. *Id.* at 8–9, quoting Moses Grandy, *Narrative of the Life of Moses Grandy, Late a Slave in the United States of America* (1844).
16. *Gutman* at 349.
17. *Id.*
18. *The Narrative of Bethany Veney: A Slave Woman* (Aunt Betty's Story), in *Collected Black Women's Narratives* 20–21 (Henry L. Gates, ed., 1988) (1902).
19. W. E. B. Du Bois, *Black Reconstruction* 57 (1935) (*Du Bois*).
20. *The Black Military Experience* 657 (Ira Berlin et al., eds., 1982) (*Berlin III*).
21. See James A. McPherson, *The Negro's Civil War* 167 (1991).
22. *Id.* at 713.
23. *Id.* at 672.
24. *Id.* at 604.
25. *Goodell* at 17.
26. *Id.* at 115–21.
27. Harriet Beecher Stowe, *A Key to Uncle Tom's Cabin* 133 (1853). Stowe writes in response to charges that family separations depicted in *Uncle Tom's Cabin* were unrealistic or atypical. Her evidence of the prevalence of slave family disruption includes eyewitness accounts of family separations resulting from slave auctions, *id.* at 137, and advertisements for the sale of slaves in South Carolina, *id.* at 134–36 and 138–42.
28. William Wells, "Family Government," *The Liberator* 192 (December 1, 1837).
29. Samuel Ward, *Autobiography of a Fugitive Negro* 15–17 (1968 ed.) (1855) (*Ward*).
30. S. F. D., "People of Color," 1 *New York's Freedom Journal* No. 7, p. 1 (April 27, 1827).
31. *Cong. Globe*, 38th Cong., 2d Sess. (1865) (Representative Creswell).
32. *Cong. Globe*, 38th Cong., 1st Sess. 1439 (1864) (Senator Harlan).

33. *Cong. Globe*, 38th Cong., 2d Sess. 200 (1865) (Representative Farnsworth).
34. *Cong. Globe*, 39th Cong., 1st Sess. 2778 (1866) (Senator Eliot, speaking with respect to the homestead provisions of the Freedmen's Bureau Bill).
35. *Cong. Globe*, 38th Cong., 1st Sess. 1479 (1864) (Senator Wilson).
36. It was not unusual at that time for divorce to be granted legislatively rather than judicially.
37. *Maynard v. Hill*, 125 U.S. 190, 211 (1888).
38. *Stanley v. Illinois*, 405 U.S. 645, 656 (1972).
39. *Loving Warriors* at 114.
40. Benjamin Platt Thomas, *Theodore Weld: Crusader for Freedom* 149 (1950) (*Thomas*).
41. *Id.* at 149.
42. *Id.* at 161.
43. *Id.* at 162–64; *Sterling* at 60–62.
44. *Sterling* at 62.
45. *Thomas* at 164.
46. *Sterling* at 62.
47. *Sterling* at 220–21.
48. *Id.* at 221. Although we do not know what words Foster spoke on that day, his marriage was regarded as a demonstration of "the possibility of a partnership of equals, neither affirming mastership, never a thought of superiority or dictation or control." *Id.* at 376, quoting Lucy Stone's remarks at Foster's memorial.
49. See *Sterling* at 266–67.
50. *Loving Warriors* at 114.
51. See *Sterling* at 220, 222.
52. *Loving Warriors* at 17. Lucy Stone received her degree from Oberlin College in 1847.
53. *Loving Warriors* at 20.
54. *Id.* at 34.
55. *Id.* at 39.
56. *Id.* at 45.
57. *Id.* at 55.
58. *Id.* at 76.
59. *Id.* at 74.
60. *Id.* at 85.
61. *Id.* at 108.
62. *Id.* at 109–10.
63. *Id.* at 123. A guest at the wedding wrote that although Stone omitted the word "obey," she did, in the event, promise to "love and honor" her spouse.
64. *Id.* at 85.
65. See *id.* at 131.
66. *Id.* at 136.

67. *Id.* at 136.
68. *Id.* at 3; *Sterling* at 301.
69. *Reynolds v. U.S.*, 98 U.S. 145 (1878).
70. *Id.* at 162–64.

Because Reynolds was prosecuted under an act of Congress, rather than under state law, the Fourteenth Amendment was not implicated. Nonetheless, the case has been used, without reference to this distinction, as authority for upholding state laws against polygamous marriage. The extent to which enactment of the Fourteenth Amendment altered the meaning of the first eight amendments (by which civil rights and liberties are protected against federal encroachment) is an intricate question, as to which, see *Amar* at 1277–79.

71. *Cong. Globe*, 39th Cong., 1st Sess. 474 (1866).
72. For a discussion of questions raised by the belief-action dichotomy, see *Tribe* at 1183–84. For a somewhat recent and highly controversial application, see *Department of Human Resources v. Smith*, 494 U.S. 872 (1990), in which the distinction was used to justify prohibition of the strictly ceremonial use of peyote in Native American religious communities. For critique and rejection of the belief-action test of First Amendment compliance, see *Torcaso v. Watkins*, 367 U.S. 488 (1961); *Follet v. Town of McCormick*, 321 U.S. 573 (1944); *Murdoch v. Pennsylvania*, 319 U.S. 105 (1943).
73. In this case, involving federal, but not state action, the relevant framers are those who conceived the Bill of Rights. The Court's discussion of the intent of the framers was, however, so broad as to be applicable in either the late 1700s or the 1860s.
74. *Id.* at 164, 166.
75. Amar & Widawsky, "Child Abuse as Slavery: A Thirteenth Amendment Response to DeShaney," 105 *Harvard Law Review* 1359, 1366 (1992), quoting *National Party Platforms 1840–1972*, at 27 (Donald B. Johnson & Kirk H. Porter, eds., 1973) (*Amar & Widawsky*). See also Orma Linford, "The Mormons, and the Law: The Polygamy Cases," 9 *Utah Law Review* 308 (1964).
76. *Id.*, quoting Sumner, "The Barbarism of Slavery, Speech in the United States Senate on the Admission of Kansas as a Free State" (June 4, 1860), in *The Works of Charles Sumner* (1872).
77. Testimony of J. B. Roudanez before the American Freedmen's Inquiry Commission, February 9, 1864, reproduced in *The Wartime Genesis of Free Labor in the Lower South* 523 (Berlin et al., eds., 1990) (*Berlin II*).
78. Testimony of Samuel B. Smith Before the American Freedmen's Inquiry Commission, November 19, 1863, reprinted in *Berlin II* at 753.
79. *Goodell* at 248–49.
80. *Ward* at 204–5.
81. *Id.* at 120.
82. *Id.*
83. *Cong. Globe*, 33d Cong., 1st Sess. 268 (App. 1854) (emphasis added).

84. Ronald Walters, *The Antislavery Appeal: American Abolitionism After 1830* 95 (1976), quoting a nineteenth-century abolitionist; Walters, "The Family in Ante-bellum Reform: An Interpretation," 3 *Societas* 221, 225 (1973).
85. *Amar & Widawsky* at 1367.
86. Linda Brent, *Incidents in the Life of a Slave Girl: Written by Herself* 26 (1861; L. Maria Child, ed., Harvest Books, 1971 edition). For a perceptive discussion of the fundamental feminist insights born of experiences of this sort, see *Giddings* at 42–45.
87. Lou Cannon, unpublished dissertation, 146–54.
88. *Id.* at 153.
89. *Essentials in Church History* 444–74 (J. Smith, ed., 25th ed., 1972).
90. *Murphy v. Ramsey*, 114 U.S. 15 (1885); *Davis v. Beason*, 133 U.S. 333 (1890); *Mormon Church v. U.S.*, 136 U.S. 1 (1890); *Cleveland v. U.S.*, 329 U.S. 14 (1946).
91. *Cleveland v. U.S.* at 26. The majority ruled, in an opinion by Justice Douglas, that religiously motivated polygamy was included in the Mann Act's prohibition of transportation across state lines for purposes of debauchery. It also rejected the claim that the act, so interpreted, interfered unconstitutionally with rights of marriage or of free exercise of religion.
92. Authorities documenting the survival of polygynous Mormon communities and official responses to their marriage practices are collected in J. Areen, *Cases and Materials on Family Law* 10–18 (1985).
93. James Madison, *Memorial and Remonstrance Against Religious Assessments* (1785), quoting Virginia Declaration of Rights.
94. *Turpin v. Locket*, 6 Call. 113 (Va., May 1804) (Tucker, J.).
95. Courts and commentators have disagreed, for example, as to whether the religion clauses of the First Amendment were motivated by an evangelical wish to protect churches from state influence, by a Jeffersonian wish to protect the state against the influence of a dominant religion, or by a Madisonian wish to guard against the tendency of each to corrupt the other. For a discussion of these strains in First Amendment history and their influence upon Supreme Court jurisprudence, see *Tribe* at 1158–66.
96. *Gutman* at 331.
97. 163 U.S. 537 (1896).
98. 347 U.S. 483 (1954).
99. *Plessy v. Ferguson* at 537, 550–52, 559.
100. James Oliver Horton, *Black Bostonians* 94 (1979).
101. David Herbert Donald, *Charles Sumner and the Coming of the Civil War* 29, 235 (1960) (*Donald*), and authorities cited.
102. The classic analysis of the United States' color-caste system is Allison Davis, Burleigh B. Gardner, and Mary R. Gardner, *Deep South* (1941), from which this definition is drawn.

NOTES   261

103. In some states, these laws were first enacted after Emancipation; in others, they were reenacted or revived. See Joel Williamson, *The New People* 91–99 (1980); Joseph R. Washington, *Marriage in Black and White* 73-80 (1993 ed.) for pieces of the confusing history of pre- and post-Civil War laws against intermarriage.

104. Section 4189 of the Code of Alabama provided that "if any white person and any negro, or the descendant of any negro to the third generation . . . , intermarry or live in adultery or fornication with each other, each of them must, on conviction, be imprisoned in the penitentiary or sentenced to hard labor for the county for not less than two nor more than seven years." *Pace v. Alabama*, 106 U.S. 583 (1883).

105. *Id.* at 583.

106. *Id.* at 585.

107. *Id.*

108. Dorothy Sterling writes that Child was "the most popular woman writer in the North until she wrote *An Appeal in Favor of That Class of Americans Called Africans*, the first book to call for immediate emancipation. The *Appeal* brought numbers of converts to the cause and swift reprisals to its author. Sales of her books dropped precipitously; subscriptions to her magazine *Juvenile Miscellany* were cancelled, and literary critics who had once sung her praises now attacked her for entering the male world of politics." *Sterling* at 39. Child subsequently served as editor of the *National Anti-Slavery Standard*. *Id.* at 126–27.

109. Lydia Maria Child, "Prejudices Against People of Color, and Our Duties in Relation to This Subject," in Louis Ruchames, *The Abolitionists: A Collection of Their Writings* 62 (1963) (*Ruchames*).

110. David Ruggles, "The 'Extinguisher' Extinguished! or David M. Reese, M.D. 'Used Up,' " quoted in *Ruchames* at 84–85.

111. *Ward* at 151–52 (1968 ed.).

112. William Jay, *An Inquiry into the Character and Tendency of the American Colonization and American Anti-Slavery Societies*, quoted in *Ruchames* at 98–99.

113. *Cong. Globe*, 39th Cong., 1st Sess. 318–22 (1866).

114. *Cong. Globe*, 39th Cong., 1st Sess. 417–20 (1866).

115. *Cong. Globe*, 39th Cong., 1st Sess. 204–5 (January 10, 1866). Rhetoric of this kind appeared in antislavery journals as well:

> This committee is opposed to "social equality and marital amalgamation." Astonishing news! The petitioners asked for the right of suffrage, and you straightway get into the turnpike of "social equality," and ride on the keen gallop into *"marital amalgamation"*—a place you seem to be well acquainted with, from your facility in getting there. How is it your imagination runs off so readily into *this* channel? Is it because you are so much more familiar than other people with this kind of amalgamation, or do you thus lug it in here as a bugbear to make the eyes of popular prejudice stick out, because you have no argument to advance in its place? Profound

Legislators! A colored man cannot ask you for the right of suffrage, without your hair sticking up in horror at the thoughts of *marital amalgamation!* Ann Arbor *Signal of Liberty,* January 30, 1843.

116. Bernard Schwartz, *Super Chief* 158–62 (1983) (reporting the Justices' deliberations concerning *Naim v. Naim,* 350 U.S. 891 [1955]) (*Schwartz*).
117. *Loving v. Virginia,* 388 U.S. 1 (1967).
118. Charles L. Black, Jr., "The Lawfulness of the Segregation Decisions," 69 *Yale Law Journal* 421, 426 (1960).
119. *Loving* at 12.
120. *Schwartz* at 669.
121. 434 U.S. 374 (1978).
122. *Id.* at 386–88. The requirement of a "substantial interference" with the right to marry served to distinguish this case and an earlier case in which the Court approved social security provisions that disadvantaged benefit recipients who married. (It also served, in later years, as one of the sources for Justice O'Connor's alternative to *Roe v. Wade's* test for determining the legitimacy of state measures that inhibit reproductive choice.)
123. *Id.* at 395–96.
124. 482 U.S. 78, 95–96 (1987).

3. "The Child Is Not the Creature of the State": Stories about Parenting

1. *Meyer v. Nebraska,* 262 U.S. 390 (1923); *Bartels v. Iowa et al.,* 262 U.S. 404 (1923).
2. *Meyer* at 397–98.
3. See *Allgeyer v. Louisiana,* 165 U.S. 578 (1897); *West Coast Hotel v. Parrish,* 300 U.S. 379 (1937).
4. See Max Lerner, *The Mind and Faith of Justice Holmes* 318–19 (1943).
5. *Meyer* at 399.
6. *Id.* at 401–2.
7. *Id.* at 402.
8. *Id.* at 403.
9. *Bartels v. Iowa* at 412–13. The difference insisted on by these two Justices would be described today as a difference in the level of scrutiny deemed appropriate in light of the importance of the right at issue. Although the dissenting Justices in the Iowa and Nebraska cases joined the opinion of the Court in *Meyer,* and can thus be said to have agreed that rights of family have special constitutional status, it is possible that they employed a "rational basis test" which would today be considered appropriate in a case involving a right with no special constitutional status.
10. 268 U.S. 510 (1925).
11. *Id.* at 534.

12. *Id.* at 535.
13. Barbara Bennett Woodhouse, "Who Owns the Child? *Meyer* and *Pierce* and the Child as Property," 33 *William and Mary Law Review* 995 (1992) (*Woodhouse*).
14. David Tyack, Thomas James & Aaron Benavot, *Law and the Shaping of Public Education, 1785–1954* 177–89 (1987).
15. *Woodhouse* at 1081–82.
16. *Berger v. United States*, 255 U.S. 22, 29, 42–43 (1921).
17. *Woodhouse* at 1070–80.
18. See *The New York Times*, January 24, 1935; Benjamin Twiss, *Lawyers and the Constitution: How Laissez Faire Came to the Supreme Court* (1962).
19. The briefs and arguments in *Meyer* and *Pierce* are reprinted in *Landmark Briefs and Arguments of the Supreme Court of the United States: Constitutional Law* vol. XXI and XXIII. Quoted passages are from p. 10 of the plaintiffs' argument in *Meyer* and p. 67 of the plaintiffs' brief in *Pierce*.
20. *Gutman* at 329–30.
21. William W. Brown, *Narrative of the Life of William W. Brown* (1848).
22. Report from Port Royal, S.C., dated June 2, 1862, reprinted in *Berlin II* at 205.
23. *Finley* at 75.
24. *Gutman* at 216–24.
25. Octavio Albert, *The House of Bondage or Charlotte Brooks and Other Stories* 3–4 (1890).
26. *Id.* at 14–15.
27. Stanley Feldstein, *Once a Slave: The Slaves' View of Slavery* 49 (1971) (*Feldstein*).
28. Deposition of J. B. Roudanez, dated February 9, 1864, reprinted in *Berlin II* at 521, 22.
29. James W. C. Pennington, *The Fugitive Blacksmith* 2 in *Five Slave Narratives* (William Lord Katz, ed., 1968) (*Five Slave Narratives*).
30. Child development specialists disagree on the question whether children need the persistent care of a single, primary caretaker or thrive equally well with the care of a consistent network of caregivers. Compare Goldstein, Freud & Solnit, *Beyond the Best Interests of the Child* (1973); Goldstein, Freud & Solnit, *Before the Best Interests of the Child* (1979); and Group for the Advancement of Psychiatry, *Divorce, Child Custody and the Family* (Mental Health Materials Center, 1980). They agree, however, that in the absence of either, a child is likely to suffer debilitating emotional harm and is at risk of failing to thrive altogether. Indeed, the emotional and developmental consequences of want of adult interaction can be fatal.
31. Jacob Stroyer, *My Life in the South* 17 (1898 ed.).
32. *Id.* at 33.
33. *Botkin* at 168–69.
34. *Id.* at 174.
35. *Pennington* at xiii.
36. *Id.* at 6–7.

37. *Id.* at 7.
38. Eric Foner, *Reconstruction: America's Unfinished Revolution, 1863–1877* 80 (1988).
39. *Id.* at 120.
40. *Id.* at 122, quoting A. D. Lewis to William W. Holden, June 5, 1869, North Carolina Governor's Papers.
41. *Id.* at 122–23.
42. *Feldstein* at 92.
43. *Id.*
44. *Botkin* at 156.
45. *Pennington* at 4.
46. Moses Grandy, *Narrative of the Life of Moses Grandy, Late a Slave in the United States of America* 6 (1844), reprinted in *Five Slave Narratives.*
47. *Bibb* at 14.
    Aptheker has assembled evidence that slaves who were hired out were "commonly treated more harshly, or with less care and attention, than those in possession of their owner." Herbert Aptheker, *American Negro Slave Revolts* 123 (1943), quoting a South Carolina judge writing in 1839. Bibb reported very harsh treatment at the hands of those who hired his services, recalling that he was forced to go without "half enough to eat," without shoes in winter and without "clothes enough to hide my nakedness" and "working under the lash." *Bibb* at 14–15. Grandy described a mixed group of employers, saying that "sometimes a slave gets a good home, and sometimes a bad one." In the bad ones, he experienced lasting injury from floggings and from working without adequate food or clothing. *Grandy* at 7.
48. *Autobiography of James L. Smith* (1881), reprinted in *Five Black Lives* 139, 166 (Wesleyan University Press, 1971) (*Five Black Lives*).
49. Aptheker, *American Negro Slave Revolts* at 325, quoting J. Bassett, *The Southern Plantation Overseer.*
50. *Brent* at 153.
51. *Bibb* at 44.
52. *Bullwhip Days* at 155.
53. *Grandy* at 5–6.
54. *Feldstein* at 59.
55. *Id.* at 60.
56. Frederick Douglass, *Life and Times of Frederick Douglass* 95–96 (1962 ed.).
57. *The Story of Mattie J. Jackson* 6–9 (1866), reprinted in *Six Women's Slave Narratives* (Nathaniel Gates, ed., 1988).
58. *Ward* at 19–20.
59. *Ward* at 12–13.
60. *Feldstein* at 59.
61. Frances Ellen Watkins Harper, *Poems on Miscellaneous Subjects* (1857); Frances Ellen Watkins Harper, *Poems* (1857).

62. *Id.* at 82.
63. *Id.* at 177.
64. James Alan McPherson, *Battle Cry of Freedom: The Civil War Era* 37 (1988).
65. *Black Women in Nineteenth-Century American Life* 226, quoting "Miss Remond's First Lecture in Dublin," 2 *Anti-Slavery Advocate* (London), 221–24 (April 1859) (*Remond Lecture*).
66. Garrison, *Declaration of Sentiments of the American Anti-Slavery Society*, adopted December 4, 1833, reprinted in *Ruchames* at 80; *The Abolitionists: Means, Ends, and Motivations* 53 (H. Hawkins, ed., 1972) (*Hawkins*).
67. *Hawkins* at 48–49.
68. John Rankin, *Letters on American Slavery* 17–18 (1838).
69. Dwight L. Drumond, "The Abolition Indictment of Slavery," in *Hawkins* at 22, 30.
70. Benjamin Quarles, *Black Abolitionists* 62 (1969).
71. *Id.* at 246.
72. *Id.* at 249.
73. *Sterling* at 284.
74. *Lerner* at 21, quoting "Testimony of Angelina Grimké Weld," in Theodore Weld, *Slavery As It Is: Testimony of a Thousand Witnesses* (1939).
75. "The Disruption of Family Ties," *Anti-Slavery Record*, March 1836, at 9 (emphasis omitted).
76. Walters, *The Antislavery Appeal* at 58.
77. Petition, dated May 25, 1774, to the Governor, the Council, and the House of Representatives of Massachusetts, reprinted in *Aptheker*, vol. I at 8–9.
78. *Id.*
79. *Id.*
80. Petition dated January 6, 1773, to the Governor, the Council, and the House of Representatives of Massachusetts, reprinted in Aptheker, *Documentary History* vol. I at 6–7.
81. *Declaration of Sentiments* at 53–55.
82. The Preamble reads:
    We the People of the United States, in Order to form a more perfect Union, establish Justice, insure domestic Tranquility, provide for the common defence, promote the general Welfare and secure the Blessings of Liberty to ourselves and our Posterity, do ordain and establish this Constitution for the United States of America.
83. Grimké, letter to Catharine E. Beecher, June 17, 1837, reprinted in *Hawkins* at 61–63 (emphasis and internal quotations omitted).
84. *Remond Lecture* at 227.
85. David W. Blight, *Frederick Douglass' Civil War* 175 (1989) (internal quotes omitted).
86. *Id.*
87. *Id.* at 242, quoting Douglass's "Mission of War" speech of 1864.

88. Benjamin Quarles, *The Negro in the Civil War* 175 (1953).
89. *Berlin II* at 7.
90. Foner, *Reconstruction* 88.
91. *Du Bois*, at 136 (quoting 39th Cong., 1st Sess., Senate Executive Document No. 2, Report of Carl Schurz).
92. *Id.* at 142, quoting Report of the Joint Committee on Reconstruction, 1866.
93. *Cong. Globe*, 38th Cong., 1st Sess. 1369 (1864).
94. *Cong. Globe*, 38th Cong., 1st Sess. 2948 (1864).
95. *Cong. Globe*, 38th Cong., 1st Sess. 2984 (1864).
96. *Cong. Globe*, 38th Cong., 1st Sess. 1479 (1864).
97. *Cong. Globe*, 38th Cong., 1st Sess. 1439 (1864).
98. *Cong. Globe*, 38th Cong., 2d Sess. 200 (1865).
99. *Cong. Globe*, 38th Cong., 2d Sess. 193 (1865).
100. *Cong. Globe* 38th Cong., 1st Sess. 1324 (1864).
101. House of Representatives Executive Document No. 118, 39th Cong., 1st Sess. (1866).
102. *Cong. Globe*, 39th Cong., 1st Sess. 1160 (1866) (quoting letter from Lieutenant Stewart Eldridge to Major General Howard, November 28, 1865).
103. *Cong. Globe*, 39th Cong., 1st Sess. 589 (1865). An example of legislation establishing this device was also offered by Senator Sumner as an illustration of the evils of the Black Codes. *Cong. Globe*, 39th Cong., 1st Sess. 93 (1865).

Similar apprenticeship arrangements were held, in an opinion by Chief Justice Chase, sitting in the Circuit of Maryland, to violate the Thirteenth Amendment. *In re Turner*, 24 F. Cas. 337 (C.C.D. Md., 1867) (No. 14,247). *Turner* has been incorrectly cited as an opinion of the Supreme Court abolishing these apprenticeship practices. See, e.g., *Gutman* at 410. The effect of *Turner* is not entirely misperceived as a result of this error. An excerpt from a subsequent district court opinion, transmitted to Congress in 1868, says of the case, "This decision . . . will govern me in all future applications of a similar character, unless a different opinion shall be pronounced by the Supreme Court." *Senate Miscellaneous Documents* No. 24, 40th Cong., 2d Sess. 6 (1868).
104. *Cong. Globe*, 39th Cong., 1st Sess. 2779 (1866).
105. See Jacobus tenBroek, "The Thirteenth Amendment to the Constitution of the United States: Consummation to Abolition and Key to the Fourteenth Amendment," 39 *California Law Review* 171, 200–1 (1951).
106. *Cong. Globe*, 39th Cong., 1st Sess. 39 (1865).
107. *Cong. Globe*, 39th Cong., 1st Sess. 42 (1865).
108. *Cong. Globe*, 39th Cong., 1st Sess. 91 (1865) (quoting regulations accompanying the 1861 proclamation emancipating the serfs of Prussia).
109. *Cong. Globe*, 39th Cong., 1st Sess. 42 (1865).
110. *Cong. Globe*, 39th Cong., 1st Sess. 474 (1866).
111. *Cong. Globe*, 39th Cong., 1st Sess. 474 (1866).
112. *Cong. Globe*, 39th Cong., 1st Sess. 504 (1866).

113. The Court used a test that does not seem particularly rigorous. It required that laws bear a "real and substantial" relationship to legitimate government ends, but also that they be the least restrictive means of achieving the government's ends. Moreover, the Court was often unwilling to consider social facts or the views of social scientists in assessing the justiciability of social welfare legislation. For a discussion of the effects of these judicial stances, see Tribe at 567–74.
114. See, e.g., Lochner v. New York, 198 U.S. 45 (1905) (invalidating a sixty-hour maximum workweek for bakers).
115. See, e.g., Jay Burns Baking Co. v. Bryan, 264 U.S. 504 (1924) (invalidating the requirement of standardized weights for loaves of bread).
116. 304 U.S. 144 (1938).
117. Id. at 146. Carolene Products was decided under the Due Process Clause of the Fifth rather than the Fourteenth Amendment, but this difference is unimportant in the present context.
118. Id. at 150 n. 3.
119. Id. at 144, 152 n. 4.
120. Tribe at 771.
121. Planned Parenthood v. Casey, 505 U.S. 833 (1992).
122. Minersville v. Gobitis, 310 U.S. 586, 599 (1940).
123. Id. at 606.
124. Peter Irons, The Courage of Their Convictions 22–23 (1988).
125. 319 U.S. 624 (1943).
126. Id. at 639–40.
127. Id. at 638.
128. Id. at 643.
129. Id. at 645.
130. Reynolds, Murphy, Maynard, Davis, Mormon Church, and Cleveland involved federal authority; Pace and Skinner were equal protection cases; Meyer and Pierce rested decision squarely on the Fourteenth Amendment. Petitioners in Buck argued and were answered by the Court exclusively in Fourteenth Amendment terms.
131. See Tribe at 567.
132. Justices Roberts and Reed, also dissenting, adhered to the views expressed in Gobitis.
133. Barnette at 639.
134. Id. at 648.
135. Id.
136. 321 U.S. 158 (1944).
137. Id. at 162.
138. Id. at 166.
139. Id.
140. See Felix Frankfurter, Child Labor and the Court, reprinted in Felix Frankfurter, Law and Politics 206–7 (1939).

268 NOTES

141. Justice Murphy would have relied upon the narrower, less controversial theory of incorporation, rather than upon the majority's sweeping statements of due process entitlement. But he would have overturned the conviction. He dissented, arguing, with a reference to the *Carolene Products* footnote, that the regulation, as applied to Ms. Prince, violated religious freedom protected by the First Amendment. Justice Jackson, joined by Justices Roberts and Frankfurter, agreed with the majority that the conviction should be affirmed, but dissented vigorously from the grounds of affirmance. In the view of the dissenting Justices, the selling of religious literature was commercial activity and, as such, outside the protection of the First and Fourteenth amendments.
142. 406 U.S. 205 (1972).
143. *Id.* at 211.
144. *Id.* at 219–20. Justice Douglas observed that this reasoning made possible the overruling of *Reynolds*. *Id.* at 247.
145. *Id.* at 232.
146. *Gobitis* at 586, 599.
147. *Yoder* at 222, 224.
148. *Id.* at 245 (opinion of Justice Douglas).
149. *Id.* at 239 (opinion of Justice White).
150. *Id.* at 247–49.
151. Letter of Major General John M. Palmer, Commander of the Department of Kentucky, to Senator Joseph C. Fowler of Tennessee, in *The Destruction of Slavery* 646 (Ira Berlin at al., eds., 1985) (*Berlin I*).
152. *Feldstein* at 69.
153. *Id.*
154. James Mars, *Life of James Mars, a Slave* 38, reprinted in *Five Black Lives*.
155. *Narrative of Lunsford Lane* 21 (1842), reprinted in *Five Slave Narratives* (*Lane*).
156. *Botkin* at 163.
157. Petition dated January 13, 1777, to the Council and House of Representatives of Massachusetts, reprinted in Aptheker, *Documentary History*, vol. I at 8–9.
158. *Bibb* at 24.
159. *Lane* at 21.
160. Aptheker, *American Negro Slave Revolts* at 58.
161. *Id.* at 58–59.
162. See Anthony E. Cook, "Beyond Critical Legal Studies: The Reconstructive Theology of Dr. Martin Luther King, Jr.," 103 *Harvard Law Review* 985, 1015–23 (1990).
163. Aptheker, *American Negro Slave Revolts* at 58.
164. *Botkin* at 27.
165. G. W. Offley, *A Narrative of the Life and Labors of the Rev. G. W. Offley* (1860), reprinted in *Five Black Lives*, 134.
166. *Gutman* at 87.
167. *Feldstein* at 178.

168. *Id.* at 173, 178.

169. *The Story of Mattie J. Jackson; White* at 127–28; *Gutman* at 222, 224–29; New Netherlands petition, 1661, reprinted in Aptheker, *Documentary History* vol. I at 1–2; Advertisement, *Gazette*, March 1, 1831, reprinted in Aptheker, *Documentary History* vol. I at 111–12; Petition to the Pennsylvania Senate and House of Representatives, January 1832, reprinted in Aptheker, *Documentary History* vol. I at 126–33; *Aunt Betty's Story, Schomburg Library of 19th Century Black Women Writers, Collected Black Women's Narratives* 20–21; *Botkin* at 161–62; Speech of Representative Henry M. Turner to the Georgia legislature, September 3, 1868, quoted in *Feldstein* at 178. The comparable dilemma of Anthony Burns, similarly resolved, is reported *id.* at 78.

170. *Giddings* at 43–44, quoting Brent, *Incidents in the Life of a Slave Girl.*

171. *Ward* at 166–67.

172. "On the Immutability of Human Affairs," 1 *New York's Freedom Journal* No. 5, p. 19 (1827).

173. *Ward* at 87.

174. *Bibb* at xi–xii.

175. Ethiop, "Afric-American Picture Gallery," 13 *Anglo-African Magazine*, February 1859, at 56–57 (emphasis in original).

176. *Rankin* at 48–49.

177. Petition to the Governor and Legislature of Massachusetts, dated May 25, 1774, reprinted in Aptheker, *Documentary History*, vol. I at 8–9.

178. *Lane* at 8. Petition reprinted in *Am I Not a Man and a Brother?* 428–29 (R. Burns ed., 1977); Statement of the pioneer National Negro Convention regarding Canadian Emigration, 1830, reprinted in Aptheker, *Documentary History*, vol. I at 103; Letter of Reverend Andrew Bryan to a Reverend Dr. Rippon, December 23, 1800, reprinted in Aptheker, *Documentary History*, vol. I at 48–49.

179. *DeShaney v. Winnebago County Department of Social Services*, 489 U.S. 189 (1989).

180. *Id.* at 195–96.

181. For an analysis of these reasons, see Davis and Barua, "Custodial Choices for Children at Risk: Bias, Sequentiality and the Law," 2 *University of Chicago Law School Roundtable* 139 (1995).

182. 405 U.S. 645 (1972).

183. *Id.* at 651.

184. 452 U.S. 18 (1981).

185. *Id.* at 27, quoting *Stanley v. Illinois*, 405 U.S. 645, 651 (1972).

186. *Id.* at 38.

187. *Id.* at 47.

188. *Santowsky v. Kramer*, 455 U.S. 745 (1982).

189. *Id.* at 753.

190. Judith Areen, *Cases and Materials on Family Law* 1985 (3rd ed., 1972), quoting letter of March 23, 1976, from Patrick T. Murphy, attorney for Peter Stanley.

191. For the facts of this matter, I rely upon Truth's autobiography, *Narrative of So-*

journer Truth) 30–40 (1993) (Truth), and Nell Irvin Painter, Sojourner Truth, a Life, a Symbol (1996) (Painter); Cheryl Harris, "Reflections on Slavery: Policing the Boundaries of Race and Gender Through Property, Patriarchy and White Supremacy," 18 Cardozo Law Review (1996); Carleton Mabee Sojourner Truth: Slave, Prophet, Legend) 16–21 (1995 ed.) (Mabee). Sources confirming Truth's autobiographical account of this incident are discussed by Mabee at 19–20.

192. Mabee reports that Truth's efforts to secure Peter's return continued for about two years, during which she first "traveled the five miles or so back and forth between her home . . . and Kingston, often barefoot, walking or trotting with a gait that was distinctly her own." She subsequently moved to Kingston so that she could pursue the child's claim more effectively. Id. at 18. It is worth noting that Mabee discusses in rather judgmental terms the fact that Truth had left Peter, as well as her other children, to reside, with their father, under the control of the master who sent Peter to Alabama, and the ways in which Truth's religious, social, and political work later occasioned absences from her husband and children. Id. at 13–15, 23–24.

193. Truth recalled in her Narrative that she had mistaken important-looking gentlemen for the "grand jury" to which she had been told to take her appeal and was ridiculed for failing to know rituals by which oaths are taken in courts of law. Truth at 33–34.

194. See Mabee at 14, citing Laws of the State of New York vol. IV, Albany, 1818, chap. 137, passed 1817, 136, 139. There is no surviving official account of the decision.

195. For a full description of the "general strike," by which slaves transferred their labor "from the Confederate planter to the Northern invader," see Du Bois, at 55–127 (1962 ed.). Du Bois estimates that the strike involved half a million people. Id. at 67. See also James M. McPherson, Battle Cry of Freedom 355–57, 497–99, 709–11 (1988); Benjamin Quarles, The Negro in the Civil War 58–77, 95, 312, 314–20 (1953); Berlin I at 3, 8. For evidence of strike activity among slaves before the Civil War, see Aptheker, American Negro Slave Revolts at 20.

196. Du Bois at 59, 62–65; Gutman at 363–431.

197. See, generally, Berlin III at 656–709 (describing the extent to which "family stood at the center of antebellum black life, slave and free," and the ways in which black soldiers fought as and for family).

198. All quoted material in this paragraph is from Gutman at 371, 383–84.

199. Testimony of Colonel Geo. H. Hanks before the American Freedmen's Inquiry Commission (February 6, 1864) in Berlin II at 517, 519.

200. Letter of Sam Bowmen to his wife (May 10, 1864) in Berlin I at 483–85.

201. Letter from Captain Wm. B. Fowle, Jr., to Major Southward Hoffman (January 14, 1863) in Berlin I at 87.

202. Gutman at 409.

203. Id. at 410.

204. Affidavit of Clarissa Burdett (March 27, 1865) in *Berlin I* at 615–16.
205. *Gutman* at 410, 404.
206. Affidavit of Amy Carrington (August 10, 1865) in *Berlin I* at 307–8.
207. Leon Litwack, *Been in the Storm So Long: The Aftermath of Slavery* 366 (1979). See also Foner, *Reconstruction* at 199; Theodore Branter Wilson, *The Black Codes of the South* (1965); *Du Bois* at 17, 173.
208. For an account of this use of the apprenticeship system, see *Bibb* at 14–16.
209. *Feldstein* at 253.
210. *Gutman* at 402–3, 410.
211. *Id.* at 407–12.
212. *Id.* at 410.
213. Rebecca Scott, "The Battle over the Child: Child Apprenticeship and the Freedmen's Bureau in North Carolina," 10 *Prologue* 101–13 (1978).
214. *Id.* at 110.
215. An ideology, as I intend the term, corresponds to what Jean-François Lyotard describes as a narrative that legitimates knowledge in a discourse such as law. Jean-François Lyotard, *The Postmodern Condition: A Report on Knowledge* 31–35 (Bennington & Massumi translation, 1984 [1979]).
216. Indeed, apprenticeship laws were, at times, tailored to restrict the amount of education the apprentice was required to receive. See *Gutman* at 402 (reporting that, in Maryland, white apprentices were to be taught a trade and educated, while black apprentices were only to be taught a trade).
217. *Truth* at 38. See also *Mabee* at 19.
218. *Truth* at 38.
219. *Truth* at 39.
220. Aptheker, *Documentary History*, vol. I at 105 (quoting D. Rowland, Senate of South Carolina, December 9, 1844, Report of the Committee on Federal Relations, p. 30).
221. Testimony of Mr. Frederick A. Eustis before the American Freedmen's Inquiry Commission (June 1863) in *Berlin II* at 246–48.
222. Edward. L. Pierce to Hon. S. P. Chase (June 2, 1862) in *Berlin II* at 205.
223. Walters, "The Family in Ante-bellum Reform" 221, 224–25.
224. The facts of this matter are taken from the following documents: Excerpts from clipping from *United Presbyterian*, March 1864, enclosed in letter from Robert George to Hon. E. M. Stanton, March 20, 1864, in *Berlin I* at 314–6; Letter from Brigadier General R. P. Buckland to M. D. Lauden, February 23, 1864 (Buckland letter), in *id.* at 316; Letter from Brigadier General Augustus L. Chetlain to Lieutenant Colonel T. H. Harris, April 12, 1864 (Chetlain letter), in *id.* at 316–17.
225. Testimony of Tobias Gibson, April 25, 1865, Smith-Brady Commission, in *Berlin II* at 611.
226. *Scott* at 107, 109–11.
227. *Gutman* at 403–6.
228. *Id.* at 406–9.

229. Testimony of Colonel Geo. H. Hanks before the American Freedmen's Inquiry Commission, February 6, 1864, in *Berlin II* at 517, 519.
230. *Cong. Globe*, 39th Cong., 1st Sess. 589 (1866).
231. *M. L. B. v. S. L. J.*, 1996 U.S. LEXIS 7647.
232. 431 U.S. 494 (1977).
233. *Id.* at 499.
234. *Id.* at 507.
235. *Id.* at 520.
236. *Id.* at 537.
237. *Id.* at 543.
238. *Id.* at 548.
239. *Id.* at 549.
240. *Id.*
241. Chief Justice Burger dissented on the ground that the Court should have avoided the constitutional issue because of Ms. Moore's failure to exhaust the remedy of application for an exemption.
242. 431 U.S. 816 (1976).
243. The most complete and influential articulations of psychological parent theory are contained in Joseph Goldstein, Albert J. Solnit, Sonja Goldstein, and the late Anna Freud, *In the Best Interests of the Child* (1996).
244. *Smith* at 863.
245. *In re Sanjivini K.*, 47 N.Y. 2d 374, 382 (New York Court of Appeals, 1979).
246. *Quilloin v. Walcott*, 434 U.S. 246 (1978). The Court declined, on procedural grounds, to consider Quilloin's sex discrimination claim. It found no unlawful discrimination by virtue of the more privileged position given married and divorced fathers.
247. 441 U.S. 380 (1979).
248. On the day of its decision in *Caban*, the Supreme Court rejected the equal protection claims of a man who was disentitled under Georgia law to recover for the wrongful death of his illegitimate son, although a similarly situated woman would have been entitled to sue (*Parham v. Hughes*, 444 U.S. 347 [1979]). Justice Powell provided the swing vote in a narrow concurrence, arguing that the state's interest in minimizing problems of proof was sufficient to justify the gender-based discrimination. The Due Process Clause received only a passing mention: the plurality said that established rights of family concerned "integrity . . . against state interference and the freedom . . . to raise . . . [one's] children" rather than a right to sue for money damages (*id.* at 358–59). In announcing this decision, the Court distinguished the equal protection standards applicable to illegitimate children and to their parents; in 1977, in a decision protecting the right of illegitimate children to inherit from their fathers, it had set a standard of intermediate scrutiny for classifications separating legitimate and illegitimate offspring. *Trimble v. Gordon*, 430 U.S. 762 (1977).

249. *Id.* at 395–97. Justice Stewart found the father's equal protection claim stronger, but, despite an expressed appreciation of the risks associated with government reliance upon gender stereotypes, he perceived differences between unwed mothers and fathers that justified the choice made by the New York legislature.

250. In 1981, a unanimous Court held that indigent putative fathers have a due process right to funds to obtain blood grouping tests in defending against state-initiated paternity claims—*Little v. Streater*, 452 U.S. 1 (1981)—recognizing in the process that the tests were reasonable in cost and provided a greater than 90 percent probability of negating paternity for erroneously accused men. *Id.* at 8.

251. 463 U.S. 248 (1983).

252. *Id.* at 261 (citations omitted).

253. Justice Scalia's opinion in the case reports that blood tests showed a 98.07 probability of Michael H's paternity. This is impossible (if the number is correct, it means the test established a 98.07 probability that the qualifying match among the three blood types was not due to chance) and rather badly exaggerates the reliability of existing tests. Either way, the evidence of paternity was overwhelmingly persuasive.

254. This is essentially the reasoning that one member of the five-person majority followed. Justice Stevens, who in *Lehr* and *Caban* had been outspoken in support of state authority to configure families in traditional ways thought to serve the needs of children, filed a narrow concurrence, and the fifth vote for denial of the claims of Michael and Victoria. He disagreed with the plurality view that Michael was without due process rights of family integrity, and he found room within California law to permit visitation between Michael and Victoria. Believing that the trial judge was free to consider Michael's request for visitation rights, he concluded that Michael had received the equivalent of the right, secured by *Caban*, to be heard concerning Victoria's best interests.

255. *Michael H.* at 127, n. 6.

256. *Id.*

257. *Id.* at 130.

258. Justice O'Connor's decision to join the majority opinion in *Bowers v. Hardwick* suggests that her unwillingness to foreclose consideration of general principles cannot be taken as an invariable commitment to consider them.

259. *Lehr* at 262.

260. *Id.* at 263.

261. *M.L.B.* at 10.

4. "They Have Not Owned Even Their Bodies": Stories about Procreation

1. *Loving* at 12.

2. *Pierce* at 535.

3. 274 U.S. 200, 201 (1927).

4. Stephen J. Gould, "Carrie Buck's Daughter," 93 *Natural History* 14 (July 1984) (*Gould*).

5. Heredity is a major causative factor in only about 5 percent of cases. *Diagnostic and Statistical Manual of Mental Disorders* 30 (3d ed., revised, 1987). See also Ferster, "Eliminating the Unfit—Is Sterilization the Answer?" 27 *Ohio State Law Journal* 591, 632 (1966).

6. For a well-documented account of the eugenics craze of the 1920s, see Ellen Chesler, *Woman of Valor: Margaret Sanger and the Birth Control Movement in America* 214–17 (1992) (*Chesler*).

7. *Gould* at 337.

8. *Buck* at 207 (citation omitted).

9. *Id.* at 201.

10. *Skinner v. Oklahoma*, 316 U.S. 535, 541 (1942).

11. *Id.* Interestingly, although the Court announced the strict scrutiny standard and took pains to justify special scrutiny in light of the nature of the right at stake, it is not clear that the majority actually found it necessary to give special scrutiny to the Oklahoma statute. The majority opinion's characterizations of the Oklahoma scheme for deciding which felons would be subject to sterilization suggest that the Justices thought the law without rational basis and therefore vulnerable even to the lax scrutiny to which the Court had limited itself in the usual case.

12. *Id.* at 544.

13. *Id.* at 546.

14. See *Stump v. Sparkman*, 435 U.S. 349 (1978) (holding a judge immune to a charge that he violated the civil rights of a young woman whom he ordered sterilized).

15. Allen Chase, *The Legacy of Malthus: The Social Costs of the New Scientific Racism* 343 (1977).

16. Daniel J. Kelves, *In the Name of Eugenics: Genetics and the Uses of Human Heredity* 116 (1985).

17. *Id.* at 118–19.

18. *Pennington* at iv–v.

19. *Ward* at 169.

20. Anon., "On the Political Tendency of Slavery in the United States, 4th Installment," 1 *New York's Freedom Journal* 1 (No. 14, 1827).

21. *Donald* at 311, 354–55.

22. Walters, *The Antislavery Appeal* 95.

23. *Du Bois* at 43.

24. *Id.* at 43–44.

25. *Feldstein* at 90.

26. *Botkin* at 161–62.

27. *Bullwhip Days* at 296–97, 147–49.

28. Anon. "The Disruption of Family Ties," *Anti-Slavery Record* March, 1836, p. 9 (emphasis in original).

29. *Declaration of Sentiments* (1833), in *Hawkins* at 53–54.

30. *Cong. Globe*, 39th Cong., 1st Sess. 474 (1866).

31. *Gutman* at 85.

32. *Chesler* at 67.

33. 367 U.S. 497 (1961).

34. *Id.* at 517

35. Justice Harlan made a similar argument, noting that the Third and Fourth amendments—prohibiting the quartering of soldiers in any house without consent of the owner, and protecting the right of security against unreasonable searches and seizures—formed the basis of a concept of individual privacy, specially prized within the confines of the home, that was fundamental to American notions of ordered liberty (*id.* at 549). The term "ordered liberty" was first used in *Palko v. Connecticut* to describe those principles of justice "so rooted in the traditions and conscience of . . . [the American] people as to be ranked as fundamental." 302 U.S. 319, 325 (1937).

36. *Id.* at 540.

37. As Justice Harlan also pointed out, the fact that due process is guaranteed by both the Fifth and Fourteenth amendments makes nonsense of arguments that the latter is limited by the terms of the former: To say that the Fourteenth Amendment Due Process Clause incorporates the Bill of Rights is to say that due process is, among other things, due process.

38. *Id.* at 542–43.

39. *Id.* at 543.

40. *Id.* at 522. Justice Douglas also thought the Connecticut statute clearly violative of the First Amendment rights of doctors. *Id.* at 513–15.

41. 381 U.S. 479 (1965).

42. *N.A.A.C.P. v. Button*, 371 U.S. 415 (1963).

43. The argument from the Ninth Amendment, relied upon by several of the Justices, drew heavily upon the scholarly work of Norman Redlich. See Norman Redlich, "Are There 'Certain Rights . . . Retained by the People'?" 37 *New York University Law Review* 787 (1962).

44. *Griswold* at 485.

45. *Id.* at 500. Justice Goldberg also wrote separately, relying on the Ninth Amendment as proof of the constitutional legitimacy of unenumerated but traditionally recognized rights. *Id.* at 492.

46. *Id.* at 503, quoting *Kovacs v. Cooper*, 336 U.S. 77, 95 (opinion of Frankfurter, J.). Justice Frankfurter was describing the opinions and philosophy of Justice Holmes with respect to the First Amendment: "[F]or him the right to search for truth was of a different order than some transient economic dogma. And without freedom of expression, thought becomes checked and atrophied. Therefore, in considering what interests are so fundamental as to be enshrined in the Due

Process Clause, those liberties of the individual which history has attested as the indispensable conditions of an open as against a closed society" came with a special momentum.

47. *Id.* at 504.

48. 402 U.S. 62, 68 (1971).

49. 405 U.S. 438 (1972).

50. *Id.* at 453. Three years earlier, Justice Marshall had used similar language, writing for the Court to strike a law that made possession of obscene materials a crime: "If the First Amendment means anything, it means that a State has no business telling a man, sitting alone in his own house, what books he may read or what films he may watch." *Stanley v. Georgia,* 394 U.S. 557, 565 (1969).

51. Bob Woodward and Scott Armstrong, *The Brethren: Inside the Supreme Court* 172 (1981) (emphasis added).

   Justice Stewart's decision to join the Court's opinion had special significance in light of his earlier vote to invalidate on vagueness grounds the statute considered in *Vuitch.*

52. Justice Douglas joined the opinion of the Court but issued a separate opinion arguing that the case could be decided exclusively on First Amendment grounds. Justice White's concurring opinion, joined by Justice Blackmun (who also joined the Court opinion), appeared to rest on narrow grounds, arguing that the case involved contraceptive distribution by an unauthorized person; that the marital status of the recipient was not established at trial; that the requirement of authorization for distribution of a spermicidal foam was unreasonable; and that the conviction was therefore invalid. Yet this chain of reasoning requires that special scrutiny be given the legislative decision to restrict the right of distribution. To give that special scrutiny is to go beyond *Griswold's* holding that the state may not impose direct regulation upon marital sex. The meaning of the rights established in *Griswold* was, then, in the minds of all of the concurring Justices, broader than the holding and terms of the *Griswold* opinions.

   Only Chief Justice Burger dissented in *Eisenstadt;* Justices Rehnquist and Powell were newly appointed and did not participate in deciding the case.

53. *Id.* at 152–53. No member of the Court disagreed that family rights were among the liberties protected by the Due Process Clause, although Justice Rehnquist, writing in dissent, hedged the question a bit. *Id.* at 173. The Court's further conclusion that laws infringing these rights required special scrutiny was rejected by Justice Rehnquist, who took the view (citing Holmes, Frankfurter, and Black) that the Due Process Clause permitted deprivations of liberty so long as they were taken with rational basis.

54. *Doe v. Bolton,* 410 U.S. 179, 221–22. He offered this additional characterization of the stakes at issue for the pregnant woman: "At the heart of the controversy in these cases are those recurring pregnancies that pose no danger whatsoever to the life or health of the mother but are, nevertheless, unwanted for any one or

more of a variety of reasons—convenience, family planning, economics, dislike of children, the embarrassment of illegitimacy, etc." *Id.* at 221.

55. *Roe v. Wade*, 410 U.S. 113, 168–69 (1973).

56. *White* at 147.

57. *Bibb* at 44.

58. *Giddings* at 46; *Gutman* at 80–82; *White* at 86–88.

59. *Feldstein* at 90.

60. *Id.* at 58.

61. *Harper* at 85.

62. *Botkin* at 154.

63. *Planned Parenthood of Central Missouri v. Danforth*, 428 U.S. 52, 92 (1976).

64. Gerald Gunther, "The Supreme Court, 1971 Term—Foreword: In Search of Evolving Doctrine on a Changing Court: A Model for a Newer Equal Protection," 88 *Harvard Law Review* 1, 8 (1972).

65. *Barnette* at 639.

66. Justice Murphy dissented alone, urging application of a test requiring grave and immediate danger and a legitimate state interest. *Prince* at 174, 176.

67. *Loving* at 11.

68. *Eisenstadt* at 447.

69. *Poe v. Ullman* at 554.

70. *Griswold* at 497, 503–4. Justice White said in *Eisenstadt* that since the prohibition of contraception sales burdened a constitutional right, it was impermissible unless "essential" to a legitimate state purpose (at 463–64), but it cannot be said, in light of the language of his other family rights opinions, that Justice White intended to apply strict scrutiny with respect to legislation burdening procreative choice.

71. *Stanley* at 651.

72. *Yoder* at 221, 230, 233.

73. *Roe* at 162.

74. A state may also choose to regulate abortion in a manner that places a state interest in women's health in opposition to a pregnant woman's, or a family's, conflicting interests in unborn life. Imagine a state regulation that forbids dangerous but potentially effective measures to cure infertility or avoid miscarriage. In this scenario, the designation of women's health as a compelling state interest raises doctrinal problems of the same kind as those raised by the designation of unborn life as a compelling state interest.

75. *Roe* at 155, 163, 164.

76. *Planned Parenthood v. Danforth*, 428 U.S. 52 (1976) (striking prohibition of abortion by saline amniocentesis); *Akron v. Akron Center for Reproductive Health*, 462 U.S. 416 (1983) (striking hospitalization requirement for all second-trimester abortions); *Planned Parenthood v. Ashcroft*, 462 U.S. 476 (1983) (striking hospitalization requirement for all second-trimester abortions, but upholding

requirement that pathologists perform tissue analysis); *Simopoulos v. Virginia*, 462 U.S. 506 (1983) (upholding requirement that second-trimester abortions be performed in licensed outpatient "hospital" facilities).

77. *Danforth* (striking a regulation imposing upon the physician performing an abortion a duty of care toward the fetus regardless of viability); *Colautti v. Franklin*, 439 U.S. 379 (1979) (striking, on vagueness grounds, a regulation imposing upon the physician performing an abortion a duty of care toward the fetus that may be viable); see also *Akron* (striking a requirement of humane disposal of fetal remains) and *Ashcroft* (upholding a requirement that second physicians be present to attend to the fetus during post-viability abortions).

78. *Akron* (striking requirement of preoperative counseling by the attending physician) and *Thornburgh v. American College of Obstetricians and Gynecologists*, 476 U.S. 747 (1986) (striking informed consent requirement with a prescribed role for the physician).

79. *Roe* at 116.

80. *Doe v. Bolton*, 410 U.S. 179, 192 (1973).

81. *Danforth* at 65–67.

82. *Akron* (concerning a provision held to discourage, rather than inform, consent, and a twenty-four-hour waiting period between consent and abortion); *Thornburgh* (striking informed consent requirement with prescribed content and twenty-four-hour waiting period).

83. *Danforth* (striking requirements of parental and spousal consent); *Belotti v. Baird*, 443 U.S. 622 (1979) (striking requirements of parental notification and parental or judicial consent for all minors); *H.L. v. Matheson*, 450 U.S. 398 (upholding requirement of parental notification as applied to minors not shown to be "mature" or in need of exemption); *Akron* (striking blanket requirement of parental or judicial consent for patients under fifteen); *Ashcroft* (upholding requirement of parental or judicial consent absent showing of maturity).

84. *Danforth* at 63–65 (upholding a definition of viability in terms of the survival capacity of the unborn); *Colautti* (striking, on vagueness grounds, a viability determination requirement).

85. *Carey v. Population Services International*, 431 U.S. 678, 685, 686, 702 (1977).

86. 432 U.S. 464 (1977).

87. In *Carey*, Justice Powell had argued that the *Roe* Framework should be applied only in cases in which access to abortion was entirely closed or significantly burdened.

88. *Maher* at 477.

89. *Id.* at 464, 474.

90. *Beal v. Doe*, 432 U.S. 438, 446 (1977); *Maher* at 473–74.

91. *Maher* at 480.

92. *Thornburgh* at 797 (dissenting opinion).

93. Bork, "Neutral Principles."

94. *Thornburgh* at 759.

95. *Id.* at 798, 814.
96. *Akron* at 461.
97. *Thornburgh* at 784.
98. 492 U.S. 490 (1989).
99. *Id.* at 515–20.
100. *Id.* at 532.
101. 505 U.S. 833 (1992).
102. The portions of the O'Connor-Kennedy-Souter opinion discussing the framework for evaluating abortion restrictions were not joined by other Justices and were not part of the opinion of the Court. Since the four dissenting Justices take views that are more restrictive than that represented by the "undue burden" test, it was clear at the time of *Casey*'s announcement that states would not be required to meet a test more rigorous than the "undue burden" test. On the other hand, since two Justices (Blackmun and Stevens) presumably continued to adhere to a test more rigorous than the "undue burden" test, it was likely that legislation failing to meet the "undue burden" test would be invalidated. Since the *Casey* decision, Justice Ginsburg (an outspoken defender of the right of abortion choice) has replaced Justice White, and Justice Breyer (whose views with respect to abortion were not clearly known at the time of his confirmation) has replaced Justice Blackmun.
103. *Casey* at 878, 883.
104. *Id.* A requirement of parental notification was also approved.
105. *Id.*
106. *Id.* at 851 (citations omitted).

5. A New Appreciation of Family Rights

1. *Du Bois* at 725.
2. *Poe* at 542–43.
3. Frank Michelman has attributed a similar view to Justice Brennan, arguing that tradition as referred to in Brennan's opinions "seems to refer to norms rather than practice," whereas tradition in the opinions of Justice Scalia "refers to the actual practice of people . . . not to their normative reflection about it." Frank Michelman [McCorkle Lecture], 77 *Virginia Law Review* 1261, 1314 (1991).
4. Hayden White, "The Value of Narrativity," in *On Narrative* (W. J. T. Mitchell, ed.) (1980).
5. *Du Bois* at 725.
6. 83 U.S. 36 (1872). Justice Swayne described the three Reconstruction Amendments as "all consequences of the late civil war," and identified their purpose as securing "to every one within . . . [the] jurisdiction [of the federal government] . . . rights and privileges . . . which, according to the plainest considerations of reason and justice and the fundamental principles of the social compact, all are entitled to enjoy." *Id.* at 123–29. Justice Bradley argued that "the mischief to be remedied"

by the Fourteenth Amendment was "slavery and its incidents and consequences; . . . [a] spirit of insubordination and disloyalty to the National Government" and violations of the civil rights of antislavery advocates. *Id.* at 120–22.

7. 163 U.S. 537, 555 (1895).

8. *Id.* at 542.

9. 83 U.S. 36, 72.

10. *Id.* at 129.

11. *Id.* at 70.

12. *Id.*

13. *Id.* at 82.

14. *Id.*

15. David A. J. Richards, *Conscience and the Constitution: History, Theory and Law of the Reconstruction Amendments* 110 (1993).

16. See *Du Bois* at 55–83 (describing a "general strike" against the slave system in which "perhaps a half million" [*id.* at 67] of the 3,953,740 slaves in the South [*id.* at 57] transferred their labor "from the Confederate planter to the Northern invader" [*id.* at 55].

17. *Richards* at 109–10 and authorities cited.

18. See Abraham Lincoln, "First Inaugural Address," in Fehrenbacher, *Abraham Lincoln: Speeches and Writing, 1858–1865* 215–24 (1964).

19. When emancipation became an articulated purpose of the war, white resistance increased. James McPherson concludes that in 1862 the attitude of the typical white Union soldier was summed up by the comment of a New York soldier who said, "We must first conquer & then its time enough to talk about the *dam'd niggers*." McPherson adds that "[I]n 1863, hostility to emancipation was the principal fuel that fired antiwar Democrats." He reports extensive antiblack violence, both by draft rioters at home and by troops in the South, and incapacitating desertions by troops unwilling to fight to free slaves. McPherson, *Battle Cry of Freedom* 497, 594–95, 609.

20. See Quarles, *Black Abolitionists* 47–50 (documenting reservations of white abolitionists regarding social equality and integration).

21. 39th Cong., 1st Sess., Senate Executive Document No. 2, Report of Carl Schurz (1805).

22. *Du Bois* at 30.

23. Joseph B. James, *The Ratification of the Fourteenth Amendment* 303 (1984).

24. *Cong. Globe*, March 11, 1867 (Representative Beck), quoted in Paul H. Buck, *The Road to Reunion* 86 (1959).

25. *Id.* at 96.

26. *Du Bois* at 331.

27. *Id.* at 332.

28. *Id.*

29. Richard L. Hume, "Negro Delegates to the State Constitutional Conventions of

1867–69," in *Southern Black Leaders of the Reconstruction Era* 130 (Howard N. Rabinowitz, ed., 1982).

30. *Id.* at 134.

31. David Levering Lewis, *W. E. B. Du Bois, Biography of a Race, 1868–1919* 15 (1993).

32. Foner, *Reconstruction* 314.

33. Kenneth M. Stampp, *The Era of Reconstruction 1865–1877* 169–70 (1965).

34. *Id.*

35. Eric Foner, *Freedom's Lawmakers: A Directory of Black Officeholders During Reconstruction* xii (1993).

36. *Du Bois* at 711–28.

37. Foner, *Reconstruction* xix–xx.

38. David Saville Muzzey, *History of the American People*, quoted in *Du Bois* at 712.

39. *Du Bois* at 717.

40. Foner, *Reconstruction* xxi.

41. *Id.* at xix.

42. *Id.* at xii.

43. See Jacobus tenBroek, "The Thirteenth Amendment to the Constitution of the United States: Consummation to Abolition and Key to the Fourteenth Amendment," 39 *California Law Review* 171, 200–1 (1951).

44. Peggy C. Davis, "Law, Science and History: Reflections on *In the Best Interests of the Child*," 86 *Michigan Law Review*, 1096, 1106–20 (1988).

45. David A. J. Richards, *The Constitution, Feminism, and Gay Rights* (unpublished manuscript); see also David A. J. Richards, *Conscience and the Constitution: History, Theory, and Law of the Reconstruction Amendments* (1993).

46. Christopher Eisgruber, *Material World* (unpublished manuscript).

47. Resort to the doctrine of substantive due process does not, of course, excuse the Court's continued neglect of the Privileges and Immunities Clause. As many scholars have complained, this rich constitutional language has not reemerged since it was unjustifiably interred by the *Slaughter-House* Court.

48. *Du Bois* at 114.

49. *Burns* at 452–53.

50. *Feldstein* at 79.

51. Foner, *The Life and Writings of Frederick Douglass* vol. I at 148.

52. H. Aptheker, *The Negro in the Abolitionist Movement* 30 (1941).

53. Aptheker, *American Negro Slave Revolts* at 223–24, quoting R. Sutcliff, *Travels in Some Parts of North America* (circa 1804).

54. W. Grimes, *Life of William Grimes* (1860), reprinted in *Five Black Lives* at 59, 62.

55. *Ruchames* at 30.

56. *Ward* at 76.

57. Wright, *The Sin of Slavery and Its Remedy: Containing Some Reflections on the Moral Influence of American Colonization*, reprinted in *Ruchames* at 58.

58. Brigadier General J. W. Phelps to Captain R. S. Davis, June 16, 1862, in *Berlin I* at 210, 211.

59. Clipping from the Cleveland *Daily Herald*, November 1862 (estimated date), in *Berlin I* at 539, 541.

60. *Cong. Globe*, 39th Cong. 1st Sess., Part I, 536.

61. *Cong. Globe*, 39th Cong. [February 5, 1866].

62. Speech by Frederick Douglass, June 16, 1861, in *The Collected Papers of Frederick Douglass*, Series One, vol. III 439 (1985).

63. Petition dated May 25, 1774, in Aptheker, *Documentary History* vol. I at 9.

64. *Ward* at 119.

65. *Brent* at 6.

66. Statement of the Pioneer National Negro Convention regarding Canadian Emigration (1830), reprinted in Aptheker, *Documentary History* vol. I at 103.

67. *Report of the Committee on Homosexual Offenses and Prostitution* 23–224 (1963).
   It must be said that the Committee's statement of legitimate state ends is rather narrow, excluding, in the absence of a generous reading of the terms "order," "decency," "offense," "injury," and "exploitation," measures designed to provide a floor of opportunity and security or an environment that enhances communal life.

68. Mary Warnock, *A Question of Life* 1, 11, 47 (1985).

69. *Poe* at 546–47, 519.

70. *Griswold* at 485.

71. 497 U.S. 261 (1990).

72. *Cruzan* at 349–50; *Webster* at 565.

73. Linda Greenhouse, "When Second Thoughts in Case Come Too Late," *The New York Times*, Nov. 5, 1990, Section A, page 14, column 5.

74. 478 U.S. 186, 196–97.

75. *Id.* at 188, 190, 196–97. The statute at issue defined sodomy as "any sexual act involving the sex organs of one person and the mouth or anus of another."

76. Jerome Bruner, *Acts of Meaning* 33 (1990).

77. Toni Morrison, *Playing in the Dark: Whiteness and the Literary Imagination* 48 (1992).

78. *Du Bois* at 29.

79. *Poe* at 542.

80. *Casey* at 851.

81. *Murphy v. Ramsey*, 114 U.S. 15, 45 (1885)

82. *Romer v. Evans*, 116 S.Ct. 1620 (1996).

83. *Smith v. O.F.F.E.R* at 833–38.

84. *Lehman v. Lycoming County Children's Services Agency*, 458 U.S. 502 (1982).

85. *Danforth* at 69, 70, 74, 93.

86. The requirements for judicial bypass proceedings are set out in *Belotti v. Baird*, 443 U.S. 622, 643–44 (1979). They were embellished or modified in *Matheson, Akron, Ashcroft,* and *Hodgson.*

87. *Id.* at 655.
88. *Id.* at 657.
89. *Id.* at 134.
90. In this vision of democracy, the state and the principles that bind the people are seen as dynamic—open to influence by minorities as minorities engage in the political process. It is a vision in which Lord Devlin's principle of preservation of a moral status quo would hold no sway. See Patrick Devlin, *The Enforcement of Morals* (1965).
91. Heymann and Barzelay, "The Forest and the Trees: *Roe v. Wade* and Its Critics," 53 *Boston University Law Review* 765, 773 (1973).

Afterword

1. Ralph Ellison, *Going to the Territory* 126 (1986).

INDEX

• ⇦═══⇨ •

abolitionists, *see* antislavery movement
abortion, 5, 8, 157, 185–90, 192–211,
 230–31; regulation of, 196–211, 214,
 244–49
abuse, parental, 156
*Akron v. Akron Center for Reproductive
 Health* (1983), 207, 277n76, 278nn77,
 78, 82
Amar, Akhil Reed, 9, 53, 55–56
American and Foreign Anti-Slavery
 Society, 37
American Anti-Slavery Society, 24, 43;
 Declaration of Sentiments of, 107, 110
American Eugenics Society, 170
American Freedmen's Inquiry
 Commission, 93, 150
*American Slave Code in Theory and
 Practice, The* (Goodell), 37, 54
Amish, 125–28, 196, 243
Amistad mutiny, 90
Anglo-African Magazine, 136
antimiscegenation laws, 5, 66–77, 195,
 215
antislavery movement, 9–10, 211n, 213,
 237, 247; breeding practices
 denounced by, 180; on brutality and
 depravity of slaveholders, 174–75; and
 Declaration of Independence, 224–26;
 family rights in ideology of, 108–11;
 on infanticide, 191; and marriage, 29,
 31, 37–38, 42–49; and miscegenation,
 68–72; and moral autonomy, 226–27;
 parent-child separations denounced
 by, 102, 105–8; polygamy linked with
 slavery by, 54–57; racism of, 65; on

right to work, 20–21; and women's
 rights, 23–25
Anti-Slavery Record, 108–9, 180
Anti-Slavery Women, 43
apprenticeship, 147–49, 153–54
Aptheker, Herbert, 131, 264n47

Baird, William, 186
Bartels v. Iowa, 262n9
Barzelay, Douglas, 248
Belotti v. Baird (1978), 245
Beloved (Morrison), 191
Berger v. United States (1921), 88
Bibb, Henry, 12, 32, 93, 100, 102, 107,
 130, 190, 234
Bill of Rights, 12, 50, 118, 119, 122,
 123, 125, 182–85, 189, 224, 226,
 259n73, 275n37; *see also specific
 amendments under* Constitution
birth control, *see* contraception
Black, Charles, 75–76, 211
Black, Hugo, 7, 77, 122, 158, 276n53
Black Codes, 114–15, 144, 146–47, 155,
 266n103
Blackmun, Harry, 137, 138, 141, 157,
 163, 165, 187, 205–6, 210, 276n52,
 279n102
Blackwell, Henry, 25, 43–49, 237
Blake, Jane, 190
Bork, Robert, 7, 124, 205
Boston Female Anti-Slavery Society, 65
Bourdieu, Pierre, 253n8
Bowers v. Hardwick (1985), 214, 231–
 33, 240, 273n258
Bradley, Joseph P., 22, 23, 42, 279n6

Bradwell, Myra, 15, 16, 18n, 22–23, 25, 27, 42, 83–85, 215
Brandeis, Louis D., 88, 254n21
Brennan, William, 127, 141, 157–59, 165, 187, 188, 196, 202, 279n3
Brent, Linda, 57, 101–2, 134, 227
Brewer, David J., 279n102
Brooks, Charlotte, 92–93
Broomall, Representative, 113
Brown, Elizabeth, 91
Brown, Henry, 103
Brown, William W., 91, 109
Brown v. Board of Education (1954), 64–67, 75, 76, 77n, 187, 188, 200, 209n, 215
Bruner, Jerome, 234, 251
Bryan, Andrew, 136, 247
Buck v. Bell (1927), 168–72, 193, 267n130
Burdett, Clarissa, 145–46
Burger, Warren, 126–28, 159, 161, 201n, 202, 203, 207, 232, 272n241, 276n52
Burgess, John W., 222, 223
Burns, Anthony, 224
Burns, Sarah, 251
Bush, George, 209
Butler, Andrew, 57
Butler, Benjamin Franklin, 17

Caban v. Mohammed (1979), 161–62, 272n248, 273n254
Calhoun, John, 183
Canada, fugitive slaves in, 70–71, 135
Captivi (Plautus), 91
Cardozo, Benjamin, 88
Carey v. Population Services International (1977), 202–3, 232n, 278n87
Carrington, Amy, 146
Catholic schools, 86–89
Chapman, Maria Weston, 25, 43
Chase, Salmon P., 23, 266n103
chattel principle, 174
Chesler, Ellen, 181
Chicago Legal News, 15, 23
Child, Lydia Maria, 69–70, 191, 261n108
child labor laws, 124–25
children: mutual aid in caring for,

among slaves, 133; public duty to protect, 137–39; see also parental rights
child welfare systems, 242–44
Christian, John, 151–52
Christian, Pauline, 151–52
Church of Jesus Christ of the Latter-day Saints, see Mormons
Civil Rights Act (1866), 50, 115–17, 148
Civil War, 4, 15, 18, 19, 22, 65, 111, 219–20, 223, 225, 237, 280n19; black children during, 145–46, 150–51; marriages of former slaves during, 35–36
Clark, Senator, 113
"clear and present danger" test, 195
Cleveland v. U.S., 260n91
Cobb, Thomas R. R., 30–31
Colautti v. Franklin (1979), 278nn77, 85
Coleman, Charlotte, 65
Columbia University, 88
common law traditions: of community protection of children, 138; in marriage, 29–30, 41, 49
communitarians, 7–8
community, dialectic between self and, 234–36
compelling state interest, 194; in fetal life, 196–203, 206, 207, 230–31, 247; right to work and, 17
Comstock, Anthony, 181
Congress, U.S., 12, 21, 24, 50, 53, 72, 216, 259n70; Reconstruction, 18, 22, 27, 38–39, 62, 112–17, 144, 147, 155, 159, 169, 218–19, 225, 243
Connecticut Anti-Slavery Society, 24
Constitution, U.S., 5–9, 21, 22, 50, 51, 55, 61, 67, 110, 111, 120, 137, 153, 164, 167–68, 188–90, 192, 198, 205, 210, 215, 232, 247; Preamble, 265n82; First Amendment, 50–52, 57–61, 121–26, 181, 184, 195, 202n, 259n72, 260n95, 268n141, 275nn40, 46, 276nn50, 52; Third Amendment, 125, 182, 275n35; Fourth Amendment, 125, 182, 254n21, 275n35; Fifth Amendment, 125, 184, 267n117, 275n37; Ninth

CPSIA information can be obtained
at www.ICGtesting.com
Printed in the USA
LVHW111820150522
718837LV00001B/59